Language & Literature

A PRACTICAL GUIDE STUDENT BOOK

Mike East
Nevine El Souefi
Graham Maclure
Chad Schwaberow

International Baccalaureate
Baccalauréat International
Bachillerato Internacional

Language and Literature: A Practical Guide (Student Book)

Published by International Baccalaureate Organization (UK) Ltd,
Peterson House, Malthouse Avenue, Cardiff Gate, Cardiff, Wales CF23 8GL
United Kingdom, represented by IB Publishing Ltd, Churchillplein 6,
The Hague, 2517JW The Netherlands
Website: www.ibo.org

The International Baccalaureate Organization (known as the IB) offers four
high-quality and challenging educational programmes for a worldwide
community of schools, aiming to create a better, more peaceful world.
This publication is one of a range of materials produced to support these
programmes.

© International Baccalaureate Organization 2014

Published 2014

The rights of Mike East, Nevine El Souefi, Graham Maclure and Chad
Schwaberow to be identified as authors of this work have been asserted by
them in accordance with sections 77 and 78 of the Copyright, Designs and
Patent Act 1988.

International Baccalaureate, Baccalauréat International and **Bachillerato
Internacional** are registered trademarks of the International Baccalaureate
Organization.

IB merchandise and publications can be purchased through the IB store at
http://store.ibo.org. General ordering queries should be directed to the Sales
and Marketing Department at sales@ibo.org.

British Library Cataloguing in Publication Data

A catalogue record for this book is available from the British Library

ISBN: 978-1-910160-02-2
Typeset by Q2A Media Services Pvt Ltd
Printed and bound in Dubai.

Acknowledgments

We are grateful for permission to reprint copyright material and other content:

p7 blocks: ©iStockphoto, tools: ©iStockphoto, plans: ©iStockphoto, house:
©iStockphoto; p9 Cultural greetings: Ujjval Panchal, Map of Greeting Body
Gestures, Computation Design project by Ujjval Panchal, Pilot Year-CIID,
Denmark; p13 children playing with blocks; ©iStockphoto; p13 Tying a
bow tie: commons.wikimedia.org/wiki/File:HowToTieBowtie_VersionB.
png; p16 garden: ©iStockphoto; p18 Macbeth: copyright Philip Buchel;
p18 Macbeth and the Three Witches by Theodore Chasseriau (1855); p19
Macbeth Et Les Sorcieres by Ary Scheffer; p19 The Three Witches from
Macbeth, by Alexandre-Marie Colin (1827); p20 Goldfish: ©iStockphoto;
p20 Okara, G. 1985. *Piano and Drums*. In *Touched with Fire: An Anthology of
Poems* compiled by Jack Hyde. UK. Cambridge University Press; p23 Anne
Bamford, quoted in "Creativity: It's Not What You Know...". May 2011. IB World.
International Baccalaureate; p25 Female Soldier: ©iStockphoto; p25 New
York in ruins: ©iStockphoto; p25 Alien: ©iStockphoto; p30 Walt Whitman:
http://upload.wikimedia.org/wikipedia/commons/8/85/Walt_Whitman_-_Brady-
Handy_restored.png; p60 Three little pigs: ©iStockphoto; p66 London:
©iStockphoto; p81 My Last Duchess: http://commons.wikimedia.org/wiki/
File:Agnolo_Bronzino,_ritratto_di_Lucrezia_de%27_Medici.JPG; p91 Police officer:
©iStockphoto; p93 Spilled milk: ©iStockphoto; p93 Rose: http://commons.
wikimedia.org/wiki/File:Starr_070402-6235_Rosa_sp..jpg; p93 Candle: http://
commons.wikimedia.org/wiki/Candle#mediaviewer/File:Einzelne_Kerze.
JPG; p93 Moon: http://commons.wikimedia.org/wiki/Moon#mediaviewer/
File:Moon_apollo12.jpg; p93 Fire: http://commons.wikimedia.org/wiki/
Fire#mediaviewer/File:FIRE_01.JPG; p105 The Good Earth: http://commons.
wikimedia.org/wiki/File:The_Good_Earth_Character_Web.png; p109 Audience:
©iStockphoto; p110 Film: ©iStockphoto; p111 Sound: ©iStockphoto; p111
Light: ©iStockphoto; p112 Composition: ©iStockphoto; p117 Corruption:
©iStockphoto; p118 Extract from speech by former US President George
W Bush, 20th Sept 2001; p118 Extract from the Obama 2008 Presidential
campaign slogan; p119 Sheep: http://commons.wikimedia.org/wiki/
File:Flock_of_sheep.jpg; p126 Teen girl room: ©iStockphoto; p126 Teen boy
room: ©iStockphoto; p130; Quote from Ian Mc Neil in An Inspector Calls,
May 30, 2001. In WriteWork.com. Retrieved from http://www.writework.
com/essay/inspector-calls-1; p153 Emily Dickinson: http://commons.
wikimedia.org/wiki/Emily_Dickinson#mediaviewer/File:Emily_Dickinson_
daguerreotype_%28cropped%29.jpg; p154 Lear: Old man with a beard, Edward
Lear: http://en.wikisource.org/wiki/There_was_an_Old_Man_with_a_beard; p160
Woman crying: ©iStockphoto; p162 Compass: http://commons.wikimedia.
org/wiki/Compass#mediaviewer/File:Compass_icon_matte.svg; p169 Romeo
& Juliet: http://commons.wikimedia.org/wiki/Romeo_and_Juliet#mediaviewer/
File:DickseeRomeoandJuliet.jpg; p173 The On the Road scroll: http://
en.wikipedia.org/wiki/On_the_Road#mediaviewer/File:Kerouac_ontheroad_
scroll.jpg; p178 Song extract: Somethin' Else by Eddie Cochran; p179
President Obama at the Mandela funeral: http://upload.wikimedia.org/
wikipedia/commons/4/44/Obama_Madiba_Memorial.jpg; p183: The last sleep
of Arthur: http://www.bestthinking.com/articles/history/europe_history/
the-unique-holy-crown-of-saint-stephen-of-hungary; p187 Highlighters:
http://commons.wikimedia.org/wiki/File:Highlighter_pen_-photocopied_text-
9Mar2009.jpg; p190 Reading room: http://upload.wikimedia.org/wikipedia/
commons/thumb/d/d3/British_Museum_Reading_Room_Section_Feb_2006.
jpg/1280px-British_Museum_Reading_Room_Section_Feb_2006.jpg; p210
Oak Grove Beach: http://southofpdx.wordpress.com/2012/09/20/oak-grove-
beach-1917-1929; p211 Rolls Royce: http://www.earlyamericanautomobiles.
com/americanautomobiles21.htm; p211 Fashionable Dresses: https://www.
pinterest.com/vtdnp/vintage-fashion-in-vermont-newspapers; p211 Jazz:
http://www.westmichmusichystericalsociety.com/eg; p221 Japan Tsunami
advertisement: ©iStockphoto, ©Shutterstock, redrawn from http://cfile30.
uf.tistory.com/image/1974C05A4D8C5DDD1E1EB0; p223 Extract from the
Ryan's Well Foundation website www.ryanswell.ca; p226 Hunger poster: Keely
Joy Photography, Inc. Feed My Starving Children, FMSC.org. https://www.flickr.
com/photos/fmsc/7267988232; p227 Hamburger stack: http://pixabay.com/
p-19264/?no_redirect; p227 bandwagon: ©iStockphoto; p227 Name calling:
http://upload.wikimedia.org/wikipedia/commons/0/05/Dope-poster.svg;
p227 Barack Obama: http://commons.wikimedia.org/wiki/File:Barack_Obama_
playing_basketball_with_members_of_Congress_and_Cabinet_secretaries.jpg;
p227 Testimonial: ©iStockphoto; p231 transfer: http://www.flickr.com/photos/
thaigov/4354187272/in/set-72157623427197612; p231 card stacking:
©iStockphoto; p235 Egyptian hieroglyphics: http://commons.wikimedia.org/
wiki/File:Maler_der_Grabkammer_der_Nefertari_004.jpg; p235 Bayeux Tapestry:
http://commons.wikimedia.org/wiki/File:Bayeux_Tapestry_scene1_Edward.jpg;
p235 Trajan's Column: http://commons.wikimedia.org/wiki/File:101_Conrad_
Cichorius,Die_Reliefs_der_Traianss%C3%A4ule,_TafelCI.jpg; p243 Stressed
student: http://www.iclipart.com/search.php?x=97&y=9&keys=167987&
andor=AND&cat=All&tl=clipart&id=111_10_3_17; p244 Shakespeare: http://
commons.wikimedia.org/wiki/File:Shakespeare_Droeshout_1623.jpg; p244
Emergency: ©iStockphoto.

continued on back page

Contents

How to use this book   v

1. Introduction to IB skills   1

2. Introducing key concept 1: communication   9

3. Introducing key concept 2: connections   15

4. Introducing key concept 3: creativity   22

5. Introducing key concept 4: perspective   27

6. Genre and conventions   33

     Topic 1: Genre conventions   34

     Topic 2: Exploring a theme in audio visual media   42

     Topic 3: Exploring a theme in articles   46

7. Structure   52

     Topic 1: Exploring openings and their functions   56

     Topic 2: Exploring structure in poetry   62

     Topic 3: Walking and talking your way through structure   68

8. Point of view   74

     Topic 1: Narrative point of view   75

     Topic 2: Can I trust the narrator?   80

     Topic 3: Bringing different points of view together   84

9. Character   88

     Topic 1: A personal approach to characterisation   93

     Topic 2: The role of speech in characterisation   98

     Topic 3: Communicating character changes and development   103

10. Theme   108

     Topic 1: Theme in video   109

     Topic 2: Theme in literature   113

     Topic 3: Theme in propaganda   117

11. Setting   122

     Topic 1: The role of setting in communicating character   124

     Topic 2: Exploring the role of setting in establishing context   130

     Topic 3: The function of setting in creating mood and atmosphere and communicating theme   135

12.	Style	143
	Topic 1: Exploring elements of style	144
	Topic 2: Writing in the same style	149
	Topic 3: Building your own style	157
13.	Intertextuality	163
	Topic 1: Using intertextuality to inspire creativity	165
	Topic 2: Using intertextuality to create humor or a larger message	174
	Topic 3: Creating credibility through literary allusion	178
14.	Purpose	182
	Topic 1: Preparing for commentaries/textual analysis	184
	Topic 2: Doing commentaries/textual analysis successfully	189
	Topic 3: Selecting elements to fit your purpose	194
15.	Context	197
	Topic 1: Context and its effect on style	198
	Topic 2: Context and literature	207
	Topic 3: Context clues	212
16.	Audience imperatives	218
	Topic 1: How audience members respond	220
	Topic 2: How creators reach different audiences	222
	Topic 3: Reaching the intended audience	226
17.	Self-expression	234
	Topic 1: The graphic novel	235
	Topic 2: Creative writing	239
	Topic 3: Creative writing: poetry	246

How to use this book

As well as introducing you to the 4 key concepts and 12 of the related concepts in the Middle Years Programme (MYP) language and literature course, this book will also help you practise all the skills you need to reach the highest level of the MYP assessment criteria.

This book has been divided into chapters on key and related concepts. Throughout the book you will find features that will help you link your learning to the core elements of the MYP.

On the first page of each of the related concept chapters you will find:

- the topics you will be focusing on
- the inquiry questions you will be considering
- a checklist of skills you will practise
- a glossary of any difficult terms
- a list of the command terms you will come across.

You will also see a list of other concepts that relate to the chapter. You should keep these in mind as you work.

Each related concept chapter is divided into three topics that help you explore the concept through a variety of activities. Some activities can be done individually while others may be done with a partner or in a group.

Here are the other features that you will come across in the book:

GLOBAL CONTEXTS
For each activity you will see an indication of a global context that is the focus of that activity. Global contexts help organize inquiry into six different areas:

- identities and relationships
- orientation in space and time
- personal and cultural expression
- scientific and technical innovation
- globalization and sustainability
- fairness and development.

These global contexts indicate how the activity is relevant to your life and the real world.

ATL SKILLS

Alongside global contexts, each topic and activity includes an ATL skills focus. There is an emphasis on the particular skill listed in each box, but you will also be using and developing other skills too.

TIP

Throughout the chapters you will see additional information to help your understanding of a topic or activity.

TAKE ACTION

These boxes suggest practical applications of a topic or activity that can make a difference in your life or the lives of others.

QUICK THINK

These boxes provide questions to challenge your thinking. Your teacher may use them for a class discussion.

INTERDISCIPLINARY LINKS

As an MYP student you are encouraged to use skills and knowledge from different subject areas in your learning. Look out for these boxes, which provide links to other subject groups.

CHAPTER LINKS

These boxes direct you to other chapters that relate to a topic or activity.

WEB LINKS

These boxes include websites and search terms for further reading and exploration.

LITERARY LINKS

These boxes provide information about books and films that relate to the topic.

Introduction to IB skills

Welcome to language and literature for MYP 4/5. In this book you will learn about learning in a language and literature context. You will find out more about writing in a variety of different text types, analysing and responding to literature, preparing for assessments and examinations, and much more.

This chapter explains what the key concepts are that relate to language and literature. It then goes on to explain the 12 related concepts that are the essence of language and literature.

Key concepts

In the Middle Years Programme (MYP), each subject area has key concepts that are used as a framework for knowledge. They are powerful ideas that we explore through different topics to try to understand the world around us. In MYP language and literature, there are four key concepts that we use as the basis for study. These concepts are:

- communication
- connections
- creativity
- perspective

Chapters 2 to 5 take each of the key concepts and explore them in greater detail.

Related concepts

There are also 12 related concepts, which are the central themes for the chapters in this book. These concepts are much more related to language and literature. In chapters 6 to 17 each related concept is looked at in greater detail. Through these related concepts, key subject skills and techniques are demonstrated and explained.

Related concepts in Language and literature		
Genre and conventions	Theme	Purpose
Structure	Setting	Context
Point of view	Style	Audience imperatives
Character	Intertextuality	Self-expression

Learning skills

You have been learning all your life. You began in settings such as your home and neighbourhood. Then, your learning became more formal as you started school. Learning in the MYP is primarily inquiry-based learning. This means that you are encouraged to ask questions in order to understand the many ways that language and literature interacts to form the world as we know it. Your learning will continually cycle through three different phases.

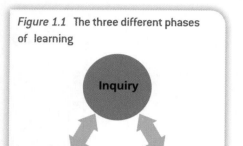

Figure 1.1 **The three different phases of learning**

Inquiry

Ask questions—it's the only way you are going to find out exactly what you want to know. Think about what you already know and what you want to know. Your curiosity is one of your best assets as a student.

Action

An important part of conceptual learning is action. Action in the MYP might involve learning by doing, service learning, educating yourself and educating others. Sometimes you may choose not to act, based on newly acquired knowledge and understandings. Remember to think of the learner profile characteristic of being principled in your actions and make responsible choices.

Reflection

As a learner, you will become increasingly aware of the way that you use evidence, practise skills and make conclusions. Reflection in your learning helps you to look at the facts from a different perspective, to ask new questions and to reconsider your own conclusions. You may then decide to lead your inquiry in a different direction.

Inquiry learning can be frustrating. There is not always a "right" answer; sometimes conclusions may be uncomfortable or may conflict with what you want to believe; and you will come to realize that there are no "endpoints" in learning. As an MYP student, learning through inquiry, action and reflection is central to your education and forms the foundation of acquiring knowledge and conceptual understanding.

Conceptual learning **is:**	Conceptual learning **is not:**
learning through inquiry	learning only through memorization
taking action to understand the world around you	trying to find the "right" answer
using knowledge to understand big ideas	passively accepting everything you read/hear/see.
making connections through concepts across different subjects.	

The characteristics of conceptual learning

The objectives covered

Both the skills and the objectives are closely related to the assessment criteria that your teacher will have made available to you. There are four assessment criteria and each one is designed to measure your skills in a different area of language and literature as follows:

Criterion A	Analysing	Maximum 8
Criterion B	Organizing	Maximum 8
Criterion C	Producing text	Maximum 8
Criterion D	Using language	Maximum 8

The objectives of any MYP subject state the specific targets that are set for learning in the subject. They define what you will be able to accomplish as a result of studying the subject.

These objectives represent some of the essential processes of language. In order to meet these objectives, you will engage in a variety of activities, continually refining your skills: listening, speaking, reading, writing, viewing and presenting. These skills are very much interactive and interrelated, though in some instances your teacher may wish to deal with them as discrete skills.

A: Analysing

This objective refers to enabling you to deconstruct texts, in order to identify their essential elements and to extract meaning from them, through demonstrating an understanding of the creator's choices, the relationships between the various components of the text, and making inferences.

Through engaging with texts, you will be required to think critically and show awareness of, and an ability to reflect on, different perspectives through your interpretations of the text. You should further be able to use the text to support your personal responses and ideas.

These last two years of the MYP should prepare you to:

i) analyse the effects and purposes of the content, context, language, structure, technique and style of texts created by others

ii) analyse the effects of the creator's choices on an audience

iii) justify your opinions and ideas, using appropriate examples, thorough explanation and accurate terminology

iv) compare and contrast works

v) connect literary and non-literary features across and within genres or texts.

B: Organizing

This objective requires you to value and demonstrate an understanding of and an ability to organize your ideas and opinions using a range of appropriate conventions for different forms and purposes of communication. You must also recognize the importance of maintaining academic integrity by respecting intellectual property rights and referencing all sources accurately.

These last two years of the MYP should prepare you to:

i) employ organizational structures that serve the context and the intention

ii) organize opinions and ideas in a sustained, coherent and logical manner with ideas building on each other

iii) use language-specific conventions to show the reason for the order of your ideas

iv) acknowledge sources according to a recognized convention

v) use a presentation style suitable to the context and intention.

C: Producing text

This objective requires you to engage in the process of text creation with an emphasis on both the creative process itself and on the understanding of the connection between you, the creator, and your audience. You will explore and appreciate new and changing perspectives and ideas. As a result, you will develop the ability to make choices aimed at producing texts that please both you, the creator, and your audience.

These last two years of the MYP should prepare you to:

i) create works that demonstrate your insight, imagination and sensitivity

ii) make choices that serve the content, context and intention, and which are designed to have an impact on your audience

iii) select relevant details and examples to justify ideas

iv) employ a range of literary techniques

v) explore and reflect critically on new perspectives and ideas arising from your personal engagement with the creative process.

D: Using language

This objective expects you to develop, organize and express yourself and communicate thoughts, ideas and information. You are required to use accurate and varied language that is appropriate to the context and intention. This objective applies to all written, oral and visual text.

These last two years of the MYP should prepare you to:

i) use accurate and varied vocabulary, sentence structures and forms of expression

ii) use an appropriate register and style that serves the context and intention

iii) use correct grammar, syntax and punctuation

iv) use correct spelling (alphabetic languages) or writing (character languages) and pronunciation

v) use appropriate non-verbal communication techniques in oral, presentation or visual work.

TIP

It may sound like an obvious thing, but many students neglect to read these criteria closely—or even the specific rubrics produced by their teachers. Carefully following the descriptors in the criteria and the rubrics that go with a specific task increases your chance of success.

Knowledge

The concept of "connections" or "perspective" isn't something you can touch but you can certainly explain it to another person using specific examples from different subject areas. This is where your knowledge of facts is essential. Without the support of specific knowledge,

Figure 1.2 The role of knowledge in supporting conceptual understanding

Knowledge, facts and examples

Related concepts

Key conceptual understanding

facts and examples, it is very difficult to understand and explain key concepts and related concepts. In the MYP, your teachers have a choice as to what facts and examples they will use to help develop your understanding of key concepts. The use of knowledge, facts and examples will be different in every MYP classroom but they will all lead you to an understanding of the key and related concepts in the subject group of language and literature.

Global contexts

Now that you know what the key and related concepts are, let's focus a little more on the knowledge, facts and examples that will help you understand, explain and analyse them. The MYP calls this part of the curriculum global contexts. The global context is the setting or background for studying the key and related concepts. It is easy to think that the global context is the choice of topic in your course of study. There are six global contexts:

- identities and relationships
- orientation in time and space
- personal and cultural expression
- scientific and technical innovation
- globalization and sustainability
- fairness and development.

> ### 🌐 GLOBAL CONTEXTS
> The choice of global context is influenced in several different ways.
> **Scale**—study of a concept on an individual, local or global level.
> **Relevance**—your education needs to be relevant for you and the world you live in, and this will influence the choice of context.
> **International-mindedness**—IB programmes aim to develop internationally minded students and this is supported through using a variety of contexts to understand concepts.

Do students have an influence over what global context is chosen? Absolutely—that's the reason why MYP language and literature courses look different all around the world. The contexts that are relevant for you may not be relevant for a student studying in another country or even in another school in your own country. What all MYP language and literature courses do have in common is the goal of deepening your understanding of the language and literature key concepts.

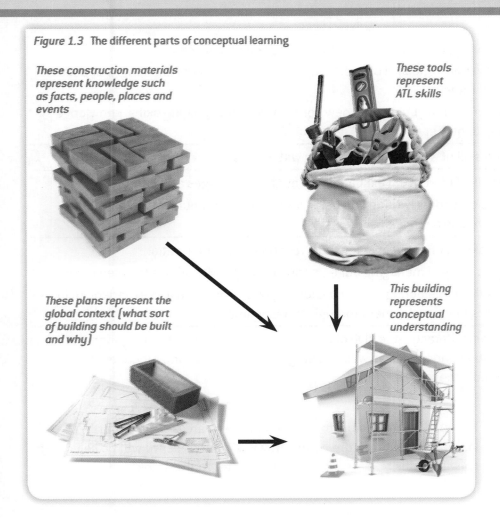

Figure 1.3 The different parts of conceptual learning

These construction materials represent knowledge such as facts, people, places and events

These tools represent ATL skills

These plans represent the global context (what sort of building should be built and why)

This building represents conceptual understanding

Approaches to learning (ATL) skills

As a learner, you are developing a range of skills to help you learn and process significant amounts of knowledge and understanding. Some skills are very specific to particular subjects while other skills are ones that you use every day in every class, and will ultimately use for life! The skills that you learn through the MYP allow you to take responsibility for your own learning. There are five groups of MYP skills:

ATL SKILLS	Communication skills
Thinking skills	Self-management skills
Social skills	Research skills

Depending on the subject, you might focus more on one or two areas than on others. As you move through the MYP and mature as a student, the focus will also move through different skills—from being taught, to practising—to consolidate your skill ability. Read through the outline of ATL skills, taking some time to reflect on where and when you have learned, practised or mastered different skills. Also, think about which skills you still need to learn, practise or master.

Thinking skills	Critical thinking—the skill of analysing and evaluating issues and ideas.
	Creativity and innovation—the skill of exercising initiative to consider challenges and ideas in new and adapted ways.
	Transfer—the skill of learning by making new connections and applying skills, knowledge and understanding to new situations.
Social skills	Collaboration—the skill of working cooperatively with others.
Communication skills	Interaction—the skill of effectively exchanging thoughts, messages and information.
	Literacy—the skills of reading, writing and using language to communicate information appropriately and write in a range of contexts.
Self-management skills	Organization—the skill of effectively using time, resources and information.
	Affective skills—the skills of managing our emotions through cultivating a focused mind.
	Reflection—the skill of considering and reconsidering what is learned and experienced in order to support personal development through metacognition.
Research skills	Information and media literacy—the skill of interpreting and making informed judgments as users of information and media, as well as being a skillful creator and producer of information and media messages.

Approaches to learning (ATL) skills

It would be impossible to focus on all these areas in just your MYP language and literature course in years 4 and 5, so we will be selecting specific skills to learn, practise and master in this book.

Summary

Look back at Fig 1.3 on conceptual learning. Remember that conceptual learning happens when you use the inquiry cycle, develop your ATL skills and increase subject knowledge. These three factors work together to develop detailed understanding of the four key concepts in language and literature: communication, connections, creativity and perspective. While the content of language and literature courses will look different in every MYP classroom, there is always the same focus on conceptual learning to construct a deeper understanding of the big ideas in life and the world around us.

CHAPTER 2

Introducing key concept 1: communication

INQUIRY QUESTIONS	
	◼ **How do we communicate and why is it important to consider this question?**
	◼ **What are some of the challenges to effective communication?**
	◼ **How does the context of our communication affect the language we use?**

SKILLS	
	ATL
	✓ Negotiate ideas and knowledge with peers and teachers.
	✓ Draw reasonable conclusions and generalizations.
	✓ Recognize unstated assumptions and bias.
	✓ Listen actively to other perspectives and ideas.
	✓ Build consensus.
	✓ Use appropriate forms of writing for different purposes and audiences.
	Language and literature
	✓ Speak and listen—discuss, role-play and use drama to explore language.
	✓ Develop reading and viewing skills through explorations of language.
	✓ Analyse and evaluate the role of language in a range of texts.

GLOSSARY

Modality the way a speaker expresses probability, usuality, obligation and inclination.

Register type of language used in a specific social context.

COMMAND TERMS

Consider think carefully about (something), before making a decision.

Discuss offer a considered and balanced review that includes a range of arguments, factors or hypotheses. Opinions or conclusions should be presented clearly and supported by appropriate evidence.

Introducing communication

How do we communicate and why is it important to consider this question?

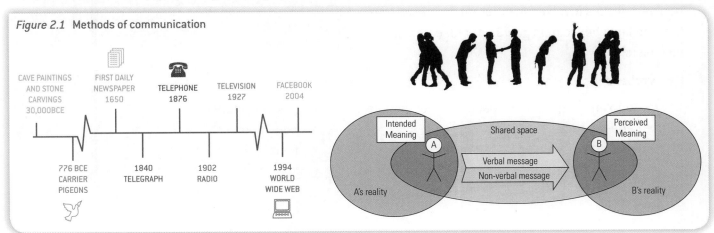

Figure 2.1 Methods of communication

CAVE PAINTINGS AND STONE CARVINGS 30,000BCE

FIRST DAILY NEWSPAPER 1650

TELEPHONE 1876

TELEVISION 1927

FACEBOOK 2004

776 BCE CARRIER PIGEONS

1840 TELEGRAPH

1902 RADIO

1994 WORLD WIDE WEB

Intended Meaning

Shared space

Perceived Meaning

A

B

Verbal message

Non-verbal message

A's reality

B's reality

The following has been adapted from the IB MYP language and literature guide:

> Communication is the exchange or transfer of facts, ideas and symbols. It requires a sender, a message and an intended receiver and a common written, spoken or non-verbal "language".

> Language is important to learning, thinking and communicating and is the basis of what makes us human and unites us all. Being a strong communicator is important for success in all societies.

One thing the images and extract here make clear is that communication is central to everything we do and the way we learn. Developing language skills in a range of contexts and situations for a variety of purposes is essential for successful communication.

Understanding the nature of communication

In these activities you will be exploring the following questions:

- What challenges does communicating across cultures create?
- What are some of the key barriers to successful communication?
- What role do verbal and non-verbal cues play in communication?
- What is the role of shared understandings in communication?
- How do our own needs, attitudes and assumptions impact on communication?

 Activity 1   **Considering cultural greetings**

Consider a common situation that focuses on the context of culture and situation—meeting and greeting people. Using the earlier images, and your own experience, brainstorm or research as many different ways of greeting people in different cultures as you can. As you do so consider specific verbal and non-verbal cues involved in different greetings. Use the web links box to help guide your research and discussion.

WEB LINKS

To learn more about cultural greetings you could research websites such as the following:

www.brucevanpatter.com Click on "Old site" and "Strange ways people greet each other".

www.ehow.com Search for "Cultural Influences on Verbal and Non-verbal Communication Styles".

Non-verbal cues

- proximity—personal space between people
- eye-contact
- gesture

- posture, stance
- body contact
- facial expression

Verbal cues

- the formality/informality of the language
- common sayings or expressions used across cultures
- how people address each other (forms of address)—title, first name, formal or informal pronouns
- the different types of language people use: questions, statements, offers and commands
- the tone of voice people adopt

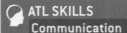
GLOBAL CONTEXTS
Personal and cultural expression

ATL SKILLS
Communication
Negotiate ideas and knowledge with peers and teachers.
Critical thinking
Draw reasonable conclusions and generalizations.
Recognize unstated assumptions and bias.

Exploring Context

The way we greet each other varies enormously both within and between different cultures or situations. It is often based on the social expectations of a culture and also how well the people involved in the greeting know each other. An awareness of context and shared understandings about how to behave often determine the success or failure of communication.

Whenever we use language there are two contexts:

1) **Context of culture**—the way things are done in a particular culture or context (ordering a meal, buying a train ticket and so on). Think about how your different classes have different cultures or ways of doing things—each with different expected behaviours.

2) **Context of situation**—three key factors:

   - The subject matter—what is being talked or written about.
   - The roles and relationships between the participants in the interaction (status, attitude, frequency of contact).
   - Whether the text is written or spoken.

Together these elements determine the language we use in any act of communication. You will be exploring these contexts in more detail throughout the coming chapters.

<aside>
QUICK THINK
What aspects of greetings are important in order to communicate successfully within a culture? How does the way we greet one another vary across cultures?
</aside>

 **Activity 2** Challenges of communication

This activity explores elements that can become barriers to communication.

STEP 1 **Pair sharing**

Think of an experience when you were unable to communicate effectively or where the message was misunderstood or misinterpreted in some way (for example, visiting a foreign country, writing an essay, explaining something in class, talking to a stranger, giving directions). Share with a partner and discuss , considering the questions below:

a) Roles—what was the status or relationship between you and your audience?

b) Mode—what was the channel of communication (written, spoken, read out, visual)?

c) How were you aware that the communication had failed?

d) How was your message interpreted differently by the other person?

e) What could you have done to make your message clearer?

f) How did you and/or the other person respond to the failure or misunderstanding?

g) What strategies did you adopt to help you communicate your message?

h) To what extent was a lack of a common understanding of the "culture"—the expected patterns of language and behaviour—the cause of the problem?

i) What would you do differently in the future to avoid similar breakdowns in communication?

j) What were the main barriers to communication?

STEP 2 With your partner, list some of the major barriers to communication. Use the headings below to organize your thoughts:

Physical barriers—noise, distractions	Emotional barriers—fear, mistrust, vulnerability, guilt
Cultural barriers—language, customs	Perceptual barriers, stereotypes, unfamiliarity
Language barriers—translation, pronunciation, **register**, **modality**	Other

🌐 **GLOBAL CONTEXTS**
Personal and cultural expression

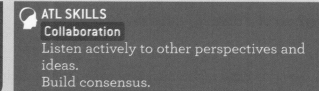 **ATL SKILLS**
Collaboration
Listen actively to other perspectives and ideas.
Build consensus.

Activity 3 | Giving instructions

Instructions can be given in different ways

This activity explores different ways of giving instructions.

STEP 1 To test your own communication skills, think of a simple task that you can give someone to do that involves them following your instructions. They must be in a classroom context.

Possible ideas to get you thinking:
- making an object out of paper—hat, boat, simple origami shape
- tying a shoelace
- tying a knot in a string or tie
- braiding hair
- juggling three balls
- opening an electronic device
- citing a reference using online help

STEP 2 Present instructions for how to complete your chosen task in three ways:

a) a written version of instructions on a sheet of paper—written

b) reading the instructions out loud as if over the phone—oral

c) a visual set of instructions outlining steps on a sheet of paper—visual.

STEP 3 Having prepared your instructions and any necessary materials, share your instructions with three different partners following the directions below.

a) Swap the written instructions with a partner and have the partner follow them.

b) Sitting back to back with a partner read out the oral instructions. They cannot ask questions but must simply follow your instructions. Be sure to speak slowly and clearly.

c) Swap the visual instructions with a partner and have the partner follow them.

STEP 4 At the end of each exchange discuss with your partner the following questions:

a) What was helpful in communicating clear instructions?

b) What prevented clear communication?

c) How could instructions have been clearer?

REFLECTION Use the following questions to reflect on the task and what you learned about communication.

- How did your language change when you had to write down the instructions?
- How did the visual images affect the clarity of the instructions?
- What does this exercise teach you about the role of context in successful communication?
- How much more difficult would this exercise have been if you were attempting an activity you did not have knowledge of or familiarity with?

This activity teaches us that success or failure of communication is determined by whether or not the recipient understands the message. It also reinforces how you need to adapt your language to suit your audience and purpose.

GLOBAL CONTEXTS
Personal and cultural expression

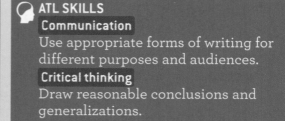

ATL SKILLS
Communication
Use appropriate forms of writing for different purposes and audiences.
Critical thinking
Draw reasonable conclusions and generalizations.

Reflection

Now that you have worked through this chapter, answer the following questions and complete the task.

a) How can you apply what you have learned about communication to different tasks you complete in different subject areas?

b) What are the biggest challenges to effective communication that you face?

c) Set yourself three SMART goals to improve your written and oral communication.

Summary

In this chapter you have explored the key concept of communication. You have looked at why it is important, how it can be used well, and the challenges we face in communicating effectively according to the context in which we wish to communicate and how this effects the language we use.

Introducing key concept 2: connections

GLOSSARY

Connections the complex relationships that are formed and developed between people and ideas.

INQUIRY QUESTIONS

- What is connected and why are connections important?
- How can analysing paintings give us insight into works of literature?
- How can analysing literary works give us insight into the paintings that have been based on them?

SKILLS

ATL

✓ Inquire in different contexts to gain a different perspective.

Language and literature

✓ Understand the development of character.

✓ Understand use of symbolism and its effects.

✓ Understand the style of an artist and how meaning is created in their work.

✓ Understand how the artwork promotes a certain reading of the play.

COMMAND TERMS

Analyse break down in order to bring out the essential elements or structure. To identify parts and relationships, and to interpret information to reach conclusions.

Comment give a judgment based on a given statement or result of a calculation.

Introducing connections

What is connected and why are **connections** important?

We live in an interrelated world in which complex relationships are in a state of continual change. Connections are the complex relationships that are formed and developed between people and ideas.

There are two main ways that the MYP encourages students to make connections outward from their subjects: learning in context and interdisciplinary learning.

Learning in context

Each of the topics you study in all of your subjects will have a global context. It provides a link between the topic and the wider world and the global dimensions of many of our current issues. It may also lead to deeper inquiry, responsible action and critical reflection, developing learner profile attributes, and finding creative solutions.

As you study a wider and wider range of global contexts you should also start to:

a) have greater global sensitivity—seeing the link between local issues and broader developments on the planet.

b) have greater global understanding—the capacity to think in flexible and informed ways about issues of global significance.

c) develop your sense of the global self—a perception of yourself as a global actor and member of humanity, capable of making a positive contribution to the world.

These three skills lead to greater global engagement.

Figure 3.1 **Each of the topics you study has a global context.**

In the Diploma Progamme there is a requirement called CAS, which means creativity, action and service. These are a range of activities alongside your academic studies to enhance your personal and interpersonal development through service projects. Engaging in service projects in the MYP will help you to develop a deeper sense of global engagement.

To conclude, global contexts comprise a range of ideas and issues that can be personally, locally, nationally, internationally and globally significant. Global contexts also:

- Make learning relevant.
- Celebrate our common humanity.
- Encourage responsibility for our shared guardianship of the planet.
- Help us become increasingly aware of our place in the world.

In addition, your teachers will also be designing topics that connect global contexts to every area of study. These topics are explained next.

Interdisciplinary learning

Interdisciplinary learning is an escape from the confining boxes on the timetable.

It can be generally defined as the process by that we come to understand bodies of knowledge and modes of thinking from two or more subject groups and integrate them to create a new understanding. It is a process that invites you to integrate concepts, theories, methods and tools from two or more disciplines to deepen your understanding of a complex topic.

You will be demonstrating interdisciplinary understanding when you can bring together concepts, methods or forms of communication from multiple established areas of expertise to explain a phenomenon, solve a problem, create a product or raise a new question in ways that would have been unlikely through single disciplinary means.

But that's enough talking. In order to understand interdisciplinary activities in practice let us do a couple.

In this activity you will be exploring the following inquiry questions:

- How can analysing paintings give us insight into works of literature?
- How can analysing literary works give us insight into the paintings that have been based on them?

INTERDISCIPLINARY LINKS
Visual art—what can we learn about literature through exploring art?

STEP 1 Study the painting on the right. It is of a famous actor playing a character in a drama.

Painted by Charles Buchel (1914)

As the subject is a protagonist in a work of literature, carefully **analyse** the work and **comment** on the following:

a) Are there any symbolic elements to the painting?

b) How are colours, light and dark used in the painting and to what effect?

c) **Comment** on outlines, lines of movement and lines of perspective (depth).

d) **Comment** on the composition of the painting, in particular the location of the central figure and the space around him.

e) What does this painting reveal about the protagonist's character?

f) The character in the painting is Macbeth. How well has the artist captured the protagonist's character based on your reading of the work?

STEP 2 Next, explore this famous scene when Macbeth and Banquo meet the three witches. Consider the paintings that follow and answer the questions about them.

WEB LINKS
Go online and enter "Act I, Scene III of Macbeth" into a search engine. You should easily be able to find the text for this scene. Read the scene and then consider the paintings that follow.

Macbeth and the Three Witches by Theodore Chasseriau (1855)

Macbeth et les sorcières by Ary Scheffer (c. 1830)

The Three Witches from Macbeth by Alexandre-Marie Colin (1827)

Answer these questions for each painting:

a) [Analyse] any symbolic elements to the painting. How are colours, light and dark used in the painting and to what effect?

b) [Comment] on the composition of the painting and where the characters are in relation to each other.

c) Which elements are being emphasized and which are being given less importance? Why do you think this is so?

d) [Comment] on outlines, lines of movement and lines of perspective (depth).

e) What does this painting reveal about how the artist wanted to portray the witches?

f) How well does this fit with the perception of witches in Shakespeare's time and with your perception of the witches' role and character?

g) Where they are present, decide on which character is Macbeth and which is Banquo. In what way are these characters presented? Does this presentation fit with your perception of their character? Justify your opinion.

h) To what extent do you consider this artist's interpretation of this scene an accurate representation of it? Justify your opinion.

GLOBAL CONTEXTS
Personal and cultural expression

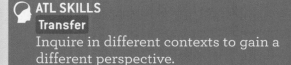

ATL SKILLS
Transfer
Inquire in different contexts to gain a different perspective.

Exercises like this can be done with all types of art. You will need to modify your questions, though, depending on the work.

TIP

For more information on studying paintings in visual arts see: Mittler, GA. 1988. "The Elements of Art". *Art in Focus*. McGraw-Hill/Glencoe.

In this activity you will study the effects of migration. As language and literature students you will read the poem *Piano and Drums* by Gabriel Okara in the context of post-colonial Nigeria. You will also view this activity from the context of Individuals and Societies. Answer the questions that follow the poem.

> **∞ INTERDISCIPLINARY LINKS**
> Your individuals and societies teacher will select a range of resources on migration and colonialism, to inform your reading of the poem that follows.

Does the impact of one culture upon another look like this?
Do you have another image in your head?

Piano and Drums by Gabriel Okara

When at break of day at a riverside
I hear the jungle drums telegraphing
the mystic rhythm, urgent, raw
like bleeding flesh, speaking of
primal youth and the beginning
I see the panther ready to pounce
the leopard snarling about to leap
and the hunters crouch with spears poised;

And my blood ripples, turns torrent,
topples the years and at once I'm
in my mother's laps a suckling;
at once I'm walking simple
paths with no innovations,
rugged, fashioned with the naked
warmth of hurrying feet and groping hearts
in green leaves and wild flowers pulsing.

Then I hear a wailing piano
solo speaking of complex ways in
tear-furrowed concerto;
of far away lands
and new horizons with
coaxing diminuendo, counterpoint,
crescendo. But lost in the labyrinth
of its complexities, it ends in the middle
of a phrase at a daggerpoint.

And I lost in the morning mist
of an age at a riverside keep
wandering in the mystic rhythm
of jungle drums and the concerto.

As you explore the poem consider the following questions:
  a) What does the piano symbolize?
  b) What does the drum symbolize?
  c) How does the narrator react to the drum?

d) How does the narrator react to the piano?

e) Describe what the moments of pain, sadness or danger reveal.

f) Describe the change of rhythm in the poem.

g) What is the poet saying about cultural difference?

From your understanding of individuals and societies consider:

h) How accurately does the poem reflect the clash of cultures that may occur during migration?

i) To what extent does Gabriel Okara echo your perceptions or experience of migration?

Now, bringing both subjects together:

j) Which has a greater impact on you, exploring the facts of migration, or the emotional response through poetry?

GLOBAL CONTEXTS
Identities and relationships

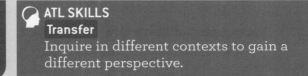
ATL SKILLS
Transfer
Inquire in different contexts to gain a different perspective.

Reflection

Look back over the chapter and think about how this interdisciplinary topic can add to, deepen and strengthen your learning. Also consider the advantage of an interdisciplinary topic here as compared to a single subject topic.

Summary

By connecting subjects we can deepen the learning as you have seen with the activities here on *Macbeth* and migration/colonialism. The following task asks you to apply the same key concept as you reflect back on these activities.

a) For the activity on *Macbeth,* choose another school subject and topic from the timetable that could further deepen your understanding of this play.

b) For the activity on migration/colonialism, choose another school subject from the timetable that could allow you to express what you have learned about this topic in a creative way.

c) Consider the units you have already explored in language and literature. What other connections could be made to other subjects from them that could potentially deepen the learning?

References

Okara, G. 1985 *Piano and Drums.* In *Touched with Fire: An Anthology of Poems* compiled by Jack Hyde. UK. Cambridge University Press.

Introducing key concept 3: creativity

INQUIRY QUESTIONS	

INQUIRY QUESTIONS

■ **How and why do we create?**

■ **How can we use the design cycle in language and literature?**

■ **How can our creativity be used to entertain others?**

SKILLS

ATL

✓ Communicate information and ideas effectively to multiple audiences using a variety of media and formats.

Language and literature

✓ Work effectively in small groups.

✓ Create original works and ideas.

✓ Organize work appropriately for your audience.

GLOSSARY

Apex the top, highest point or summit.

Gamebooks fiction where the reader makes choices that affect the plot of the story.

Pun a play on words that uses words with the same or similar meanings or sounds, usually for humorous effect.

COMMAND TERMS

Create to evolve from one's own thought or imagination, as a work or an invention.

Organize Put ideas and information into a proper or systematic order.

Introducing creativity

How and why do we create?

Creativity is the process of creating something new and original, approaching an idea or issue in a different way. It is characterized by expressiveness and imagination.

Creativity may include recombination or building upon the ideas of others. If this is the case, you should acknowledge your sources, by creating a bibliography.

If you completed the quick think activity here, you have taken part in the creative process, just as you have done many times before across several subjects. If the creation is a painting, a piece of music or an invention it most probably lies outside of the scope of language and literature; however, activities such as creative writing are very important in this subject.

QUICK THINK

Search online for "Homonym: nearly 150 words with more than one meaning" or simply research homonyms. Try to think of an original (and clean) joke that uses homonyms. Make a **pun**. Tell your joke to the class and vote on the best ones.

The importance of creativity

Anne Bamford, Director of the Engine Room project at the University of the Arts London, says:

> *Creativity is a way of thinking. If you ask "What's three plus three?" the answer is always six. But if you ask "What is six?" you're turning the task around to get to a different way of thinking that goes beyond the subject. It could be two plus four. It could be half a dozen eggs to make a pavlova. It could be anything.*

To give you an idea of how important creativity is, there is a pyramid-shaped model used in education called Bloom's Taxonomy that defines learning objectives (figure 4.1).

Creativity is at the top of the diagram. Or, we could say, at its **apex**.

As an MYP student, being creative can be seen as the ultimate expression of educational achievement. It is also part of what it means to be human.

Simply the way a question is phrased can change creative thinking. A lot depends on how you look at things.

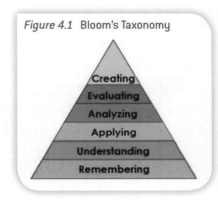

Figure 4.1 Bloom's Taxonomy

 Activity 1   **Creative writing: gamebooks**

In **gamebooks** you enter the world of the author's imagination. Your decisions change the plot and allow for multiple endings. As gamebooks often take you into dangerous imaginary situations, you must choose wisely or terrible things can happen to you.

Many people see creativity as an individual thing. This activity treats creativity as a class project.

In this activity you will be creating an adventure novel using the following stages:

Investigate: You will read a range of gamebooks and analyse them, breaking them down into their separate parts.

Plan and create: You will then construct one of your own role-playing/adventure novels in an electronic format using programs of your choice. This will include characters, plot and the creation of a convincing genre/setting for the adventure. You will break down your e-novel into parts with different individuals responsible for creating different sections in the chosen program.

Create (continued): You then present this e-novel to an MYP 1, 2 or 3 group, who will then attempt to complete it successfully.

Evaluate: The MYP 1, 2 or 3 students will complete a survey on their reactions to the e-novel. You can then make changes before the final assessment.

STEP 1 **Investigate**

Analyse one or more gamebooks/adventure novels. Consider the following questions:

a) Which genre did the adventure novel use?

b) How convincing was it?

c) How well-developed was the protagonist/main character?

d) Explain why this worked/did not work.

e) How well-developed was/were the antagonist(s)/villains?

f) Explain why this worked/did not work.

g) Which parts of the plot/action were well done? Why?

h) Which parts of the plot/action were disappointing/poorly done? Why?

STEP 2 **Plan and create**

You will now construct one or more of your own gamebooks in the chosen electronic format. Elements to include:

- An opening—set the scene.
- The setting—this must be realistic, convincing and accurate to the genre you have created. For example, a vampire hunt might be set in the Carpathian Mountains of Romania.
- Outline your hero/heroes. Try to develop them a little as the story unfolds. Make sure you invent them—no new adventure for Harry Potter, for example.
- The plot—the story will have dead ends and failure. There may be one way to reach the end, or more.
- Reward clever thinking—design the choices so that those completing your adventure advance if they think carefully.
- Punish silly decisions—if the readers make unconsidered choices, send them back to the start to begin again.
- Balance—don't make it too difficult, or too easy.
- The ending/resolution—conclude the story for those who will reach the end. Praise their success.

Now assign different sections of the story to different members of your group.

STEP 3 **Create and present**

You may choose to illustrate your work with images from the Internet, though be careful that they are consistent. Work through your e-novel with the target group.

STEP 4 **Evaluate**

Use the same survey questions for those who complete your adventure that you used to review the published adventure novel (from Step 1).

Example of an adventure novel

Here is an example of what one group chose to do:
A sole surviving member of an elite US unit…

…is battling across a modern-day New York in ruins, to destroy a mysterious space portal that has opened up on Wall Street, the home of the New York Stock Exchange.

All types of alien creatures, some flying, some walking, some crawling, are coming out of the portal. Among them is an intelligent species with technology superior to that on Earth.

On the way, our heroine meets all types of monsters, who mostly want to eat her.

⃝⃝ INTERDISCIPLINARY LINKS

Instead of using images from the Internet to illustrate your e-novel, you could create your own images in visual art instead. Perhaps they could be done in the style of a black and white cartoon. Alternatively, you could compose some atmospheric music to be playing in the background as you present your adventure to your audience.

Continuing with the example, six students decide to work on this project and they divide the work as follows:

Beginning

- Student 1 writes the introduction to the character and the scenario.

Middle: crossing New York

- Student 2 writes about the journey through Brooklyn to the East River.
- Student 3 writes about the choice to try to cross the East River by boat.
- Student 4 writes about the choice to cross over the Brooklyn Bridge.
- Student 5 writes about the choice to try to go through the subway tunnels of Clark Street Station to Wall Street Station (during a power cut).

End

- Student 6 writes about the final confrontation at the alien portal.

 **TAKE ACTION**

After you have presented your story within your school, consider whether you could present it to children in the wider community, perhaps as part of a service programme.

GLOBAL CONTEXTS
Personal and cultural expression

ATL SKILLS
 **Media literacy**
Communicate information and ideas effectively to multiple audiences using a variety of media and formats.

Reflection

Check your understanding of this key concept. Has it inspired you to be creative? How successful was your e-novel? Consider the following questions.

    a) What were the main challenges in writing an adventure novel?

    b) How effectively did you organize yourselves as a group?

    c) What would you do differently next time?

Summary

In this chapter we have looked at the concept of creativity, how and why it is important, and how you can use it to communicate with and entertain a range of audiences using a variety of different mediums. Thinking creatively can be applied to a range of contexts and problems, not just the obvious creative industries who inspire and engage with their application of creative flair on a daily basis. As you apply the creative skills you have explored in this chapter you will begin to discover how creativity can expand how you look at approach problem solving and equip you with the tools and confidence to think outside the box.

Introducing key concept 4: perspective

INQUIRY QUESTIONS	▪ **What is the difference between sympathy and empathy?** ▪ **How does your perspective colour your view of the world?** ▪ **How much empathy and perspective is necessary to live in today's world?**
SKILLS	**ATL** ✓ Recognize unstated assumptions and bias. ✓ Consider ideas from multiple perspectives. ✓ Listen actively to other perspectives and ideas. ✓ Consider ethical, cultural and environmental implications. ✓ Practise empathy. ✓ Use a variety of speaking techniques to communicate with a variety of audiences. ✓ Gather and organize relevant information to formulate an argument. ✓ Access information to be informed and inform others. **Language and literature** ✓ Evaluate evidence and arguments. ✓ Seek a range of perspectives from multiple and varied sources.

GLOSSARY

Empathy the skill of having a good sense or understanding of what another is going through.

Stooge one who allows oneself to be used for another's profit or advantage; a puppet.

Sympathy recognizing a person's suffering and offering emotional support or assistance.

COMMAND TERMS

Discuss offer a considered and balanced review that includes a range of arguments, factors or hypotheses. Opinions or conclusions should be presented clearly and supported by appropriate evidence.

Justify give valid reasons or evidence to support an answer or conclusion.

Summarize abstract a general theme or major point(s).

Try a new strategy! Try using role-play and debate as a study technique. For example, if you are reviewing your notes on World War II, why not get together with classmates and stage your own debate? Become Stalin, Churchill, Mussolini, Hitler and Truman (or add other world leaders from the time). You will have to use perspective and, most importantly, you will practise the highest levels of Bloom's Taxonomy (analysis, evaluation and synthesis) while increasing your understanding.

Introducing perspective

What is perspective and why is it important?

The Middle Years Programme will require you to form your own perspective on a variety of issues and viewpoints across your disciplines. For example, you might have to debate the impacts of Science from a variety of viewpoints, "get into character" in a dramatic performance, compare different definitions of "healthy" in Physical and Health education, or analyse sources in Individuals and Societies to determine whose perspective is most reliable.

The key concept of perspective is critical to a language and literature learner since so many of the related concepts rest upon this conceptual foundation. You cannot determine an author's purpose very successfully if you cannot move from the perspective of a reader to the perspective of a writer. This is a critical shift when creating a thesis statement for literary analysis. Additionally, you cannot discuss an author's plot construction in nearly as much depth if you cannot see the perspectives of various characters.

However, as you enter into the Action phase of the Inquiry Cycle, you will have to recognize different perspectives in order to successfully collaborate, plan and reach your goal.

Without a sense of perspective, it is difficult to understand other people in a deep and meaningful way. There is the risk of only understanding them in a superficial (surface) or stereotypical (conventional) way. A vital skill in understanding perspectives is **empathy**.

Though complete empathy is impossible, it is a deeper feeling than **sympathy**. With sympathy we may feel sorry for a person's problems, whereas when we have empathy with someone it is more of an active process of understanding how they feel and identifying with their situation. As empathy is a skill, it is something that we can continually refine and improve in.

Empathy is not just about understanding the lives of other humans, it is also an intimate awareness with the other creatures we share this planet with, many of whom are increasingly threatened by humans encroaching into their habitats.

Activity 1   The difference between empathy and sympathy

Watch the video in the web links box and answer the following questions:

a) How can empathy help us survive as a species?

b) What does the video mean by 'to empathise is to civilise'?

c) Why are nations 'fictions'?

d) Can technology extend empathy worldwide?

WEB LINKS
Go to www.thersa.org and enter "The Empathetic Civilisation" into the search box. Alternatively go to www.youtube.com and enter "RSA Animate — The Empathetic Civilisation" into the search box.

GLOBAL CONTEXTS
Globalization and sustainability

ATL SKILLS
Critical thinking
Recognize unstated assumptions and bias. Consider ideas from multiple perspectives.

 **Activity 2**   Why is consideration of perspective so important when acting to better a community?

Background

What follows is an example of a 16-year-old from Pakistan whose action involved taking on a group she deemed to be terrorizing her school and limiting her educational opportunities. This eventually made her a candidate for the Nobel Peace Prize for 2013—the youngest candidate in the history of the award.

Malala Yousafzai has been hailed as a hero for surviving a Taliban gun wound to the head and writing a book designed to guarantee the right of education in her community. She has appeared on many international news networks and media. But, as the *New York Times* investigated further into the story, they found that, though Malala has been well received in the west, there are those from her own community and country who see her as a "western **stooge**" and question what she has done for their hometown.

Directions

STEP 1 In common groups, read or view one of the three articles/videos on Malala Yousafzai shown in the web links box.

STEP 2 Discuss your article for understanding and determine what perspectives you would offer to a group who has not read/viewed it.

STEP 3 Move into heterogeneous (diverse) discussion groups with members representing each of the three articles/videos.

STEP 4 In your discussion, focus on the guiding question on perspective for the activity as well as the questions that follow. Compare your different points of view on the issue.

a)  the main idea of your article/video and the perspective(s) it gave on Malala.

b) Justify: Is Malala a hero? What is a hero and what do you think a person should have to do to win the Nobel Peace Prize?

c) To what extent does the perspective and purpose of each news source impact upon the message we received?

🔗 **WEB LINKS**

1) *The Daily Show* with Jon Stewart, October, 2013. Go to www.youtube.com and search for "The Daily Show: Extended Interview: Malala Yousafzai".
2) *The New York Times*, October 2013. Go to www.nytimes.com and search for "Pakistani Girl, a Global Heroine After an Attack, Has Critics at Home".
3) *Huffington Post*, July 2013. Go to www.huffingtonpost.co.uk and search for "Malala Yousafzai and the White Saviour Complex".
(Extension Reading: Go to medidiversified.org and search for "A Reply to: Malala Yousafzai and the White Saviour Complex", October, 2013).

🌐 **GLOBAL CONTEXTS**
Identities and relationships

🧠 **ATL SKILLS**
Collaboration
Listen actively to other perspectives and ideas.
Reflection
Consider ethical, cultural and environmental implications.

👥 **Activity 3**   **Dead Poet's Society and standing on a new desk**

STEP 1 Watch the two-minute scene from the film *Dead Poet's Society* (see the web link box). The scene shows the teacher, played by Robin Williams, pushing his English class to 'look at things in a different way'—pushing them to seek different perspectives. His main point is that, as you explore the views of others and seek to understand them, you are more likely to find your own voice. MYP students who firmly develop an understanding of the key concept of perspective will be blessed with greater empathy for others and greater understanding of themselves.

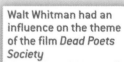
Walt Whitman had an influence on the theme of the film *Dead Poets Society*

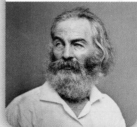

🔗 **WEB LINKS**
Watch the clip from *Dead Poet's Society*. Go to www.youtube.com and search for "The Universe is wider than our views of it (Thoreau)".

STEP 2 **Stand on a new desk**

Today after class, move to a new perspective or viewpoint that you have not considered previously. For example, move to a different view of the cafeteria, or your neighbourhood. Or interview someone you have never spoken to before, but who you see often. Sketch, photograph, describe or summarize what you saw. Be ready to offer your new perspective when you return to class.

STEP 3 **Demographic grid**

Create this Demographic grid in your notebook or computer and fill out your demographic details then describe a time when this has impacted upon your perspective, either influencing your perspective on a situation or someone else's perspective on you.

Example: My socio-economic level is middle class. But, my father lost his job when I was a child and we had to go without a lot of the comforts we had previously experienced. It wasn't so much hardship, but I could see how the financial strain put a lot of added pressure on my parents during that time period and it built some empathy for classmates whose parents had to deal with that pressure all of the time.

My demographic details		
Gender	Ethnicity	Socio-economic background
Nationality	Generation	Religion (optional)
Time when this impacted upon my perspective:		

STEP 4 **60-second sharing**

Be ready to share your experiences with members of the class who differ from you in terms of their demographics.

Follow up questions:

a) How much do our demographics define us?

b) How often do we presume a person's perspective based upon their background?

c) Are there better ways to find out and understand a person's perspective?

STEP 5 **Taking action through a "stand on your own desk" oral presentation**

Structure:

The oral assignment takes the structure of a presentation given to fellow students. Your teacher can give you more information about how it can be assessed.

- Part one: Address a viewpoint that you have long held without investigating an alternative perspective.
- Part two: Inquire into and present an alternative perspective with a particular focus on overcoming personal bias and building empathy.

GLOBAL CONTEXTS
Identities and relationships

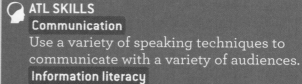

ATL SKILLS
Communication
Use a variety of speaking techniques to communicate with a variety of audiences.
Information literacy
Access information to be informed and inform others.

Reflection

Now that you have worked through this chapter, consider the following questions:

a) Whose perspectives do you understand most in society? Whose do you struggle to be open-minded about?

b) What is the difference between empathy and sympathy?

c) How much empathy and perspective is necessary to live in today's world? Can too much empathy be a bad thing?

Summary

In this chapter you have learnt about the importance of perspective in shaping and colouring how you as an individual view the world and your relation to it. You have also explored sympathy and empathy and how it is necessary to apply these to your daily encounters and problems so that you may understand the people, environment and challenges you encounter in a meaningful way.

CHAPTER 6

Genre and conventions

INQUIRY QUESTIONS

TOPIC 1 Genre conventions

- **How can the type of genre used affect the message delivered through it?**

TOPIC 2 Exploring a theme in audio/visual media

- **How can we choose a stand from different perspectives delivered through audio/visual media?**

TOPIC 3 Exploring a theme in articles

- **How can we choose a stand from different perspectives delivered through articles?**

SKILLS

ATL

✓ Read critically and for comprehension.

✓ Demonstrate awareness of media interpretations of events and ideas.

Language and literature

✓ Analyse the content, context, language, structure, technique and style of text(s) and the relationships among texts.

✓ Analyse the effects of the creator's choices on an audience.

✓ Evaluate similarities and differences by connecting features across and within genres and texts.

✓ Write and speak in a register and style that serve the context and intention.

✓ Use appropriate non-verbal communication techniques.

OTHER RELATED CONCEPTS

Context   **Style**   **Theme**

GLOSSARY

Diary entry a diary entry is intimate and introspective, not meant to be read by anyone else but the writer. A diary is used to express feelings and is reflective and often emotional. The language of a diary will reflect some of these aspects.

Fiction genres drama, fable, fairytales, short stories, legends, poetry and science fiction.

Non-fiction genres autobiographies, biographies, essays, informational texts, narrative non-fiction and speech.

Review a review should not retell the plot, but should include an amount of information about the film, book, play. Opinion and evaluation should be given, concluding with a recommendation, which might be implicit or explicit.

COMMAND TERMS

Compare to estimate, measure, or note the similarity or dissimilarity between.

Interpret explain the meaning of.

Introducing genre and conventions

Differentiating between different genres (or text types) is very important in language and literature. If you want to communicate any piece of information, you have to express it in a certain way in order to deliver the message you intended. Genre writing challenges you to consider everything that's interesting and difficult about writing; it pushes you to think about:

- the purpose of your message
- the person you are delivering it to
- the content of the message
- the situation you are in.

These things affect the way you approach your own writing, your tone or voice and your choice of words and sentences.

The term most synonymous (compatible) with genre is text types. When you study genre you study different types of texts whether oral, visual or written. Genre refers to a type of literature and can be categorized into **fiction** and **non-fiction**. Non-fiction genres include types like autobiographies, biographies, essays, informational texts, narrative non-fiction and speech. While fiction genres include types like drama, fable, fairytales, short stories, legends, poetry and science fiction. Genres are identified by their own features. Each genres has specific features that identify it and make it unique in delivering its message.

TOPIC 1

Genre conventions

Genres are identified by their own conventions. Each genre has specific conventions that identify it and make it unique in delivering its message. Conventions are linguistic and non-linguistic features that identify a certain genre.

To master writing different genres you have to be able to identify and use different genre features.

In this topic you will be exploring four narrative texts that all have the same theme, "What is beauty?" Each text has different features to match the genre it belongs to.

Diary entries

The following information will help you when analysing or writing a **diary entry**.

Diary entries make use of certain genre features

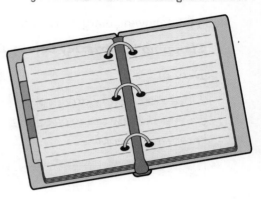

Social purpose

The purpose of a diary entry is to express your attitude towards a certain event that happened through the day.

Structure

- A topic sentence indicating what the paragraph is going to speak about could be good to keep your ideas organized.

- It can start with an orientation providing information about who, what, where and when.

- It usually recounts events in chronological order, but a flashback about something that happened before it could be useful.

- There are a lot of personal comments and/or evaluative remarks interspersed throughout the diary.

- At the end there is a "round-off" for the event.

Grammar and style

- Usually informal literary style.

- Use of action verbs to refer to events. For example: browse, pick, take.

- Use of past time tenses. For example: the next shop I visited, she told me, she came.

- Use of time connectives in order to organize the sequence of events. For example: In the meantime, then, after that, first.

- A lot of idiomatic expressions and use of everyday language. For example: check out, in fact, not to mention.

- Use of descriptive language and descriptive details, which include:

  o very detailed description of a certain action

  o a lot of adjectives to describe the place, the people or the events involved

  o use of senses to describe something thoroughly.

TIP

Idiomatic expressions are combinations or collocations of words that when put together give another meaning. The meanings of those expressions are common and well known by users of the language. There are both formal and informal idiomatic expressions. Phrasal verbs and idioms, for instance, are regarded as idiomatic because the meaning cannot be worked out from the definitions of the individual words.

Read the following diary entry and answer the questions that follow.

Shopping in Paris: My Beauty Diary, a website by the New York Times Company

Dear diary,

I love Paris. Every day I spend here I discover something new. Today I did not join the group. Instead I spent the day alone <u>checking out</u> new products, sipping latte, <u>people watching,</u> and meeting interesting people.

My first stop was at an interesting little shop called "Crabtree and Evelyn". There were so many interesting items, I hardly knew where to start; <u>in fact,</u> I could have browsed all day. The displays in the store are <u>artfully arranged</u> and I found myself taking a tour of the space at least twice, trying to choose what products I would <u>leave the store with</u>. Maria Thomas, the store's manager, was extremely helpful and took time to explain about the hair care line that the <u>store carried</u> and offered three generous samples to try.

So what did I leave the store with?? Two bars of soap that I can't wait to try. I love the scent of fresh roses and lily of the valley and these two soaps were as close to the scent of fresh flowers as <u>you can possibly get</u>. And, the Rosewater soap also contains cold cream. Does <u>this sound like luxury</u> to you??

Enchante, this was the next shop I visited. It was a tiny shop but it <u>was wall to wall perfumes!</u> The scent alone will <u>lure you into</u> this interesting little shop, <u>not to mention</u> the feast of colors that will overwhelm you. <u>Within seconds</u>, a very nice young lady by the name of Anita was <u>at my side</u>, offering help. She told me the new line called "Mechanics for Women" offers several products to choose from. I <u>picked out</u> three that looked interesting to me and Anita was extremely helpful . I asked her for the hottest scents of the summer and she <u>pointed me</u> to "Romance" by Ralph Lauren, "J'Adore" by Christian Dior, and "Allure" by Chanel.

After two hours of shopping, I wanted to have something to drink in an outdoor caffe' where I can watch people walking along the street. A <u>50ish year</u> old woman who was probably dark haired in her youth and was trying to duplicate the same color as she aged. <u>Didn't work.</u> It was too evident that the color came from a bottle and her hair cut was too severe for her features. She should have picked a dark brown instead of the black and she needed a softer hair style. Remember dear diary ....as we age, we need to go lighter with our hair color. In most cases, black simply doesn't work!

I was not only <u>dazzling around</u> shops and products, but I also met some interesting people. A young Asian woman that I spotted in Fairview Mall amazed me by her long gorgeous black hair with scarlet (not red) streaks in her hair. It looked fabulous. While this style is not going to work for all of us it really worked with her coloring!! I came closer to her and started a conversation saying; "Hello mam, I am sorry, but I <u>couldn't miss</u> your unique hair style. Did you manage to get such a beautiful hair style in Paris." She turned to me and we soon started a conversation about hair styles, cloths, fashion, <u>you name it</u>. Unfortunately, she had to leave after half an hour, as she was just on a lunch break and had to go back to work.

That was all for today dear diary. Tomorrow the group wants to go to more site seeing. I don't know if I will join them. You know I'm not the type.

Answer the following questions. Support your answers with evidence from the text.

a) What is this type of writing (genre)?

b) What is its purpose?

c) What is the level of formality?

d) What do the shaded sentences have in common?

e) The underlined words are idiomatic expressions. How do they affect the author's expression of ideas?

f) Choose three idiomatic expressions that you would use in your own diary entry.

GLOBAL CONTEXTS
Personal and cultural expression

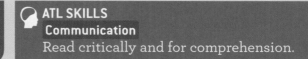
ATL SKILLS
Communication
Read critically and for comprehension.

News reports

The following information will help you when analysing or writing news reports.

Social purpose

The purpose of a news report is to document a series of events that happened and evaluate their significance.

Structure

- Usually starts with an orientation providing information about who, what, where and when.

- A record of events that is usually recounted in chronological (time) order.

- Personal comments and/or evaluative remarks interspersed throughout the record of events.

- A reorientation which rounds off the sequence of events.

Grammar and style

- Serious, informative, formal style or semi-formal style depending on the type of audience.

- If formal it would have advanced vocabulary and sentences in the passive.

- Use of action verbs to refer to events.

- Use of past time tenses.

- No literary style.

- Description is factual.

Read the following news report then answer the questions that follow.

Actress dies after plastic surgery heart accident by Simon de Bruxelles

AN ASPIRING actress died when her heart was accidentally punctured during cosmetic surgery to correct her protruding chin. The eight-hour operation to correct the alignment of 20-year-old Alexandra Mills's upper jaw had been summoned as a success by surgeons. But, unknown to the medical team, a fine tube inserted to monitor her blood pressure had pierced the wall of her heart. When Ms Mills was given an injection of potassium the next day to aid her recovery the drug leaked through the hole in her heart and triggered a cardiac arrest that led to irreversible brain damage.

Alan Crickmore, the Gloucestershire Coroner, said that Ms Mills's death had been a "terrible coincidence", for which doctors were not to blame. After the hearing her mother, Jane Mills, said: "She'd always wanted to go on the stage. When she was little she was teased at school because of her chin, so she didn't want to let it stand in the way of her career."

The operation was part of a long-term surgical plan to correct her jaw line. In June 2002 she had eight teeth removed, then in February last year she underwent the main procedure to break and reset her jaw line. The operation was carried out at Cheltenham General Hospital. John Harrison, a consultant surgeon, said that the procedure had been carried out successfully for 25 years. He added: "The procedure was to separate her upper jaw from the rest of her facial bone so that the teeth met in the correct position. There were no problems during surgery and we were all pleased at that stage with the result." However, at some time during surgery or Ms Mills's recovery, the central venous line that had been inserted into her heart moved and caused a small tear. The next day, while Ms Mills was still heavily sedated, the potassium injected to restore an imbalance in her blood flooded the area around her heart and stopped it.

She suffered massive brain damage and died four days after the operation. A postmortem examination showed the cause of death to be oxygen shortage to the brain due to an arrhythmia in the heart, caused by the potassium.

Recording a verdict of accidental death, Mr Crickmore said that there had been "no human control" over the death. "She was the unfortunate victim of an unusual event — the terrible coincidence created by the beating of her heart and the potassium acting against the best interests of her heart."

a) Match the formal vocabulary (underlined in the text) with a substituting informal word:

1)	aspiring	a.	sticking out
2)	punctured	b.	knocked out
3)	protruding	c.	poured out
4)	summoned	d.	pierced
5)	leaked	e.	called upon (called as)
6)	aid	f.	would-be
7)	triggered	g.	huge
8)	irreversible	h.	help
9)	sedated	i.	lasting
10)	massive	j.	caused

b) Find how many of the following connecting words are in the news report:

after – but – due to – then – the next day – however

c) [Compare] the news report above to the diary entry in the previous activity. Decide whether the following features are the same or different.

i) Purpose:  same different
ii) Audience: same different
iii) Level of formality: same different
iv) Outline and organization of ideas: same different
v) Type of sentences: same different
vi) Idiomatic expressions: same different

d) What is this type of writing (genre)? Support your answer with evidence from the text.

e) What is its purpose? Support your answer with evidence from the text.

f) What is the level of formality? Support your answer with evidence from the text.

g) Is formal vocabulary used in the quotations? Why/why not?

h) Look at the sentences that have been shaded. Describe them and say why you think they are formed this way.

🌐 **GLOBAL CONTEXTS**
Personal and cultural expression

💭 **ATL SKILLS**
Communication
Read critically and for comprehension.

Short Stories

The following information will help you when analysing or writing short stories.

Social purpose

The purpose of a short story is most probably to entertain through a piece of writing that contains literary elements like characters, setting, plot and so on.

Structure

- Paragraphs are not a regular length or type. Sometimes you find a dialogue, then a short paragraph of description, then maybe a telling of a series of events and so on.

- It can start with an orientation providing information about (the setting) who, what, where and when, but it could change this order by starting with a dialogue between two of the characters or a description of one of the characters' feelings, for example. Also there could be flashbacks.

Grammar and style

- Usually informal, literary style.
- Use of action verbs to refer to events.
- Use of past time tenses.
- Use of descriptive language and descriptive details, which include:
  - very detailed description of a certain action
  - a lot of adjectives to describe the place, the people or the events involved
  - use of senses to describe something thoroughly.

 Activity 3   **Exploring short stories**

Read the following short story then answer the questions that follow.

A Happy Ending **by Rebecca Ashmore**

At 10:25, Kim got out of her chair and <u>paced across</u> the examining room for at least the tenth time. She was clearly nervous, frightened. She grabbed the ties of the blue-checked bathrobe she was wearing and pulled them tight, then crossed her arms and hugged them to her chest.

Kim had every right to be nervous. She was about to have a face lift and eyelid surgery. It's not just the surgery that she feared, although that's scary enough, but the change. It was, after all, her face—her self, <u>in a way.</u> How will she look? What will people say? Will she wish she hadn't done it? It's so permanent, so drastic! Will she like whom she becomes?

The room was cold, despite the August day gathering steam outside, but the temperature was not her main concern. She looked at the nurse sitting on her stool in the corner.

"I'm scared," she said. "Should I be scared?"

"Of course," the nurse said.

"Everyone's scared. It's only sensible to be scared. If you weren't scared, we'd be worried about you." Sandy, the nursing supervisor, came into the room. Kim asked her the same question and got <u>more or less</u> the same answer.

"In fifteen minutes," Sandy said, "this is all going to look a lot better."

Kim went into the operation room for four hours. Dr. Wallace was telling stories as he worked, joking with the technicians. Finally he left to consult with new patients. The technicians finished the last of the sewing, putting in the fine touches just below the lower eyelashes.

Kim was beginning to wake up. The nurses found her clothes, <u>stuffing her into</u> the loose knit pants and shirt in which she arrived early this morning. They held up her legs, first one, then the other, as they dressed her, and then found her shoes. Julie and Martha wrapped her head in a large absorbent dressing, with another one across her eyes. She looked a bit like a mummy.

Kim said "What time is it?" They told her, almost 3 o'clock. "Ooooh, that long?" she said.

Martha and Julie <u>sat her up</u>, warning her about possible dizziness. She was fine, and so they put her into a wheelchair and wheeled her into the hall. Her sister was there to <u>pick her up.</u> She was given explicit instructions on how to care for Kim and what to do if there are any problems.

Dr. Wallace sat tiredly on a stool at the nurses' station, turned to the sister and said, "She did fine. We did a really nice job on her." The doctor took her hand and squeezed it. "That's my girl!" he said. "Go home and heal. Leave Kim's story here."

a) Read the short story *A Happy Ending* and compare it to the diary entry and the news report in the two previous activities. Decide whether the following features are the same or different.

   i) Purpose: same   different
   ii) Audience: same   different
   iii) Level of formality: same   different
   iv) Outline and organization of ideas: same   different
   v) Type of sentences: same   different
   vi) Idiomatic expressions: same   different

b) What do you think is the difference between a diary entry and a story? Support your answer with evidence from the text.

c) What do the two shaded sentences have in common?

d) What do the underlined words have in common?

 **GLOBAL CONTEXTS**
Personal and cultural expression

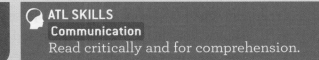 **ATL SKILLS**
Communication
Read critically and for comprehension.

Reflection

Consider the following:

- What did you learn by exploring different genres?

- How did it add to your knowledge and understanding of language and literature?

- How are you going to use what you learned in your own work?

TOPIC 2

Exploring a theme in audio visual media

Authors have their own perspective in seeing a certain theme. Each author chooses the genre that best delivers what needs to be communicated to the audience. It is the ability of the author in using genre features effectively that lets the audience see what they see. In this topic you will explore how different genres can approach a certain theme differently. The theme is "Life perception and career choices". The theme is about how people see life choices differently. For example, some see it as a choice and others see it as destiny, some believe in hard work while others believe in enjoying life. In this topic you will study how this theme has been tackled in the audio/visual media of films and songs.

 Activity 4   **The theme in songs**

STEP 1   Listen to the song in the web links box and answer the questions that follow.

a) What is the songwriters' perception about life and career choices?

b) How do the following words and phrases reinforce the song writers' perception about life and career choices? I am dreaming – faith is shaking – keep my head held high – uphill battle – the climb – I'm not breaking – keep going – got to be strong.

c) What other genre (song) features, like music, rhythm, and so on contribute to reinforcing the theme here?

> **WEB LINKS**
> Go to www.youtube.com and search for "The Climb by Miley Cyrus".
> Songwriters: Jessi Alexander; Jon Mabe

STEP 2   Listen to the next song in the web links box below and answer the questions that follow.

a) What is the songwriters' perception about life and career choices?

b) How do the following words and phrases reinforce the song writers' perception about life and career choices? Seize the moment – tomorrow's gonna come your way – beautiful life – walk in the park when you feel down – lift you up – laughing child – someone to guide you.

c) What other genre (song) features, like music, rhythm, and so on contribute to reinforcing the theme here?

d) How does the song portray life? Is this portrayal of life the same or different to the theme of the previous song "The Climb"?

> **WEB LINKS**
> Go to www.youtube.com and search for "Beautiful Life by Ace of Base".
> Songwriters: Jonas Berggren, John Ballard

After listening to the two songs consider the following:

a) Did the music add to the clarification of the theme? How?

b) Did the music video add to the clarification of the theme? How?

c) What can be the genre features (elements) of an audiovisual genre?

GLOBAL CONTEXTS
Personal and cultural expression

ATL SKILLS
Media literacy
Demonstrate awareness of media interpretations of events and ideas.

 Activity 5 The theme in the film *Jerry Maguire*

In this activity you will be analysing quotes and an extract from the 90s film *Jerry Maguire.*

STEP 1 Read the following quotes from the film and interpret what the main themes of the film could be.

Quotes by the main character:

- *I'm cloaked in failure! I lost the number one draft* pick the night before the draft! Why? Let's recap: Because a hockey player's kid made me feel like a superficial jerk. I ate two slices of bad pizza, went to bed and grew a conscience!*

- *I will not rest until I have you holding a Coke, wearing your own shoe, playing a Sega game featuring you, while singing your own song in a new commercial, starring you, broadcast during the Superbowl*, in a game that you are winning, and I will not sleep until that happens.*

- *We live in a cynical world. A cynical world. And we work in a business of tough competitors.*

Quotes by other characters:

- *Hey... I don't have all the answers. In life, to be honest, I have failed as much as I have succeeded. But I love my life. I love my wife. And I wish you my kind of success.*

- *It's not "show friends." It's "show business".*

TIP

Terms you need to know:
Draft: a process by which sports teams select new players.
Superbowl: the annual championship game of the National Football League, the highest level of professional American football in the United States, culminating a season that begins in the late summer of the previous calendar year.

Read the film **review** and make notes on what you like about the plot of the film and the concepts and issues it discusses. Then answer the questions that follow the review.

Review of the film *Jerry Maguire* by James Berardinelli

Every time I think Hollywood has slipped beyond redemption, someone in the system produces a film like Jerry Maguire that renews my faith. Apparently, creativity is not dead in the mainstream movie market — not entirely, at least. This is the kind of movie that reminds me why I started reviewing in the first place. Jerry Maguire is magic on celluloid—fresh, funny, romantic, and upbeat. You'll leave the theater with a smile on your face and perhaps a tear in your eye.

Personally, I never really bought Tom Cruise as the action lead in Mission Impossible. Here, however, the actor is playing to his strength, which lies in an arena that demands less testosterone. Leave the stunts and explosions to Schwarzenegger and Stallone. Cruise is best when he stays low key and flashes the occasional smile. And, in this picture, surrounded by a superlative supporting cast, his ability shines. Jerry Maguire works because we root for the title character, and it's Cruise's performance that forges the link between his screen personae and the audience.

As the movie opens, super sports agent Jerry Maguire is facing a crisis of conscience (that he still possesses one after working in such a cynical, materialistic business is something of a miracle). He wonders what he has become — "Just another shark in a suit?" He realizes that he hates himself and his place in the world, and laments that, although he has a lot to say, no one will listen. So, late one night, he writes a Mission Statement called "The Things We Think and Do Not Say: The Future of Our Business". The essay attacks the sports agency business, advocating a more humane approach. The next day, a copy is distributed to everyone in the office. And, although Jerry's co-workers applaud his courage ("Somebody finally said what had to be said"), his bosses are offended, and he loses his job. Only one client, unremarkable Arizona Cardinals wide receiver Rod Tidwell (Cuba Gooding Jr.), elects to remain with Jerry as he strikes out on his own. Also joining him is a 26-year old single mother, Dorothy Boyd (Renee Zellweger), who is so moved by Jerry's Mission Statement that she's willing to throw away a safe job to be part of his new venture.

In an era of downsizing and force reductions, it's easy to understand what happens to Jerry. He speaks his mind, crying out for compassion and caring, only to be slapped down. He is branded as a loser because he dares to swim against the heartless, prevalent business currents. Jerry finds himself in deep, uncertain waters, but his indefatigable spirit, bolstered by tireless support from Rod and Dorothy, helps him navigate the most dangerous eddys.

Jerry Maguire is about redemption and love. It's about finding one's heart and soul in a business climate that attempts to rip both away. Writer/director Cameron Crowe, who previously helmed Say Anything and Singles (in addition to scripting Fast Times at Ridgemont High), brings both a strong sense of verisimilitude and a lively wit to his film. Even as Jerry Maguire reaches out to the heart, it tickles the funny bone.

For anyone who has forgotten the feelings that a wonderful movie can trigger, Jerry Maguire provides a welcome reminder.

a) List the ideas discussed in the review that are connected to the theme of "Life perception and career choices" and how the reviewer interprets it.

b) Do you agree or disagree with the reviewer's points of view? Why? Why not?

c) What is the tone of the review? Give examples from the text.

d) What is the best thing you like about the review? Why?

STEP 3 Watch clips from the film *Jerry Maguire* on YouTube and write your interpretations about the following:

a) Was Jerry Maguire right to make the choices he made?

b) What do you follow when you make such choices? Duty, heart, money and why?

c) How do you think the new Mission Statement he writes is going to be accepted in his corporation?

d) What would you do if you were in his shoes, and why?

 **GLOBAL CONTEXTS**
Personal and cultural expression

ATL SKILLS
Media literacy
Demonstrate awareness of media interpretations of events and ideas.

 Activity 6   The theme in the film *The Pursuit of Happyness*

STEP 1 Watch clips from the film *The Pursuit of Happyness* on YouTube and find a synopsis online to give you an overview of the story.

Answer the questions below:

a) How would you interpret the title of the film? (what do you think it means?)

b) What is the theme of the film?

c) Did the main character in the film leave his future to destiny or did he have a dream to achieve?

d) What did it take to achieve his dream?

e) The film deals with some idealistic concepts. Which do you agree with and which do you have some doubts about? Why?

f) The following quotes are from the film. Choose the one you like best and mention the reason.

- When he sees the man in the expensive red car (Ferrari).

  "Sir, I have two questions for you: 'What do you do?' and 'How do you do it?'"

- When he is speaking to his son.

  "Don't ever let somebody tell you you can't do something. Not even me. All right?... You got a dream... You gotta protect it. People can't do somethin' themselves, they wanna tell you you can't do it. If you want somethin', go get it. Period."

- After he was accepted as an employee in the company, going down the stairs.

  "This part of my life... this part right here? This is called 'happyness'."

STEP 2 After exploring the two songs and the two films in this topic, answer the following questions:

a) Mention in one statement how each song and film tackles the themes of life, careers and the future.

b) What is common in their perceptions and what is different?

c) According to how each song/film perceives life, what would be the meaning of happiness to them?

d) Which do you agree with? Why?

GLOBAL CONTEXTS
Personal and cultural expression

ATL SKILLS
Media literacy
Demonstrate awareness of media interpretations of events and ideas.

Reflection

Consider the following:

- What did you learn about by doing this comparison?

- What don't you understand?

- What is your next step?

TOPIC 3

Exploring a theme in articles

This topic continues to explore the same theme of "Life perception and career choices" in the genre of written media. You will explore the theme in social media articles and magazine articles. Through social media articles you will be able to see a different view of the theme. Social media articles are more personalized with a strong sense of authenticity. Magazine articles often present a stand about an issue. This genre uses features of well-chosen words to appeal to readers.

 Activity 7 The theme in social media articles

STEP 1 End in mind:

Imagine it is your 70th birthday where all the people you know are around you, what would you want to hear from them when they talk about you? You might think about the following people being there:

- Family members: Sisters and brothers, Sons and daughters, Aunts and uncles.
- Friends: Close, Not close.
- People you work with: Employees, Colleagues, Boss.

If one of those people were to write a Facebook article about you at 70, how do you think you would be described?

STEP 2 The following is an article written by a former student about her teacher who has died. Read the article and then answer the questions that follow.

Article about teacher by Noran Shafey

I didn't realize until today how much I'd learnt from him. A strict science teacher in school with a ringing voice that caught you even before making a mistake, what could be scarier to a teenage girl.

Today I read that he'd passed away earlier in the morning, after paying my respects on Facebook, I found that I couldn't stop thinking of him. How we were taught to address him as Sir, not Mister, and how our British teachers would explain that we couldn't address him as Sir Wali though, as he had not received a Knighthood! But looking back, I think he deserved more than that title.

Discipline and punctuality; dare any of us be lingering outside class before his lesson, or not have our books ready on our desks, or not stand in attention as he crossed the classroom threshold. Never! He'd walk in and look down at us ignorant creatures of the magical world of science.

The Periodic Table and Mendeleev, atomic numbers, valencies, elements, oh I can remember just now when he explained how oil was formed, and what the Shell on the gas stations represented. His neat handwriting on the blackboard, the labeled diagrams in multi-colored chalk, and us while copying everything down as neat as possible.

The best treat was the visit to the lab, and us walking behind him down the corridors, and up the stairs in a perfect line, to sit behind the wooden benches, and Mr. Wali upfront, where fuming miracles materialized right before our wondering eyes. I remember feeling so proud, and so grown up, coming home to my parents and telling them that we'd been to the lab that day.

Preparing for Speech Day was a time of excitement, missing lessons for the choir and prize winners, learning how to curtsy for girls, and bow for boys. Directions of walking to the stage, then back again. On the day of the big event, no nonsense was allowed, just one look from Mr. Wali looming at the side was more than enough to set us straight and stop our silly giggles midway. I doubt that our parents had that effect on us.

Then sometime, when we were in senior school, we heard that Mr. Wali was ill, and that he would be traveling to England for a heart checkup, as far as I recall. Was that why he was being so sweet and kind to us all of a sudden? He traveled for a short while, and came back healthy, and Boom! There he was shouting at the top of his lungs, chasing all those chatterboxes back in class.

Yes, if there was any organizing to be done, it was better done with Mr. Wali in the background. Like the first day of school, when lines were set straight for the saluting of the flag in the patio. The pattern would be repeated daily, and we had to move quickly and quietly up to our classrooms. No time wasted. I can still see him with his silver grey hair and stern look, one arm crossed against his chest leaning on the other, which was raised with one finger resting on his cheekbone. Yes, we had to learn it properly from the first day.

In 2001, my class celebrated our 25th year of graduation, by having as a Silver Jubilee reunion in our school dining room. We were over forty students, with their families, and most important of all many of our teachers were present, including Mr. Wali. We lovingly sang "Pioneers", souvenirs were distributed, cheers were called out, and teachers couldn't believe the naughty boys turned out into fine young men. That was the last time I saw Mr. Wali, and I'm almost certain I caught a look of pride in his eyes as a few of us stood beside him for one of the pictures.

Dear Sir,

Please allow me to salute you one last time;
Three cheers for Mr. Wali!
Hip Hip, Horray!
Hip Hip, Horray!
Hip Hip, Horray!

Your forever grateful student,
Noran Shafey

a) What kind of person was Mr Wali? Support with evidence from the text.
b) How did he make his personal decisions? Support with evidence from the text.
c) How did the author of the article make us view Mr Wali? What descriptive language was used to make a vivid image of his character?
d) Why do his students remember him even now? Support with evidence from the text.

GLOBAL CONTEXTS
Personal and cultural expression

ATL SKILLS
Media literacy
Demonstrate awareness of media interpretations of events and ideas.

 Activity 8   The theme in magazine articles

Read the extract and answer the questions that follow.

Happiness is freedom to choose by NZ Herald

<u>**Their**</u> *climate is a cause for despair and their high tax rates would be a <u>turn-off</u> to most, but the people of Denmark have found <u>a happiness elixir</u> .*

That, at least, is the conclusion of two studies published this year. The first, by Leicester University researchers, proclaimed the Scandinavian nation the happiest in the world, and now that finding has been echoed by the United States Government-funded World Values Survey.

In the latter, New Zealand finished 15th, a respectable if not resounding rating that, at least, made it a happier place than the US, Australia and Britain.

*Why Denmark? The study director, Ronald Inglehart of the University of Michigan's Institute for Social Research, points to **its** prosperity, democracy, social equality and peaceful atmosphere.*

Yet New Zealand, to a fairly large degree, shares the same attributes. Why, then, are New Zealanders not as happy as the Danes? The answer may lie in the Danes' more modest expectations of life, allied to their willingness to acknowledge what they have and cherish it. They expect less and, therefore, are apt to appreciate what they have.

*Perhaps **that** also explains the relatively modest position occupied by the United States. Americans are prosperous and their country also ranks relatively well in social equality and political freedom. But they strive to achieve many things. Their expectations are high, and their lives can become cluttered and complicated. It seems that a failure to achieve success in all these pursuits <u>erodes the happiness quotient</u>.*

The surveys' main conclusion is that the most important determinant of happiness is the extent to which people have free choice in how to live their lives. This is the more relevant given that last-placed of the 52 countries analysed is Zimbabwe. Prosperity, democracy and peace have become alien concepts there as Robert Mugabe's thuggish regime clings to power.

The study, in fact, proves a reply to those who claim money cannot help to buy happiness. People of rich countries tend to be happier than those of poor countries.

The researchers also found that, globally, happiness had risen substantially, thanks in no small part to unprecedented economic growth in low-income countries such as China and India. Money <u>that lifts people out of poverty prompts</u> a sense of wellbeing.

Other factors have helped this global trend. Many medium-income nations have become democracies, and there has been a sharp rise of gender equality and tolerance of minorities in developed societies.

According to the study, democratisation and rising tolerance have more impact than economic growth. But, when stacked together, all three provide people with a wider range of choice in how to live their lives. They become genuinely and perpetually happy. This is not the short-term joy produced by crass consumerism or winning Lotto but a more deep-seated contentment.

*All this will not exactly enchant those who decry the diminution of traditional values or predict societal disintegration. **They** perceive only unhappiness. Nor will it impress those who romanticise poverty. Doubtless, they will say <u>too broad a brush has been applied</u>.*

Even if this is so, it remains impossible to overlook the message about the importance of freedom of choice.

It is one for all seasons, and for all countries.

a) What is the meaning of the following phrases underlined in the text?

   i)   turn-off: ……………………………………………………………………………………

   ii) a happiness elixir: …………………………………………………………………………

   iii) erodes the happiness quotient: ……………………………………………………………

   iv) that lifts people out of poverty: …………………………………………………………

   v) too broad a brush has been applied: ………………………………………………………

b) How did those phrases better clarify the message of the article?

c) What do these bold and underlined words in the text refer to? The first one is done for you.

   i)   Their: *the people of Denmark*

   ii) its: …………………………………………………………………………………………

   iii) that: …………………………………………………………………………………………

   iv) They: ………………………………………………………………………………………

d) How did those reference words better clarify the message of the article?

🌐 **GLOBAL CONTEXTS**
Personal and cultural expression

🧠 **ATL SKILLS**
Media literacy
Demonstrate awareness of media interpretations of events and ideas.

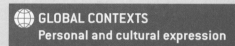 **Activity 9**   **Assess your understanding**

STEP 1   Get into pairs or groups. With your pair/group choose one of the following interactive oral tasks.

Task 1: A television talk show with a focus on a topic under the theme "Life perceptions". Choose either "Do dreams or destiny drive our future?", or "What is happiness?".
In this oral task the talk show is done by 4–6 students where each group member adopts a character that is relevant to the topic discussed. For example the host, a life coach, a film producer, a book author. This activity should last approximately 20 minutes.

Task 2: An interview with the director of the film *Jerry Maguire* or *The Pursuit of Happyness*.
The interview is done by two students, one playing the interviewer and the other the director. This activity should last approximately 20 minutes.

Task 3: A debate between two groups with opposing ideas.
One group is to be for "Destiny" the other for "Decisions". The debate can be done by 6–8 or more students. You divide yourselves in two groups each adopting an opposing idea. This activity should last approximately 20 minutes.

STEP 2   After you have chosen your scenario, you should each prepare independently and then come together to do the interactive activity spontaneously.

GLOBAL CONTEXTS
Personal and cultural expression

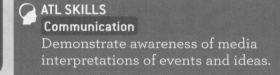
ATL SKILLS
Communication
Demonstrate awareness of media
interpretations of events and ideas.

Reflection

- What did you learn about by exploring written media?

- What don't you understand?

- What is your next step?

Summary

Through the related concept "Genre" any theme can be explored
in different contexts and from different perspectives. The author's
choice of genre and its conventions frame ideas and thoughts to
give it the form that suits the audience and situation. In this chapter
exploring different genres written about the same theme showed how
the use of genre conventions helps in delivering the message in a
manner that suits the context.

- Consider how this chapter helped you develop your ATL skills.

- What are the ATL skills you worked on most in this chapter?

- How can you share them to help peers who need more
  practice?

- What will you work on next?

References

Berardinelli, J. 1996. Review of the film *Jerry Maguire*. http://www.
reelviews.net/movies/j/jerry.html.

De Bruxelles, Simon. May 5, 2006. "Actress Dies after Plastic Surgery
Heart Accident". Times Newspapers Ltd.

Happiness Is Freedom to Choose. 2008. APN New Zealand Limited.
Herald, NZ. Retrieved from http://www.nzherald.co.nz/opinion/news/
article.cfm?c_id=466&objectid=10520043.

Huss-Ashmore, R. Spring 1999. "The Real Me: Therapeutic Narrative in
Cosmetic Surgery". *Expedition Magazine*. Vol 41, number 1.

Shafety, N. 2009. Retrieved from Facebook EGC all Generation page.

The Beauty Diary. 2009. *Shopping in Paris:* My Beauty Diary. The
Beauty and Health Site ©2009 About.com, a part of The New York
Times Company.

CHAPTER 7 Structure

KEY CONCEPT FOCUS COMMUNICATION

INQUIRY QUESTIONS

TOPIC 1 Exploring openings and their functions
- **What are the functions of openings?**

TOPIC 2 Exploring structure in poetry
- **How can you use structure in poetry to help communicate purpose and message?**

TOPIC 3 Walking and talking your way through structure
- **What are the key elements of the structure of a text at sentence and word level?**

SKILLS

ATL
- ✓ Use appropriate forms of writing for different purposes and audiences.
- ✓ Draw reasonable conclusions and generalizations.
- ✓ Recognize unstated assumptions and bias.
- ✓ Use a variety of speaking techniques to communicate with a variety of audiences.
- ✓ Write for different purposes.
- ✓ Use existing works and ideas in new ways.
- ✓ Read critically and for comprehension.
- ✓ Organize and depict information logically.
- ✓ Evaluate evidence and arguments.

Language and literature
- ✓ Articulate thoughts and ideas in a variety of ways.
- ✓ Articulate thoughts and writing skills by organizing ideas and information using a range of text types.
- ✓ Employ organizational structures that serve the context and intention.

OTHER RELATED CONCEPTS

Connections   Character   Style

GLOSSARY

Caesura a break or pause within a line of poetry made by a comma, full stop or line break. The purpose of a caesura is to add emphasis, suggest balance, or create a change in pace.

Denouement the conclusion of a plot (resolution of conflicts, misunderstandings or unsolved mysteries).

Flashback the depiction of a scene or event in the past through memory, speech, dream, narration or description.

Foreshadowing something that gives an indication or hint as to what may occur later in the text.

COMMAND TERMS

Analyse break down in order to bring out the essential elements or structure. To identify parts and relationships, and to interpret information to reach conclusions.

Create to evolve from one's own thought or imagination, as a work or an invention.

Discuss offer a considered and balanced review that includes a range of arguments, factors or hypotheses. Opinions or conclusions should be presented clearly and supported by appropriate evidence.

Examine consider an argument or concept in a way that uncovers the assumptions and interrelationships of the issue.

List give a sequence of brief answers with no explanation.

Introducing structure

Structure is central to the way we organize our ideas, it even reflects our thinking patterns. Structure comprises a number of elements and can be considered on different levels. For example:

- text structure
- sentence structure
- word structure.

As you discovered in chapter 2 on communication, the structure of a text varies according to:

- the context of culture and situation
- the purpose of our communication
- the audience and method of communication.

 Activity 1   **Considering texts you read, write and view**

Through your studies in language and literature, as well as in other subject areas, you will produce and analyse a range of spoken, written and visual texts. Look at the table that follows and think about different text types and how they are structured. While the texts listed are discrete texts, many of the texts you encounter are made up of a range of text types and forms. For example, a science practical write-up could involve a procedure or recount of the experiment, an explanation of the process, an analysis of results, and a discussion of the conclusions reached.

Think of different types of texts for each intended writing purpose. Add them to the far right hand column. The table shows both factual text types and their forms, and response text types and their forms. Some examples have been included to get you started.

Purpose of writing	Text type	Specific purpose	How are these texts structured?	Examples (Subjects/Texts/Activities)
Instruct or record	Procedures	To show how to carry out an experiment or procedure.	◼ Goal ◼ Materials needed ◼ Methods in series of staged steps	◼ Design (instructions for a project) ◼ _____ ◼ _____
	Procedural recounts or records	To record procedures or results.	◼ Aim ◼ Record of events ◼ Results ◼ Conclusion	◼ Science (write-up of a practical) ◼ _____ ◼ _____

Recount	Personal recount (factual)	To record personal events in the past chronologically to entertain or reflect.	● Orientation ● Record of events in order ● Evaluation	● Any subject (journal or memoir entry) ● _____ ● _____
	Historical or biographical recount (factual)	To record events about individuals or groups in the past.	● Background ● Record of events ● Deduction or evaluation	● Visual arts (research project on artistic movement) ● _____ ● _____
Explain	Sequential explanation (mechanical, technological or natural systems)	To explain the phases of a process. To show how and why the phases occur in that order.	● Phenomenon identification ● Explanation sequence	● Sciences (diagram or description of life cycle of an animal) ● _____ ● _____
	Causal/ Consequential (explaining why)	To explain reasons or consequences relating to an outcome or event.	● Outcome ● Occurrence ● Reasons ● Consequences ● Review ● Review	● Geography (water cycle) ● _____ ● _____
Entertain	Narrative	To entertain or instruct reader.	● Orientation ● Complication ● Resolution	● Language A (short story) ● _____ ● _____
Report or Organize	Taxonomic classification into types (subclasses)	To describe the parts of a group or system. To present information about the living or non-living world, or to explain how and why something occurs.	● General classification (class/unit) ● Description (type/part)	● Science (classification of mammals) ● _____ ● _____
Argue or Persuade	Analytical (persuading "how")	To put forward a point of view to argue one side of an issue and to justify it.	● Thesis ● Argument for one position ● Reinforcement of thesis or summing up position	● History (political speech) ● _____ ● _____

Discuss or Persuade	Interpretative (persuading "how")	To present case for different points of view, concluding with a recommendation based on consideration of the evidence.	<ul><li>Issue</li><li>Series of arguments or perspectives</li><li>Judgment, position, recommendation</li></ul>	<ul><li>Language A (essays)</li><li>_____</li><li>_____</li></ul>
Challenge or Persuade	Evaluative (persuading "how")	To argue against another person's point of view.	<ul><li>Position challenged</li><li>Arguments against</li><li>Antithesis</li></ul>	<ul><li>Any subject (debate speech for one side of the argument)</li><li>_____</li><li>_____</li></ul>
Respond	Personal response	To articulate an individual response to a work of literature or art.	<ul><li>Orientation</li><li>Text description</li><li>Comment</li></ul>	<ul><li>Performing arts (reflection on peer or own performance)</li><li>_____</li><li>_____</li></ul>
	Reviews	To assess the appeal and value of a work of literature or art.	<ul><li>Context</li><li>Text description</li><li>Judgment</li></ul>	<ul><li>Book or film reviews</li><li>_____</li><li>_____</li></ul>
	Interpretations	To interpret the message of a work of literature or art.	<ul><li>Text evaluation</li><li>Text synopsis</li><li>Reaffirm the text evaluation</li></ul>	<ul><li>Language A (literature circles)</li><li>_____</li><li>_____</li></ul>
	Critical responses	To analyse or evaluate the message in a work of literature or art.	<ul><li>Text evaluation</li><li>Text deconstruction</li><li>Challenge the text evaluation</li></ul>	<ul><li>Language A (written or oral commentary on a poem or prose extract)</li><li>_____</li><li>_____</li></ul>

GLOBAL CONTEXTS
Personal and cultural expression

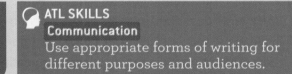

ATL SKILLS
Communication
Use appropriate forms of writing for different purposes and audiences.

Exploring openings and their functions

Openings in texts are essential in order to establish the context of a text and engage the reader's interest. It is essential that you capture your reader's interest, whether you wish to write a newspaper headline, the introduction to a critical analysis or the opening scene of a novel. The opening of a text performs a number of functions, which include:

- introducing characters and relationships
- introducing a conflict
- establishing the time and place
- explaining anything that happened before the action began
- introducing symbols or motifs
- establishing a mood or atmosphere.

 Activity 2   **Analysing openings**

In this activity you will analyse the openings of a variety of different texts taken from both fiction and non-fiction texts. In preparation, you will need to find some different text types. You can use examples from this book or any texts you are studying in class.

In pairs or a small group, study the openings of the fiction or non-fiction texts you have chosen and answer the questions below:

a) How does the title of the text preview what follows?

b) How does the opening engage your interest and make you want to read on?

c) How do subheadings give further clues as to the text's structure?

d) How are visuals used to add context to the text? What clues do they offer?

e) Which people or character(s) are introduced and what are their relationships to each other? How do you learn about them (directly from what they say or do, or indirectly from what others say about them)?

f) Who is speaking? From what point of view are events presented (first person or third person)?

g) How are the setting, mood and atmosphere established and communicated?

h) What potential conflict or conflicts are established?

i) Are events described in chronological or non-chronological order? Give reasons why the writer may have made this decision and explain its impact on the rest of the text.

j) How effective is the opening in communicating the text's purpose and message?

> **TIP**
>
> Examples of non-fiction texts are newspaper articles, editorials, web pages, film reviews and story openings.

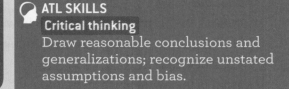

GLOBAL CONTEXTS
Personal and cultural expression

ATL SKILLS
Critical thinking
Draw reasonable conclusions and
generalizations; recognize unstated
assumptions and bias.

 Activity 3   Death and the Maiden

Read the opening of the play *Death and the Maiden* and use the questions that follow to determine whether
it fulfills the criteria of a good opening.

Death and the Maiden by Ariel Dorfman

Sound of the sea. After midnight.

*The Escobars' beach house. A terrace and an ample living/dining room where dinner is laid out on
a table with two chairs. On a sideboard is a cassette recorder and a lamp. Window walls between
the terrace and the front room, with curtains blowing in the wind. A door from the terrace leading
to a bedroom. Paulina Salas is seated in a chair on the terrace, as if she were drinking in the light of
the moon. The sound of a faraway car can be heard. She hurriedly stands up, goes to the other room,
looks out the window. The car brakes, its motor still running, the lights blasting her. She goes to the
sideboard, takes out a gun, stops when the motor is turned off and she hears Gerardo's voice.*

GERARDO (*voice off*): You sure you don't want to come in? Just one for the road (*muffled reply*) . . . .
Right then, we'll get together before I leave. I've gotta be back by . . . Monday. How about Sunday?
(*muffled reply*) . . . . My wife makes a margarita that will make your hair stand on end. . . . I really want
you to know how much I appreciate . . . (*muffled reply*) See you on Sunday then. (*He laughs*)

*Paulina hides the gun away. She stands behind the curtains. The car drives off, the lights sweeping the
room again. Gerardo enters.*

GERARDO: Paulie? Paulina?

*He sees Paulina hidden behind the curtains. He switches on a light. She slowly comes out from the
curtains.*

GERARDO (*cont'd*): Is that...? What're you doing there like that? Sorry I took this long to... I....

PAULINA (*trying not to seem agitated*): And who was that?

GERARDO: It's just that I...

PAULINA: Who was it?

GERARDO: ...had an—no, don't worry, it wasn't anything serious. It's just that the car—luckily a man
stopped—just a flat tire. Paulina, I can't see a thing without...

He puts on another lamp and sees the table set.

GERARDO (*cont'd*): Poor little love. It must've got cold, right, the—

PAULINA (*very calm, till the end of the scene*): We can heat it up. As long as we've got something to
celebrate, that is. (*Brief pause.*) You do have something to celebrate, that is.

STEP 1 Answer the following questions:

a) What is the setting of the play and how is the setting established?

b) How is dramatic tension created through a range of dialogue, stage directions, and visual and aural devices?

c) What is the mood and atmosphere and how are they communicated?

d) How are characters and their relationships introduced?

e) What is the key conflict and how does the playwright leave the audience asking questions?

f) What verbal and non-verbal devices are used to create tension?

g) What key props and symbols are introduced?

h) Having read the whole text, are any aspects of plot **foreshadowed**?

STEP 2 Look at the openings of other texts and make a list of techniques you could use to make your own openings engaging and interesting.

GLOBAL CONTEXTS
Personal and cultural expression

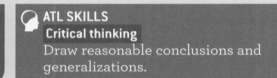
ATL SKILLS
Critical thinking
Draw reasonable conclusions and generalizations.

👥 Activity 4   Exploring narrative structure through improvisation

Examine Freytag's triangle below. Work with a partner to create a basic narrative plot that follows each of the stages on the outline of the triangle from beginning to end.

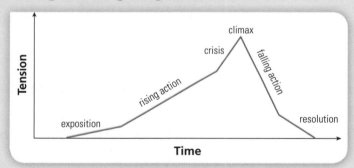

Exposition	<ul><li>Introduce the characters – their roles and relationships</li><li>Establish the setting in time and place</li><li>Introduce the conflict faced by the character(s)</li></ul>
Rising action	<ul><li>Develop the conflict and build tension</li><li>Create a moment of crisis with a climax - the point of highest emotional intensity. This is the turning point in the action</li></ul>
Falling Action	<ul><li>Show how the protagonist's fortunes change for the worse</li></ul>

With a partner **create** two improvised scenes using the following dialogue. When performing your dialogue you could choose from the following scenarios below or create (command term style) another scenario of your choosing.

Dialogue

A: Hello

B: Hi

A: What are you doing?

B: Not much

A: Anything interesting?

B: Not really

A: Bye

B: See you later

Scenarios

- A teacher discovers a student with a cheat sheet in an exam.
- A man waits for his date in a restaurant and sees an attractive girl. His date, who is a different person, enters.
- A shopkeeper sees a customer trying to steal something.
- An office worker is late for a meeting. The manager is waiting.

Before you begin your scene decide how you will do the following:

Orientation	■ establish who your characters are (their roles and relationships) ■ establish where the scene is taking place
Rising action	■ create a complication that creates tension ■ create a moment of climax
Denouement	■ create a resolution

TIP

Follow Freytag's triangle structure. You will need to think about how you can use verbal and non-verbal cues (such as miming actions and gestures) during your scene.

TIP

If you are creating a dialogue, be sure to stick to the lines and words listed in the dialogue above. If you are working with a scenario, use language and vocabulary appropriate to the scenario you have chosen.

GLOBAL CONTEXTS
Personal and cultural expression

ATL SKILLS
Communication
Use a variety of speaking techniques to communicate with a variety of audiences.

Newspapers and magazines use headlines and opening paragraphs to grab the reader's attention and create a sense of excitement and interest.

With a partner, write a sensationalized newspaper headline and opening paragraph. Use the plot from one of the scenarios you created in Activity 4. It should engage your reader's interest by communicating key information about the plot and conflict, and highlight key elements of the narrative.

Your headline must:

- fit the story and tell the reader what it is about
- make the reader interested in the story and want to read on
- be visually striking enough to grab the eye of readers
- fit into a very limited space (aim for about six words)
- capture the reader's attention using:
  - sensational language
  - emotive language
  - puns or a play on words
  - the present tense for recent past
  - no definite and indefinite articles.

The opening paragraph should try to answer as many of the five W + H questions as possible (Who? Where? When? What? Why? and How?).

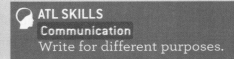

🌐 **GLOBAL CONTEXTS**
Personal and cultural expression

🧠 **ATL SKILLS**
Communication
Write for different purposes.

Filmmakers and writers often use structure to shape the reader's or viewer's experience. Many films and texts do not run in chronological order of events, rather they begin just before the moment of climax and then use **flashbacks** to explain how events lead to the climactic moment.

To illustrate this point look at the children's story *The Three Little Pigs*. If you examine the basic structure of *The Three Little Pigs* and show it visually, it would look like Figure 7.1.

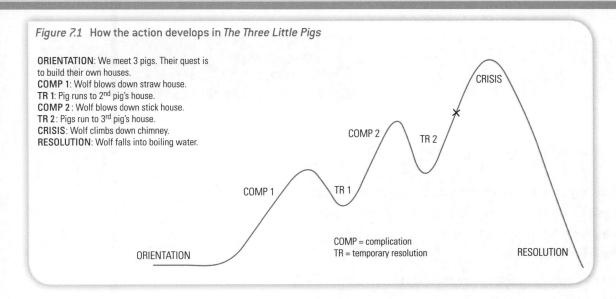

Figure 7.1 How the action develops in *The Three Little Pigs*

ORIENTATION: We meet 3 pigs. Their quest is to build their own houses.
COMP 1: Wolf blows down straw house.
TR 1: Pig runs to 2nd pig's house.
COMP 2: Wolf blows down stick house.
TR 2: Pigs run to 3rd pig's house.
CRISIS: Wolf climbs down chimney.
RESOLUTION: Wolf falls into boiling water.

COMP = complication
TR = temporary resolution

ORIENTATION · COMP 1 · TR 1 · COMP 2 · TR 2 · CRISIS · RESOLUTION

Imagine a movie version of the story that begins at point X on the diagram above. The action of the story would start with two pigs heading towards the third pig's house with the wolf in hot pursuit. The movie could then flashback to how the characters got to point X.

 Activity 6   **Manipulating the structure**

Take a narrative text you are studying in class and think about how you can manipulate the text's structure to produce an engaging opening for a movie. You can move the plot around to create tension and grab the reader's or viewer's interest.

STEP 1   Using the template below, **create** a series of 5–10 shots that outline the opening scenes of your movie. Make notes under each shot using the table as a guide.

Shot #:		Seconds:
	Draw your shot here	
Action		
Sounds/music/dialogue		
Camera shot/angle/movement		
Lighting/other effects		
Effect on viewer		

STEP 2   Write a brief description of your movie opening for the class. Use the headings in the table to structure your summary.

 **GLOBAL CONTEXTS**
Personal and cultural expression

 **ATL SKILLS**
Creative thinking
Use existing works and ideas in new ways.

QUICK THINK

Another good way to explore the narrative structure of your text is to write a condensed one-minute version. To do this you need to think about the elements you want to communicate. These might include some of the following:

- key conflicts or the problems the character(s) need to overcome. These could include:
  - person vs person
  - person vs self
  - person vs nature
  - person vs supernatural
- key characters and their relationships
- key symbols or motifs
- key themes or ideas
- key moments of tension or turning points
- key incidents that affect the plot.

Begin by moving through the text and selecting key lines that summarize the action of the chapters or acts.

WEB LINKS

For an example of a condensed version of a plot, search www.youtube.com for "The 32 second Macbeth".

Reflection

- How does the opening of a text affect the way a reader perceives the material?

- Is the opening of a text more important than its conclusion?

- How can you use what you have learned in your own production and analysis of texts?

TOPIC 2

Exploring structure in poetry

The ability to analyse how poets organize their ideas to suit their message and purpose can help you develop your own creative and critical responses to reading and writing poetry. Thinking about the decisions a poet might make can help you better understand the craft of poetry and the impact these can have on the reader.

Activity 7 Considering structure and form

In the following activity you will explore how structural features of poetry play a role in communicating the message, purpose and mood in a poem.

> **TIP**
>
> Some common structural features found in poems are: rhyme scheme, line length, sentence organization, stanza layout and punctuation.

STEP 1 Study the table of possible themes and list of possible poem structures (A–H), which present some different visual layouts of poems. Look at the themes and ideas listed in the table and write possible poem structures next to each theme. Which one best communicates the concepts, ideas and themes in the table? To help you determine where each poem structure could go consider:

- How the overall organization can create a sense of order, control, regularity and logic, or a sense of disorder, irregularity, freedom and chaos.
- How the rhyme scheme can reflect opposition, harmony and balance, or chaos, disorganization and freedom.
- How punctuation affects the pace and flow, reflecting the fluid or stilted movement of thoughts and people, or of ideas or actions.
- How **caesura** can be used to create a sense of balance or division.
- How sentence length can create a sense of order and regularity, add emphasis and highlight a change of pace or mood (such as building tension).
- How stanza organization can imply a sense of brevity, fleetingness or order, or reflect changes in ideas, time and place.

Concepts, themes, ideas	Possible poem structures	Concepts, themes, ideas	Possible poem structures
conflict, opposition		routine, order, discipline and logic	
independence, freedom of movement or thoughts		brevity, fleetingness or snapshots	
chaos, disorder and disruption, rebellion		shifting, restless movements, ebb and flow	
balance and harmony		stilted, stumbling movement	
unity, cohesion and harmony		a change, a turning point	

Poem structure A		Poem structure B

Poem structure A

_____ - _____ ; _____ a
_____ , _____ b
_____ a
_____ ; _____ . b

_____ ; _____ c
_____ ! _____ d
_____ . _____ c
_____ ; _____ d

Poem structure B

_____ a
_____ b
_____ c
_____ , d

_____ e
_____ f
_____ . g

Poem structure C

_____ a
_____ b
_____ b
_____ a

_____ c
_____ , _____ . c

_____ d
_____ e
_____ d
_____ e

_____ c
_____ , _____ . c

_____ f
_____ g

Poem structure D

_____ a
_____ b
_____ . a

_____ c
_____ ; d
_____ ! c

_____ e
_____ f
_____ . e

_____ ; g
_____ . g

Poem structure E

————————————————————— , a
————————————————— , b
————————————————————— , a
————————————————————— , b
————————————————— , c
————————————————————— , d
————————————————— , c
————————————————— , d
————————————————————— , e
————————————————— , f
————————————————— e
————————————————————— , f
————————————————————— , g
————————————————————— . g

Poem structure F

———— , ———————————————— , a
————————————————— : ———— b
————————— : ——— , ———— , ———— , b
————————— , ———————————— , a
————————————————————— a
————————————— . ———————— ; b
—— ! ——————— , ——————————— ; b
———————— , ———— , ———— , ———— . a
————————————————— , ———— ; c
————————————————————— d
———————————— , ———— , —— , c
————————————————————— , d
————————————— ; ————————— c
————————————————————— . d

Poem structure G

————————————————————— a
————————————————— b
————————————————————— , a
————————————————— b

————————————————— c
————————————————————— , d
————————————— c
————————————————————— . d

Poem structure H

—————— , —————————— , —————————— ; a
—————— , —————————— ; ——————— , b
——————— . ————— , —— ; ———————— : c
——————— , ——————————— ,! ————— : d

——————— , ——————— , ——————— e
—————— , ————————————— : f

———————————— . ————————— ; g
—————— , ————————————— . ———— . h

Think about other poem forms or structures you have seen and how they could communicate different aspects of a poem's content and message. Consider what other concepts, themes or ideas might be represented by the structures in this activity.

🌐 **GLOBAL CONTEXTS**
Personal and cultural expression

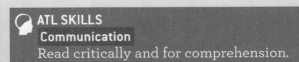
🗨 **ATL SKILLS**
Communication
Read critically and for comprehension.

Consider the role that structure plays in the meaning and interpretation of poetry.

STEP 1 The following text is a poem by William Blake called *London*. It has been written here as one long paragraph. As a group read through the lines and arrange them into a poetic form. You will need to think about how you organize the lines in order to highlight:

- key words, phrases or ideas
- transitions in time or place
- a change of topic, idea or concept
- a turning point in the action or a change in the character(s).

Make sure you vary the pace and flow of the lines.

London by William Blake

I wander thro' each charter'd street, near where the charter'd Thames does flow, and mark in every face I meet marks of weakness, marks of woe. In every cry of every Man, in every Infant's cry of fear, in every voice, in every ban, the mind-forg'd manacles I hear: How the Chimney-sweeper's cry every black'ning Church appalls, and the hapless Soldier's sigh runs in blood down Palace walls; but most thro' midnight streets I hear how the youthful Harlot's curse blasts the new born Infant's tear, and blights with plagues the Marriage hearse.

STEP 2 Now search online for the original version and **discuss** the impact the organization of the text has on the meaning and message of the poem as a whole.

STEP 3 Poets tend to manipulate the structure of sentences in order to create emphasis on certain words. Read Wordsworth's poem about London and discuss how he plays with sentence structures in order to highlight key words or phrases.

Composed Upon Westminster Bridge by William Wordsworth

Earth has not anything to show more fair:
Dull would he be of soul who could pass by
A sight so touching in its majesty:
This City now doth, like a garment, wear
The beauty of the morning; silent, bare,
Ships, towers, domes, theatres, and temples lie
Open unto the fields, and to the sky;
All bright and glittering in the smokeless air.
Never did sun more beautifully steep
In his first splendour, valley, rock, or hill;
Ne'er saw I, never felt, a calm so deep!
The river glideth at his own sweet will:
Dear God! the very houses seem asleep;
And all that mighty heart is lying still!

STEP 4 Consider the content and structure of each poem and how the two work together and add your ideas to the table below. Some ideas have been added to start you thinking.

London by William Blake	*Composed Upon Westminster Bridge* by William Wordsworth
Content <ul><li>attitude: negative</li><li>focus on the people</li><li>focus on suffering, misery, social and political problems</li><li>focus on sounds</li><li>_____</li><li>_____</li><li>_____</li></ul>	**Content** <ul><li>portrayal: positive</li><li>focus on buildings and landscape</li><li>focus on beauty, splendour</li><li>focus on sights</li><li>_____</li><li>_____</li><li>_____</li></ul>
Structural elements and how they reflect content <ul><li>rigid stanza structure reflects idea of control of church and state</li><li>_____</li><li>_____</li><li>_____</li></ul>	**Structural elements and how they reflect content** <ul><li>lines organized to highlight physical aspects of the scene (ships, towers, domes, the river)</li><li>_____</li><li>_____</li><li>_____</li></ul>

STEP 5 Answer the following questions:

a) Both poets use a regular form to describe the city. How do the different forms help communicate the different aspects of the city?

b) Why does Wordsworth use a sonnet form in his poem?

c) How does Blake use the structure of his poem to communicate the sense of control and restriction he sees inflicted on the people of London?

d) How does Blake use structure to communicate the lack of imagination and freedom of expression he sees in the people of London?

e) How does Blake use repetition to express the universality of suffering he sees in the people of London?

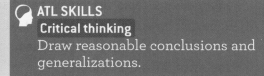

GLOBAL CONTEXTS
Personal and cultural expression

ATL SKILLS
Critical thinking
Draw reasonable conclusions and generalizations.

With a partner, discuss the following:

- How can a detailed consideration of structure help you in your understanding of poets' messages and how they communicate them?
- How can you use these analytical techniques to improve your own writing?

If you are keeping an e-portfolio, write a brief creative or critical analysis of your own or another poem.

Reflection

- To what extent do you feel poets make conscious decisions about how they organize their ideas?
- How important is it to consider structure and its impact when you read and write poetry?

TOPIC 3

Walking and talking your way through structure

A methodical approach to analysing texts will help you plan your own writing. In the following activities you will look at some ways to analyse texts and think about the planning process. You can use this to ensure you present your ideas clearly and coherently to an audience, using a range of features at text, sentence and word level.

 Activity 9   Organizing your writing

In this activity you will analyse the way texts are constructed by writers. This will help you to develop strategies to organize your writing in a clear, logical manner. You could try this activity on any text you are working on.

> **STEP 1** **Reconstructing text**
> a) Select a text (an article, an explanation of a process, a discursive essay, a speech, a scientific report, a poem or an extract from a novel, for example).
> b) Cut up your text into sections and mix up the sections so that you can no longer see its original order.
> c) Swap texts with a partner and take it in turns to rearrange each other's text back into the correct order using clues in the language. Think about how aspects of the text such as subheadings, topic sentences and discourse markers give you language clues.
> d) Once you have reconstructed the text, share the strategies you used to reconstruct the text back in to its correct order. **Discuss** any areas of uncertainty and why you may have been unsure of the order of ideas.

> **STEP 2** **Exploring paragraphs**
> a) If the text has no subheadings think of summaries for each paragraph. Try to summarize the paragraph in one word or a short phrase.

b) Underline the topic sentences of each paragraph. Remember that while the topic sentence summarizes the main idea of the paragraph, it may not always be placed at the very beginning. It should however be very close to the beginning.

c) [Analyse] the focus of the topic sentence and how it helps the reader to read the text. What is its focus? Is it the cause or result of something? Or perhaps it is the victim or agent of an action or decision? How does this focus affect how the reader interprets the text?

d) Use a highlighter pen to mark specific examples or evidence given to support a point. How brief and precise are the references? How well chosen and effective are the examples? Are they referenced correctly?

e) In the margin write the letters EG wherever a specific example is given. Write GEN in the margin alongside text that uses general terms about the point being discussed, but without giving evidence. This should give you an overview of how much supporting evidence is used in relation to the amount of general comment.

f) Highlight any transitions (phrases such as furthermore, also, but, however, in contrast) that help link paragraphs and guide the reader through the text.

g) [List] the key features of a well-constructed paragraph.

> **TIP**
>
> Point e) is especially important to consider when writing argumentative, persuasive or analytical essays where good examples and evidence add weight and interest to arguments and discussion points.

STEP 3 **Exploring introductions**

a) Read the introductory paragraph closely and consider the following questions:
    i) If an essay, to what extent does the introduction put the essay into context?
    ii) If an essay, to what extent does it outline the key ideas of the essay?
    iii) To what extent does it answer the questions: Who, What, When, Where, Why and How?
    iv) To what extent does it express the writer's opinions?
    v) To what extent does it grab the reader's attention or interest?

b) [Discuss] with a partner the role of an introduction in:
    i) texts in general
    ii) the particular text you are working on.

STEP 4 **Exploring conclusions**

a) Read the conclusion and consider the following questions:
    i) To what extent does the conclusion summarize the main arguments?
    ii) To what extent does the conclusion offer a solution to a problem?
    iii) To what extent does the conclusion end with a clear statement of the writer's position?
    iv) To what extent does the conclusion make an impact on the reader? How does it do this?

b) [Discuss] with a partner the role of a conclusion in:
    i) texts in general
    ii) the particular text you are working on.

c) [List] the ingredients of a successful conclusion.

Exploring visuals

Analyse any visuals (charts, graphs, photographs, images) and think about the following questions:

a) To what extent do the visuals help clarify the communication?

b) Has the visual been referenced in the text?

c) To what extent does it complement the writing in the text?

d) To what extent does it contradict the writing in the text?

e) To what extent does it help offer context and add clarity?

f) To what extent does it create an impact on the reader?

g) How does its position on the page affect the message of the text or paragraphs nearby?

GLOBAL CONTEXTS
Personal and cultural expression

ATL SKILLS
Communication
Organize and depict information logically.

 **Activity 10**   **Walking and talking your way through a discussion essay**

In your final two years of the IB Middle Years Programme you will be asked to produce essays, speeches and articles that persuade or argue a case. Arguments tend to put forward one side of a case while discussions present both sides of an argument and end with the writer saying which side they agree with. Review the chart at the beginning of the chapter. Remind yourself of the key elements of text types and forms.

TIP

One way to clarify ideas in your head before you start writing is to talk your ideas through with someone. It is also a good test to see if you are ready to write. If you cannot explain your arguments clearly you are not ready to begin writing.

STEP 1   **Talking through your arguments**

As a class, choose a topic or statement. Think of as many arguments as you can for and against the topic or statement you have chosen. Try to think of concrete examples to support your arguments.

Your teacher will now select one observer. If you are selected as the observer, you will need to walk around the class and observe the groups as they work through the next two steps.

a) Get into groups of five. In your groups consider one side of the debate. There should be roughly the same number of groups on each side of the debate for this activity to work. In your group of five, agree on the best five arguments or opinions to support your case and divide them among your group. Take one point each and come up with a specific example to support and illustrate your point. If you can, and your group is bigger than five, think of further arguments to develop the point.

b) Use the writing frame below to write a short 3–4 line paragraph which states the point succinctly and includes an example as supporting evidence.

Introducing the point	Introducing the example	Explaining the example
A reason why … is … An argument for … is Some people argue … They claim…	This is seen for example when…	that shows/suggests/implies/proves/supports the idea that …

c) As a group, listen to each other's arguments and evidence. Decide on the order in which you would like to present your arguments to the class. Think about which arguments will make the greatest impact on your audience.

STEP 2 **Walking through the arguments**

All groups should now come back together and form two lines (see diagram below). Each line needs to represent one side of the argument. Make sure your group lines up in the order you decided on in c) above, and is facing the opposing group. This will create a corridor 1–2 metres wide.

NOTE: Depending on the size of your class you may have more or fewer groups than is shown in the diagram.

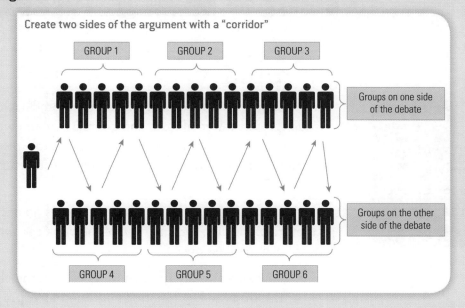

Create two sides of the argument with a "corridor"

GROUP 1   GROUP 2   GROUP 3

Groups on one side of the debate

Groups on the other side of the debate

GROUP 4   GROUP 5   GROUP 6

a) The student who was observing the groups earlier will now move down the corridor. This person represents the reader moving through the essay, listening to arguments on both sides as they progress.

b) When the "reader" reaches you, you should deliver your point and support it with evidence.

c) Once the "reader" has moved all the way down the corridor and heard all of the arguments, he or she should decide which perspectives are most convincing.

If you are the "reader", you will need to begin by saying, "In conclusion, …" and state your perspective and why you chose it. The aim is to make this closing phrase sound like the conclusion of the essay.

REFLECTION

For the "reader":

- How did you feel as you were moving down the corridor hearing the different arguments?
- Which were the strongest arguments you heard and what made them convincing?
- To what degree did the order in which you heard the arguments influence your conclusion?
- Would you have ordered the arguments differently? If so, what changes would you have made and why?

For the group:

- How did the exercise help teach you to structure and write an essay?
- What, if anything, have you learned about your own process for constructing arguments?
- What, if anything, have you learned about how to improve the language of your essays?

GLOBAL CONTEXTS
Personal and cultural expression

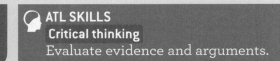
ATL SKILLS
Critical thinking
Evaluate evidence and arguments.

Summary

In this chapter you have analysed and explored aspects of structure used in a wide range of texts and genres, in your own and others' writing. You have become more aware of the role of structure in communicating a writer's purpose, and how structure can help reflect the writer's thinking.

QUICK THINK

How could you apply either of the strategies in the previous activities to improve the way you organize your thoughts and ideas on paper?

To test your understanding of these concepts go back and review the structure of the chapter, and then of the book as a whole, and answer the following questions:

- How effective are the openings of both the chapter and book in fulfilling the key functions outlined in Topic 1?

- How effective is the organization of images and text in reinforcing the thinking and ideas outlined in the chapter and the book?

- What improvements could be made to the overall structure and layout of text and images?

References

Blake, W. *London*. The Poetry Foundation. Available at: http://www.poetryfoundation.org/poem/172929.

Dorfman, A. 1994. *Death and the Maiden*. Penguin Books; Reprint edition.

Wordsworth, W. *Composed Upon Westminster Bridge*. The Poetry Foundation. Available at: http://www.poetryfoundation.org/poem/174783.

Point of view

**KEY CONCEPT FOCUS
PERSPECTIVE**

INQUIRY QUESTIONS

TOPIC 1 Narrative point of view
- ■ **How does the narrator's point of view influence the reader's perspective?**

TOPIC 2 Can I trust the narrator?
- ■ **How do critical readers analyse texts according to who is narrating?**

TOPIC 3 Bringing different points of view together
- ■ **How can bringing together different perspectives lead to positive action?**

SKILLS

ATL
- ✓ Draw reasonable conclusions and generalizations.
- ✓ Analyse complex concepts and projects into their constituent parts and synthesize them to create new understanding.
- ✓ Read critically and for comprehension.
- ✓ Consider ideas from multiple perspectives.
- ✓ Listen actively to other perspectives and ideas.

Language and literature
- ✓ Understand and identify different points of view and narrators.
- ✓ Analyze the effects of the narrator on a story and consider what perspectives have not been represented.
- ✓ See and utilize Bloom's Taxonomy and its thinking levels applied to the learning of a concept.
- ✓ Plan effective action by bringing together different perspectives.

OTHER RELATED CONCEPTS

Structure   Intertextuality   Character

GLOSSARY

Colloquial speech used in ordinary conversation and not used in formal or literary situations.

Narrator a person who narrates something, especially a character who recounts the events of a novel or narrative poem.

Objective not influenced by personal feelings or opinions in considering and representing facts.

Omniscient all-knowing.

COMMAND TERMS

Analyse breakdown in order to bring out the essential elements or structure. To identify parts and relationships, and to interpret information to reach conclusions.

Apply use knowledge and understanding in response to a given situation or real circumstances. Use an idea, equation, principle, theory or law in relation to a given problem or issue.

Contrast give an account of the differences between two (or more) items or situations, referring to both (all) of them throughout.

Introducing point of view

As defined in the MYP language and literature guide, point of view is "the particular perspective brought by a composer, responder or character within a text to the text or to matters within the text. It also entails the position or vantage point from which the events of a story seem to be observed and presented to us. When exploring this concept, students will, for example, consider positioning, voice and tone." Given the obvious cross-over to the key concept of perspective, this chapter will focus predominantly on narrative point of view (literature), or the point of view a story is told from. It will then move into journalistic and historical point of view, still focusing on understanding the person recounting the nonfiction (language).

TOPIC 1

Narrative point of view

Narrative point of view is something that we recognize from childhood. We can recognize when books speak directly to us, when the **narrator** has a funny voice, when a book starts with "Once upon a time" or when we determine right from the start that an unknown story teller is about to tell us something that they once experienced.

Once a reader moves towards literary analysis, the necessary choices of an author and their effects becomes slightly more complicated, but children's books are a great way to define the concept of point of view. This chapter is structured to move up the pyramid of Bloom's Taxonomy to demonstrate the different levels of the thinking ATL and to give context for the command terms.

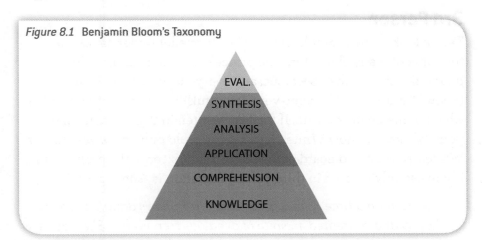

Figure 8.1 Benjamin Bloom's Taxonomy

- EVAL.
- SYNTHESIS
- ANALYSIS
- APPLICATION
- COMPREHENSION
- KNOWLEDGE

1st Person

First person narration uses "I" or "we" and puts us in the mind of our narrator. We are involved in the story, no matter where the storyteller takes us, and we can often "hear" the thoughts behind their actions.

The advantage of reading first person narration is that we really get to know the character speaking—the whole story is written from their viewpoint. We get to know their voice, both out loud and in their thoughts. The example below, taken from *Where the Red Fern Grows* by Wilson Rawls, shows these advantages. Notice how the diction or the choice of words or phrasing, and the sentence structure are **colloquial** (*"Along about then..."*). What are the effects of having the narrator's voice tell the story? Also, the reader is able to experience the moment of realized personal growth as the narrator realizes it for himself. Contrast how this would be different if it had been written in 3rd person, with a narrator telling the reader that "Billy realized he had become a full-fledged raccoon hunter"?

> *I was a proud boy as I walked along in the twilight of the evening. I felt so good even my sore hands had stopped hurting. What boy wouldn't have been so proud? Hadn't my little hounds treed and killed their first raccoon? Along about then I decided I was a full-fledged raccoon hunter.*

2nd Person

In the example below, you can see the power of speaking directly to the reader (you). Children in particular love this because it makes them part of the story. Whilst this is not used as often in adolescent literature, it is still used in speeches, plays, dramatic poems, and in a variety of situations for this same effect.

> "You're off to Great Places!
> Today is your day!
> Your mountain is waiting,
> So... get on your way!"

3rd Person

Take a look at the example below. The storyteller understands the thoughts of many characters: the prince's daughter (Snow White) is happy, the stepmother is jealous, and everyone was "quite sure she (Snow White) would become very beautiful." The narrator even knows what the magic mirror said. If this was written in 1st person, from the point of view of Snow White, the narrator could only know what Snow White had seen and heard personally. In this excerpt, the pronoun that is consistently utilized in third person narration is *"she"* or *"her"*.

> *"Once upon a time . . . in a great castle, a Prince's daughter grew up happy and contented, in spite of a jealous stepmother. She was very pretty, with blue eyes and long black hair. Her skin was delicate and fair, and so she was called Snow White. Everyone was quite sure she would become very beautiful. Though her stepmother was a wicked woman, she too was very beautiful, and the magic mirror told her this every day, whenever she asked it."*

Using the narrative point of view to gain insight

As you can see from the video mentioned at left, point of view can be assigned to two areas of classification: the "grammatical person" used in the text and "Level of Insight" of the narrator.

The grammatical person is shown by pronouns used:

- 1st Person: I or We
- 2nd Person: You
- 3rd Person: He, She, or It, broken down based on level of insight.

The level of insight can be shown on a scale, with **objective** on one end and **omniscient** on the other.

- Objective: Like a video camera, dictating events through what can be seen and heard. No hidden thoughts or information are shared. This is the level of insight a journalist generally wants to aim for, since it does not inadvertently insert bias into the reporting and just tells what happened. Also known as the "fly on the wall" point of view.

- Limited Omniscient: The narrator only knows one character's point of view, but presents other characters externally. This viewpoint is in the middle of the spectrum, giving more freedom to a writer than first person or 3rd person objective, but not as much as 3rd person omniscient.

- Omniscient: Simply defined, this equals "all knowing", meaning the narrator knows everything that is going on and tells the readers everything they need to know from the viewpoint of many characters.

WEB LINKS

Go to www.youtube.com and enter "Narrative point of view" into the search box to find a video by Mr Turner's English.

WEB LINKS

You can find an in-depth level of discussion and analysis on narrative point of view as you research, even hearing directly from a variety of authors. This web link is a starting place: blog.nathanbransford.com. Search for the post on "Third Person Omniscient vs Third Person Limited".

QUICK THINK

Look at the short extract below. Analyze how Terry Pratchett uses the 3rd person point of view in *Wyrd Sisters* for comedic effect. Look at the chapter on Setting if you would like to see the intertextuality shown here, derived from the scene in Shakespeare's *Macbeth*.

Wyrd Sisters by Terry Practchett

The night was as black as the inside of a cat. It was the kind of night, you could believe, on which gods moved men as though they were pawns on the chessboard of fate. In the middle of this elemental storm a fire gleamed among the dripping furze bushes like the madness in a weasel's eye. It illuminated three hunched figures. As the cauldron bubbled an eldritch voice shrieked: "When shall we three meet again?"

There was a pause.

Finally another voice said, in far more ordinary tones: "Well, I can do next Tuesday."

Applying and analysing narrative point of view

1) Identify the point of view used in each passage below and 2) **analyse** the effect it has on the narration of the story.

1. *PRIDE AND PREJUDICE* by Jane Austen

Mr. Bingley had soon made himself acquainted with all the principal people in the room; he was lively and unreserved, danced every dance, was angry that the ball closed so early, and talked of giving one himself at Netherfield. Such amiable qualities must speak for themselves. What a contrast between him and his friend! Mr. Darcy danced only once with Mrs. Hurst and once with Miss Bingley, declined being introduced to any other lady, and spent the rest of the evening in walking about the room, speaking occasionally to one of his own party. His character was decided. He was the proudest, most disagreeable man in the world, and everybody hoped that he would never come there again.

2. *THE IDIOTS* by Joseph Conrad

We were driving along the road from Treguier to Kervanda. We passed at a smart trot between the hedges topping an earth wall on each side of the road; then at the foot of the steep ascent before Ploumar the horse dropped into a walk, and the driver jumped down heavily from the box. He flicked his whip and climbed the incline, stepping clumsily uphill by the side of the carriage, one hand on the footboard, his eyes on the ground. After a while he lifted his head, pointed up the road with the end of the whip, and said: "The idiot!" I was startled by his outburst.

3. *RIKKI-TIKKI-TAVI* by Rudyard Kipling

Rikki-tikki heard them going up the path from the stables, and he raced for the end of the melon patch near the wall. "I was not a day too soon," he said; for he could see the baby cobras curled up inside the skin, and he knew that the minute they were hatched they could kill a man or mongoose. He bit off the tops of the eggs as fast as he could, taking care to crush the young cobras. Nagaina spun clear round, forgetting everything for the sake of her eggs. She saw she had lost her chance of killing Teddy, and the last egg lay between Rikki-tikki's paws.

4. *WHITE FANG* by Jack London

They spoke no more until camp was made. Henry was bending over and adding ice to the bubbling pot of beans when he was startled by the sound of a sharp snarling cry of pain from among the dogs. Henry grunted with a tone that was not sympathy, and for a quarter of an hour they sat on in silence, Henry staring at the fire, and Bill at the circle of eyes that burned in the darkness just beyond the firelight. An icy wind circled between them and the fire.

5. *CAMPING OUT* by Ernest Hemmingway

To be really rested and get any benefit out of a vacation a man must get a good night's sleep every night. The first requisite for this is to have plenty of cover. It is twice as cold as you expect it will be in the bush four nights out of five, and a good plan is to take just double the bedding that you think you will need. An old quilt that you can wrap up in is as warm as two blankets.

6. *THE TELL-TALE HEART* by Edgar Allen Poe

And every night, about midnight, I turned the latch of his door and opened it—oh so gently!

7. *ANIMAL FARM* by George Orwell

Three nights later old Major died peacefully in his sleep. His body was buried at the foot of the orchard.

This was early in March. During the next three months there was much secret activity. Major's speech had given to the more intelligent animals on the farm a completely new outlook on life. They did not know when the Rebellion predicted by Major would take place, they had no reason for thinking that it would be within their own lifetime, but they saw clearly that it was their duty to prepare for it.

8. *MISS BRILL* by Katherine Mansfield

Oh, how fascinating it was! How she enjoyed it! How she loved sitting here, watching it all! It was like a play. It was exactly like a play. Who could believe the sky at the back wasn't painted?

9. *HARRY POTTER AND THE CHAMBER OF SECRETS* by J.K. Rowling

"Do I look stupid?" snarled Uncle Vernon, a bit of fried egg dangling from his bushy mustache. "I know what'll happen if that owl's let out."

He exchanged dark looks with his wife, Petunia.

Harry tried to argue back, but his words were drowned by a long, loud belch from the Dursleys' son, Dudley.

Creating point of view – your turn

Are you ready to reach the top of Bloom's pyramid of thinking?

In this last challenge, write about or create a brief but exciting moment in your own life. The length should be about the same as the longer examples in numbers 1–9. See if you can narrate your story from three different points of view. After writing, share with a classmate or your teacher and evaluate the advantages and limitations of each point of view.

Options: First Person, Second Person, 3rd Person Objective, 3rd Person Limited, 3rd Person Omniscient

---

REFLECTION

1. What are the possible points of view?
2. What are the advantages and limitations of each?

GLOBAL CONTEXTS
Personal and cultural expression

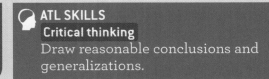
ATL SKILLS
Critical thinking
Draw reasonable conclusions and generalizations.

Can I trust the narrator?

Narrators are not always trustworthy. This is the next level of understanding in terms of narrative point of view—authors will purposely choose a narrator that should be more closely analysed by the reader. Just as archetypal characters have been defined in the chapter on characterization, so too have unreliable narrators been classed into a list of repeated styles. Most of these types fall into first person narrators. Why do you think that is?

The titles of these unreliable narrators are not well known or universally accepted. However, the types are a good guide to the unreliable narrators you might encounter. You may want to ask your teacher for help in explaining the terms used here or the examples listed:

- The Pícaro: a narrator who is characterized by exaggeration and bragging. Example: Walter Mitty

- The Madman: a narrator who is either experiencing mental defense mechanisms, such as post-traumatic-dissociation and self-alienation, or severe mental illness, such as schizophrenia or paranoia. Examples include Franz Kafka's self-alienating narrators, noir fiction and hardboiled fiction's "tough" narrator who unreliably describes his own emotions

- The Clown: a narrator who does not take narrations seriously and consciously plays with conventions, truth and the reader's expectations.

- The Naíf: a narrator whose perception is immature or limited through his or her point of view. Examples include Huckleberry Finn and Holden Caulfield.

- The Liar: a mature narrator of sound cognition who deliberately misrepresents himself, often to obscure his unseemly or discreditable past conduct. Example: John Dowell in Ford Madox Ford's *The Good Soldier*.

Analyse the poem below for the use of an unreliable narrator.

Lucrezia di Cosimo Painted by the Italian artist Bronzino (1503–1572).

WEB LINKS
You can search for an audio reading of *My Last Duchess* on www.poets.org.

My Last Duchess by Robert Browning

Ferrara

That's my last Duchess painted on the wall,
Looking as if she were alive. I call
That piece a wonder, now: Fra Pandolf's hands
Worked busily a day, and there she stands.
Will't please you sit and look at her? I said
"Fra Pandolf" by design, for never read
Strangers like you that pictured countenance,
The depth and passion of its earnest glance,
But to myself they turned (since none puts by
    the curtain I have drawn for you, but I)
And seemed they would ask me, if they durst,
How such a glance came there; so not the first
Are you to turn and ask thus. Sir, 'twas not
Her husband's presence only, called that spot
Of joy into the Duchess's cheek: perhaps
Fra Pandolf chanced to say "Her mantle laps
Over my lady's wrist too much," or Paint
Must never hope to reproduce the faint
Half flush that dies along her throat":
    such stuff
Was courtesy, she thought, and cause enough
For calling up that spot of you. She had
A heart—how shall I say?—too soon made glad,
Too easily impressed; she liked whate'er
She looked on, and her looks went
    everywhere.
Sir, 'twas all one! My favor at her breast,
The dropping of the daylight in the West,

The bough of cherries some officious fool
Broke in the orchard for her, the white mule
She rode with round the terrace—all and each
Would draw from her alike the approving speech,
Or blush, at least. She thanked men—good!
    but thanked
Somehow—I know not how—as if she ranked
My gift of a nine-hundred-years-old name
With anybody's gift. Who'd stoop to blame
This sort of trifling? Even had you skill
In speech—which I have not)—to make your will
Quite clear to such a one, and say, "Just this
Or that in you disgusts me; here you miss
Or there exceed the mark"—and if she let
Herself be lessoned so, nor plainly sether wits
    to yours, forsooth, and made excuse
—E'en then would be some stooping; and
    I choose
Never to stoop. Oh sir, she smiled, no doubt
Whene'er I passed her; but who passed without
Much the same smile? This grew; I gave
    commands;
Then all smiles stopped together. There she
    stands
As if alive. Will't please you rise? We'll meet
    the company below, then. I repeat
The Count your master's known munificence
Is ample warrant that no just pretense
Of mine dowry will be disallowed
Though his fair daughter's self, as I avowed
At starting, is my object. Nay, we'll go
Together down, sir. Notice Neptune, though,
Taming a sea horse, thought a rarity,
Which Claus of Innsbruck cast in bronze for me!

Discussion Questions:

Answer these questions on your own first. Then create final answers with a small group of classmates.

Comprehension: What is the poem about?

Analysis

- What are the hints that Robert Browning gives us to show that the narrator is not trustworthy? Cite key quotes or lines.
- What type of unreliable narrator from above do you think Ferrara would represent? Why?
- What overall effect does using an unreliable narrator have on both the poem and the reader?
- How would you characterize the narrator? Do you know anyone in today's society who has a similar character?

 **GLOBAL CONTEXTS**
Orientation in space and time

ATL SKILLS
Critical thinking
Analyse complex concepts and projects into their constituent parts and synthesize them to create new understanding.

 **Activity 3**

The TRUE Story of the Three Little Pigs *connected to an experience that you retold*

For another narrative example, look at the story of the "The Three Little Pigs" mentioned in the chapter on Structure. What if the point of view was changed in a very familiar story? Jon Scieszka explored this idea when he wrote *The TRUE Story of the* **Three Little Pigs**.

> "Everybody knows the story of the Three Little Pigs. Or at least they think they do. But I'll let you in on a little secret. Nobody knows the real story, because nobody has ever heard my side of the story." —A. Wolf

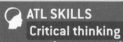 **WEB LINKS**
You can find a video Retelling of *The True Story of the Three Little Pigs* on www.youtube.com. Enter the story title into the search box.

1. Re-write the opening of another fairy tale from a different point of view. Think about the key elements that you need to change in order to show that other viewpoint. What if you switched to an unreliable narrator? What emotions or motives would drive their unreliable response?

2. Retell an event that you were involved with at school or in a co-curricular activity from the first person point of view of one of the other participants. What are some key elements that you changed to show that other viewpoint? What if you switched to an unreliable narrator? What emotions or motives would drive their unreliable response?

 **GLOBAL CONTEXTS**
Orientation in space and time

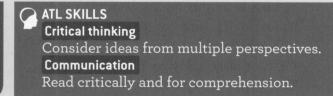 **ATL SKILLS**
Critical thinking
Consider ideas from multiple perspectives.
Communication
Read critically and for comprehension.

 **Activity 4**   Additional practice on point of view

Option 1: Creative Writing
Choose your favorite novel, story or any piece of narrative writing and write a vital page from the first person point of view of a different character. How does the story change? What are the advantages and disadvantages?

Option 2: Hot Seating Group Oral
1. As a group, choose a controversial moment or topic in a novel, play, movie, historical period, etc. and select key characters.
2. Create a television talk show scene where a host and studio audience grill the characters/personalities in a dramatic manner, with the student actors maintaining their character throughout. Focus on each character's point of view and highlight how they differ.

🌐 **GLOBAL CONTEXTS**
Orientation in space and time

🧠 **ATL SKILLS**
Collaboration
Listen actively to other perspectives and ideas.

 Activity 5   Reflection activity

Read the excerpt below. Use what you have learned about point of view to **analyse** the story.

It was a dark autumn night. The old banker was pacing from corner to corner of his study, recalling to his mind the party he gave in the autumn fifteen years before. There were many clever people at the party and much interesting conversation. They talked among other things of capital punishment. The guests, among them not a few scholars and journalists, for the most part disapproved of capital punishment. They found it obsolete as a means of punishment, unfitted to a Christian State and immoral. Some of them thought that capital punishment should be replaced universally by life-imprisonment.

"I don't agree with you," said the host. "I myself have experienced neither capital punishment nor life-imprisonment, but if one may judge a **priori***, then in my opinion capital punishment is more moral and more humane than imprisonment. Execution kills instantly, life-imprisonment kills by degrees. Who is the more humane executioner, one who kills you in a few seconds or one who draws the life out of you incessantly, for years?"*

"They're both equally immoral," remarked one of the guests, "because their purpose is the same, to take away life. The State is not God. It has no right to take away that which it cannot give back, if it should so desire."

Among the company was a lawyer, a young man of about twenty-five. On being asked his opinion, he said:

"Capital punishment and life-imprisonment are equally immoral; but if I were offered the choice between them, I would certainly choose the second. It's better to live somehow than not to live at all."

There ensued a lively discussion. The banker who was then younger and more nervous suddenly lost his temper, banged his fist on the table, and turning to the young lawyer, cried out:

"It's a lie. I bet you two millions you wouldn't stick in a cell even for five years."

"If you mean it seriously," replied the lawyer, "then I bet I'll stay not five but fifteen."

"Fifteen! Done!" cried the banker. "Gentlemen, I stake two millions."

"Agreed. You stake two millions, I my freedom," said the lawyer.

So this wild, ridiculous bet came to pass...

REFLECTION

1. What point of view is this text written in?
2. What level of insight has been chosen?
3. Looking at the overall idea or premise of the story, what advantages would this point of view have in this scene? What advantage do you think this point of view will have as the story continues?

GLOBAL CONTEXTS
Orientation in space and time

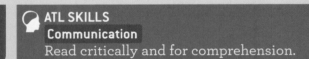

ATL SKILLS
Communication
Read critically and for comprehension.

TOPIC 3

Bringing different points of view together

If all stories are told from a point of view and there is the chance that the narrator of those stories is unreliable, how can this concept be applied beyond just thinking about the narrator when you read a novel? So far this chapter has focused on the narrative point of view. But how do you apply understanding of point of view to the stories that are told outside of fiction?

As one *Al Jazeera International* news cameraman once said, "There is no unbiased news in the world. As soon as you point your camera in one direction rather than another, you have created some degree of bias."

There is no story without a storyteller. All stories are told by someone, and that person has a background and inevitably a bias.

You can easily see this concept in action when there is a major incident in a school. Principals separate the involved parties and have each write what occurred. Invariably, if the group has had no time to discuss what occurred, each account has elements that were not included in other versions. Principals then use all of the materials to determine "what really happened".

 TAKE ACTION

As interconnections across the world have grown, so has the concept of point of view and the power it can hold – not just identifying different points of view, but also in bringing them together. Whether someone is organizing a Model United Nations conference, creating immigration policies for a country, or working in business recruitment, the value of involving different viewpoints to create greater synergy, or a situation in which the whole is greater than the parts, is a well-known collaborative strategy.

One example is when young Pakistani and Indian students came together at the Seeds of Peace conference in the U.S. state of Maine in 2005. The students noticed that the disagreements that had existed between people in their oft-estranged countries were as deeply rooted as the textbooks that they used in school. This meant that the historical foundation for discussions of peace was unsound from the beginning, since they had such different views of what had occurred in the past.

Think about examples of this in your locality or country. What could you do to identify where this has happened and put it right?

 **Activity 6**   **Creating a mutual history**

Read the 2 textbook excerpts below. Can you determine which textbook was used in India and which was used in Pakistan?

In 1947, when Hari Singh, the ruler of Kashmir, opted to stay independent, Pakistani armed intruders from Pakistan attacked Kashmir. Hari Singh then signed an agreement to join India, and the Indian army was sent in to defend Kashmir.

Hari Singh started a brutal campaign to drive out Muslims from Kashmir. Over 200,000 people in the princely State, supported by the tribesmen of the Northwest Frontier Province, were successful in liberating a large area of Kashmir from the Maharaja's control. So Hari Singh was forced to turn to India for help and in return acceded to India.

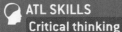 **GLOBAL CONTEXTS**
Identities and relationships

ATL SKILLS
Critical thinking
Analyse complex concepts and projects into their constituent parts and synthesize them to create new understanding.
Communication
Read critically and for comprehension.

What is the value of having a common source that has been written to include a variety of viewpoints? What are some of the considerations the authors would have had to write a book that schools would use in each country? What point of view would they need to write in?

TAKE ACTION

The students involved in Seeds of Peace published a common textbook, to be used in both countries, in 2012 as part of The History Project. They hoped that establishing a common history, representing various viewpoints, would help to create the bridge necessary to end division between their countries.

Can you think of any type of action that you can take that would help to bring important viewpoints in your community together to understand one another? Not only is it in line with the IB mission to "understand that other people, with their differences, can also be right," but it is also an important role for young people in a community since they are often less mired (stuck) in the issues surrounding the conflict.

Reflection

1. What is the value of understanding point of view?
2. How does the narrator's point of view influence the reader's perspective?
3. How do critical readers analyse texts according to who is narrating?
4. Are there other nonfiction books, articles, movies, etc. that you have watched without thinking about the point of view? How did this impact your opinion on the matter being discussed?
5. How can bringing together different perspectives lead to positive action?

Summary

This chapter has focused primarily on narrative point of view and on the many ways that a creator can choose to tell a story. It then moved to being able to analyse the effects of point of view on an audience and to provide the necessary points of view to bring about an open dialogue towards peace in the world. Finally, you were asked to apply this understanding to make a difference in your community.

References

Austen, J. 1870. *Pride and Prejudice*. Clarendon Press.

Browning, R. *My Last Duchess*. Extract from: http://www.poetryfoundation.org/poem/173024.

Checkhov, A. *The Bet*. Extract from: http://www.eastoftheweb.com/short-stories/UBooks/Bet.shtml.

Conrad, J. 2007. *The Idiots* (included in *The complete short stories of Joseph Conrad*). Barnes & Noble.

Grimm, J. & Grimm, W. Snow White. 1812. Extract from: http://www.fpx. de/fp/Disney/Tales/SnowWhite.html.

Hemingway, E. 1920. *Camping Out*. Extract from: http://grammar.about. com/od/classicessays/a/campinghemingway.htm.

Kipling, R. 2012. *RIKKI-TIKKI-TAVI,* SMK Books.

London, J. 1991. *White Fang*. Dover Publications; Unabridged edition.

Mansfield, K. *Miss Brill*. Extract from: http://www.eastoftheweb.com/ short-stories/UBooks/MissBril.shtml.

One story two sides. Textbook extracts from http://www.thehindu.com.

Orwell, George. 1945. *Animal Farm*. Extract from Project Gutenberg: http://gutenberg.net.au/ebooks01/0100011h.html.

Orwell, G. 1950. *1984*. Signet Classic.

Poe, E. 1843. *The Tell-Tale Heart*. Extract from: https://www. poemuseum.org/works-telltale.php.

Pratchett, T. 2004. *Wyrd Sisters*. Corgi.

Rawls, W. 2011. *Where the Red Fern Grows*. Random House.

Riggan, W. 1981. *Pícaros, Madmen, Naïfs, and Clowns: The Unreliable First-person Narrator*. Univ. of Oklahoma Press: Norman.

Rowling, J.K. Reprint edition 2013. *Harry Potter and the Chamber of Secrets*. Scholastic Inc.

Scieszka, J. 1996. *The TRUE Story of the Three Little Pigs*. Puffin; Reprint edition.

Seuss, Dr. 1990. *Oh, the Places You'll Go!* Random House.

Character

INQUIRY QUESTIONS

TOPIC 1 A personal approach to characterisation
- ■ **What techniques do writers use to present a character?**

TOPIC 2 The role of speech in characterisation
- ■ **How do our words define us?**

TOPIC 3 Communicating character changes and development
- ■ **How do characters change and how can we represent those changes visually?**

SKILLS

ATL

- ✓ Consider ideas from multiple perspectives.
- ✓ Interpret and use effectively modes of non-verbal communication.
- ✓ Use and interpret a range of discipline-specific terms and symbols.
- ✓ Make inferences and draw conclusions.
- ✓ Make unexpected or unusual connections between objects and/or ideas.
- ✓ Generate metaphors and analogies.
- ✓ Give and receive meaningful feedback.
- ✓ Draw reasonable conclusions and generalizations.
- ✓ Read critically and for comprehension.
- ✓ Organize and depict information logically.
- ✓ Create original works and ideas; use existing works and ideas in new ways.

Language and literature

- ✓ Explore verbal and non-verbal communication through speaking and listening – drama, role play, discussion.
- ✓ Read and view texts to explore the impact of writers' choices.
- ✓ Be creative and critical in exploration of characters and characterisation using a range of media for different purposes and audiences.

OTHER RELATED CONCEPTS

Perspective   Audience imperatives

Self-expression

GLOSSARY

Characterisation the process by which the writer reveals the personality of a character.

Connotation something suggested or implied by a word, phrase or portion of a text.

COMMAND TERMS

Analyse break down in order to bring out the essential elements or structure. To identify parts and relationships, and to interpret information to reach conclusions.

Explore undertake a systematic process of discovery.

Introducing character

When thinking about **characterisation**, a good place to start is to think about yourself. Understanding how you present yourself to the world, and how you communicate your physical and emotional states, can help you explore techniques of characterisation used by writers to present their fictional characters.

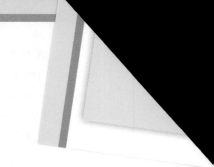

QUICK THINK

One of the first questions a stranger might ask you is your name. Think about what your name tells people about you:

- where you are from and your cultural background
- your age and the generation or time when you were born
- your personality (you can use an internet search to find out the meanings of your names)
- associations with people with that name in historical, cultural, religious, sporting or other contexts.

 Activity 1   What's in a name?

STEP 1 Writers also use characters' names to reveal aspects of their personality. You will look at this again in Chapter 17, Self-expression. Think about what the following famous names in fiction may suggest about the personalities of the characters behind them:

- Mr Gradgrind – a hardware merchant and politician in Charles Dickens's novel *Hard Times*
- Piggy – a boy in William Golding's novel *Lord of the Flies*
- Shylock – a Jew in William Shakespeare's play *The Merchant of Venice*
- Crooks – a stablehand in John Steinbeck's novel *Of Mice and Men*
- Inspector Goole from J.B Priestley's play *An Inspector Calls*
- Biff and Happy – two brothers from Arthur Miller's play *Death of a Salesman*

STEP 2 Let's look at the first character mentioned in the list, Mr. Thomas Gradgrind, from Charles Dickens's novel *Hard Times*. Mr. Gradgrind is a successful hardware merchant who embodies the spirit of the Industrial Revolution, treats people as machines and emphasizes rational thought. Find a hard or electronic copy of *Hard Times*, read Chapter 1, and analyze how Dickens uses Gradgrind's name and the description of him to convey his personality. Use the questions below to guide your analysis.

- Why is his name not mentioned here?
- What associations can you make with his name?
- How does Dickens use his name to embody his belief and attitude towards education?
- What is the narrative voice's attitude towards Gradgrind? How can you tell?
- What is the impact of repetition in the description of Mr. Gradgrind and in his own speech?

- How does his speech reinforce the impression of him as a rigid, hard rationalist?
- What interesting comparisons does Dickens use to develop Gradgrind's character?
- What associations do you make with the square shape that is used to describe him?
- How does the setting and comparisons of the schoolroom to a factory and a vault reinforce the sense of Gradgrind's character?
- How does the dialogue reinforce his dry, dictatorial character?
- What is the effect of comparing the children to vessels?

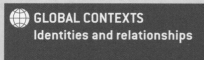 **STEP 3** Now look back at the adventure story you created in Chapter 4 on Creativity. Think about the names of the protagonists in your story.
- Did their names reflect any aspects of their personalities? If not, how could you change their names to give your readers a better sense of their personalities?

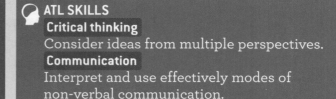

🌐 **GLOBAL CONTEXTS**
Identities and relationships

💭 **ATL SKILLS**
Critical thinking
Consider ideas from multiple perspectives.
Communication
Interpret and use effectively modes of non-verbal communication.

In addition to exploring characters' names, studying how they are addressed by other characters is also important in establishing their roles and relationships with other characters. In Shakespeare's *The Merchant of Venice*, for example, Shylock is only addressed by his name six times in the play but called "Jew" twenty-two times, something that highlights how others regard him more as a member of the Jewish community than as an individual.

In this chapter you will explore the following questions:

- How can you use your own life to investigate writers' presentation of fictional characters?

- How do writers' choices about how they present characters influence your responses to them?

- What are the different forms of direct and indirect techniques of characterisation that writers use?

- What are symbols and how do writers use them to communicate characters?

- How can you use your own creativity to show an understanding of characters and their portrayal by writers?

Considering techniques of characterisation

To further explore aspects of characterisation, continue thinking about yourself. If an investigator knew your name, what other strategies might he or she use to find out information about you – where you go, your motivations, passions, fears, interests, movements? The investigator could:

- Speak to people who know you well – friends, neighbours, parents, teachers

- Speak to people you have had regular contact with

- Visit your house – your room

- Speak to you in person

- Visit your Facebook page to see who you know and your hobbies and interests

- Read a journal or online blog that you wrote.

Writers use similar strategies or techniques of characterisation when presenting characters to a reader. With a partner, look at the following table and see what other techniques you can come up with. You might want to ask your teacher to clarify some of the words or terms listed here.

Figure 9.1 Investigating character: thinking like a detective

What they say and how they say it	• Do characters have specific speech patterns or use certain expressions or language that sets them apart or defines them? • How do characters alter their speech when talking to different people? • To what extent do they make / use statements, questions, commands, exclamations? How do these convey their tone or mood? For example, someone asking lots of questions may be doubtful, uncertain, or concerned. • Turn-taking / interruptions – do they interrupt to agree and show solidarity or do they interrupt other characters to demonstrate their authority? • Do they dominate the conversation and/or dictate the subject matter? • What forms of address do they use in dialogue and how do these convey the status and relationships between characters? (e.g. calling people by first name terms or by their title)
What they don't say / pauses / gaps and silences	Ignoring a question or a person and playing a passive role in conversations can reveal as much about a character as what they do say.
What others say about them	Do we see other characters making comments about them when they are present or absent from the scene? Having other characters describing or discussing your protagonist before you meet them can shape your expectations about them.
What they think	Describing a character's thoughts gives you yet another insight into their mind. They may be thinking differently from how they are behaving outwardly. Soliloquies in drama and free indirect discourse are some ways of presenting a character's thoughts.

Their interactions with other characters	Seeing a character interacting with other characters (through speech, actions, and behaviour) can reveal different aspects of their personality. Are characters contrasted with another character? In dialogue, look at forms of address, subject matter discussed, turn-taking, tone and volume, which all convey power relationships.
Their appearance	How characters dress, the sort of clothes they wear, even their hairstyles can say something about their moods, status, or situations.
Their facial expressions	By describing a character's facial expressions you can communicate how that character feels. It is better to show the reader in images rather than telling them (e.g. instead of writing "he was angry," you could write "the veins in his temples grew more pronounced and his face turned redder by the second.").
Their movements / actions / posture / stance / gestures	The way characters stand, move and use gestures can reveal their moods and their relationships with the people they are interacting with (e.g., "He stood, towering over the boy at the desk, shaking his fist." Or "The girl shuffled into the bus station and curled up on the hard plastic bench.").
Their relationship to their surroundings / different settings	Seeing a character in different settings (intimate private settings, public settings, work/school setting or at home) can reveal different aspects of their personality. Do they behave differently in different settings? Do they seem comfortable, uncomfortable in different places? Does the setting reflect their character (an isolated setting may reflect a desire to be alone or the fact a character feels alienated)?
Their relationship to a symbol(s)	Are characters seen with a particular object or prop (e.g. constantly looking at their watch, always with their dog, sitting by a fire) which reveals something about their personality?

Table 9.2 Techniques of characterisation

We could summarize these under the following heading: SMART PASS

Is the character presented mainly through:

- What they say? **S**PEECH
- How they move? **M**OVEMENTS
- What they do? **A**CTIONs
- How they interact with other characters? **R**ELATIONSHIPS
- What they think (but may not always say)? **T**HOUGHTS
- Through their own lens or the lens of someone else? **P**ERSPECTIVE
- How they look? **A**PPEARANCE
- Through their relationship to their surroundings? **S**ETTING
- Through their relationship to a symbol? **S**YMBOLISM

Another way to explore techniques in characterisation is by dividing techniques into two distinct types:

- DIRECT – telling the audience about the character
- INDIRECT – showing the audience aspects of character that reveal their personality.

Sometimes indirect methods of characterisation are summarized by the mnemonic STEAL:

- **S**peech – what characters say and how they say it
- **T**houghts – a character's attitudes, beliefs and motivations are revealed through the private and public expression of their feelings
- **E**ffect on others – how others react to and interact with the character reveals their personality
- **A**ctions – what a character does and how they behave
- **L**ook – the physical appearance of the character – the way they dress and what they look like

Let us now move on to further explore these and some other techniques of characterisation:

TOPIC 1

A personal approach to characterisation

The comparison of Mr. Gradgrind to a square in Dickens' description of him highlighted another key technique writers use to present their characters: symbolism. By connecting characters to symbols and their symbolic and metaphorical associations, writers can expand the picture of their characters in the minds of their audience.

Figure 9.3 Symbols are all around us – what other key symbols can you think of?

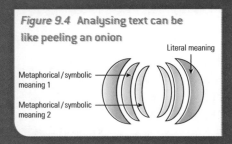

Figure 9.4 Analysing text can be like peeling an onion

Literal meaning

Metaphorical / symbolic meaning 1

Metaphorical / symbolic meaning 2

TIP

Use a dictionary of idioms to help you, or look online. Look up a symbol and see how many expressions are used about them. For example, if we look up "hands", you will find the following expressions:

- Cooperation: they worked hand in hand.
- Experience: he's an old hand at it.
- Involvement: to play a hand in.
- Inheritance: to hand down (inheritance, possession).
- Guilt/responsibility: my hands are clean, it's out of my hands.
- Fate: he was dealt a poor hand in life.
- Point of view: on the one hand, on the other hand.

In these activities you will explore the following questions:

- What are some of the key symbols used in literature and what are their common associations?
- How do writers use symbolism to communicate character?

A symbol is a concrete object that represents an abstract idea. Symbolism is a device used by writers and artists where an object, person or event represents something beyond its literal meaning.

Many symbols in different cultures have agreed meanings and associations. However, these may vary between cultures.

As a society we have already created several layers of meaning for words and images through the many written, verbal and visual texts we have produced over the ages.

In pairs, consider the following words and their **connotations** or associations. Remember to think about cultural, historical and religious associations and also about texts you have read and symbols they have featured.

Symbol group	Common symbols	Associations / Connotations
Time of day / year	Sunrise, sunset, seasons, sun, moon	
Weather and temperature	Warmth, cold, snow, rain, fog	
Animals	Lion, dove, snake, cat, lamb	
Nature / trees / plants	Rose, roots, apple tree, river, mountain	
Body parts	Hands, head, eyes	
Colours / shades	Light, dark, black, blue, white	
Shapes	Circle, triangle, square, rectangle	

Symbols, associations and connotations

Sometimes characters themselves are seen as symbols representing a given idea or concept within a text. Many characters are seen as saviour or redemption symbols, for example. Gradgrind symbolizes capitalist greed and ambition, or innate evil.

Many writers use these symbols in their writing to compare characters with different objects and symbols. Repeated symbols are called motifs. By tracking a character's relationship to a symbol you can trace their development in a text. For example, fire as a symbol in William Golding's *Lord of the Flies* conveys how the boys drift away from civilization and thoughts of rescue, and become more primitive and evil, as order breaks down on the island.

As well as symbols and their associations, writers use comparisons when describing characters. Most common are similes and metaphors (both forms of comparison) and allusions (indirect references) which create images in the reader's mind, helping form clearer mental images of the fictional characters.

Consider the following lines from Wilfred Owen's poem "Dulce et decorum est". It describes World War 1 soldiers marching back to their trenches from the front line.

> Bent double, like old beggars under sacks,
>
> Knock-kneed, coughing like hags, we cursed through sludge,
>
> Till on the haunting flares we turned our backs
>
> And towards our distant rest began to trudge.
>
> Men marched asleep. Many had lost their boots   5
>
> But, limped on, blood-shod. All went lame; all blind;
>
> Drunk with fatigue; deaf even to the hoots
>
> Of tired, outstripped Five-Nines that dropped behind.

Owen uses verbs and adverbs to communicate the soldiers' exhausted and dilapidated condition and how they move. Think of how these comparisons work on several levels. You can use a Venn diagram:

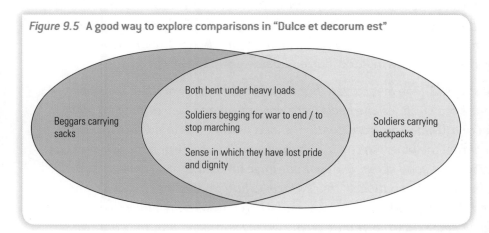

Figure 9.5 A good way to explore comparisons in "Dulce et decorum est"

Beggars carrying sacks

Both bent under heavy loads

Soldiers begging for war to end / to stop marching

Sense in which they have lost pride and dignity

Soldiers carrying backpacks

TIP

Terms you

Hags: old

Flares: ro
sent up to
glare to light up men and
targets in the area between the
front lines.

Distant rest: a camp away
from the front line where
exhausted soldiers might rest
for a few days, or longer.

Hoots: the noise made by the
shells rushing through the air.

Outstripped: outpaced,
the soldiers have struggled
beyond the reach of these
shells which are now falling
behind them as they struggle
away from the scene of battle.

Five-Nines: 5.9 calibre
explosive shells.

QUICK THINK

What associations are created by comparing the soldiers to the following?

■ Beggars	■ Hags
■ Drunks	■ Marching asleep

Draw Venn diagrams similar to the one shown and explore associations and connotations.

What impact was Owen intending to create in his audience with these unusual comparisons?

nds by Sarah Key (IB Graduate)

"Kids high-five but grown ups shake hands. You need a firm handshake, but don't hold on too tight, but don't let go too soon, but don't hold on for too long."

The excerpt that follows describes people by focusing on a key symbol, in this case, another body part: feet. Read it carefully and answer the questions that follow. Remember that while you are focusing on the writer's use of imagery and symbolism you should also be alert to other forms of characterisation. Refer to the list of techniques of characterisation earlier in this chapter to identify different ways in which the characters are presented.

> **CHAPTER LINK**
> Think back to Activity 1 about cultural greetings in Chapter 2, Communication. Think about the gestures you make when meeting and greeting people.

Reading in the Dark by Seamus Deane

The plastic tablecloth hung so far down that I could only see their feet. But I could hear the noise and some of the talk, although I was so crunched up that I could make out very little of what they were saying. Besides, our collie dog, Smoky, was whimpering; every time he quivered under his fur, I became deaf to their words and alert to their noise.

Smoky had found me under the table when the room filled with feet, standing at all angles, and he sloped through them and came to huddle himself on me. He felt the dread too. Una. My younger sister, Una. She was going to die after they took her to the hospital. I could hear the clumping of the feet of the ambulance men as they tried to manoeuvre her on a stretcher down the stairs. They would have to lift it high over the banister; the turn was too narrow. I had seen the red handles of the stretcher when the glossy shoes of the ambulance men appeared in the centre of the room. One had been holding it, folded up, perpendicular, with the handles on the ground beside his shiny black shoes, which had a tiny redness in one toecap when he put the stretcher handles on to the linoleum. The lino itself was so polished that there were answering rednesses in it too, buried upside down under the surface.

They were at the bottom of the stairs. All the feet moved that way. I could see my mother's brothers were there. I recognised Uncle Manus's brown shoes: the heels were worn down and he was moving back and forward a little. Uncle Dan and Uncle Tom had identical shoes, heavy and rimed with mud and cement, because they had come from the building site in Creggan. Dan's were dirtier, though, because Tom was the foreman. But they weren't good shoes. Dan put one knee up on a chair. There was scaffold oil on his socks. He must have been dipping putlocks[1] in oil. Once he had invited me to reach right into the bucket to find a lock that had slipped to the bottom and when I drew it out, black to the upper muscle, the slick oil swarmed down my skin to corrugate on my wrist. I sprinkled handfuls of sawdust on it, turning my arm into a bright oatmeal sleeve that darkened before Dan made me wash it off.

But it was my mother's and father's feet that I watched most. She was wearing low heels that needed mending, and her feet were always swollen so that even from there I could see the shoe leather embedded, vanishing from that angle, into her ankles. There was more scuffle and noise and her feet disappeared into the hallway, after the stretcher, and she was cough-crying as my father's workboots followed close behind her, huge, with the laces thonged round the back. Then everybody went out, and the room was empty.

Use the following prompts to consider techniques of characterisation used in this excerpt

- How are characters defined in this text through the description?
- How are characters defined by their stances?
- How are characters defined by their movements and gestures?
- How are characters defined through their thoughts?
- How are characters defined through their actions?
- How are characters defined by their appearances (clothing, facial expression etc.)?
- How are characters defined through comparison with other characters (similarities and/or differences)?
- What symbols are they associated with?
- How do their relationships with the symbols change during the text?
- How does the writer create an emotional connection with the speaker in the excerpt?

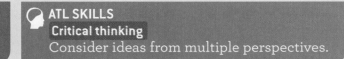

GLOBAL CONTEXTS
Identities and relationships

ATL SKILLS
Critical thinking
Consider ideas from multiple perspectives.

 **Activity 3**   A symbol of you (creating)

Having explored how writers use symbols to communicate character, use your creativity to design a symbol that represents you. Think about all the elements and associations that will communicate your character and personality. Use any of the associations from the earlier table or others you have read about. **Analyse** and research different symbols and their connotations that could be incorporated into the visual image. See Chapter 10, Theme, for more ideas.

TIP

When designing your symbol, stay away from concrete objects that represent what you are like (e.g. a ball because you like to play football). Instead, think about characteristics, beliefs and your personality, and come up with abstract symbols that reflect these aspects of you.

GLOBAL CONTEXTS
Identities and relationships

ATL SKILLS
Creative thinking
Make unexpected or unusual connections between objects and/or ideas.
Generate metaphors and analogies.
Communication
Use and interpret a range of discipline-specific terms and symbols.

Reflection

- Which techniques of characterisation do you use most often in your own writing?

- How can you create more convincing characters in your own writing using symbolism and imagery?

TOPIC 2

The role of speech in characterisation

Another key technique of characterisation is speech. In this series of activities you will explore the following questions:

- How do your words define you?

- What role do verbal and non-verbal communication play in your speech?

- How can you use drama to creatively interpret and represent characters and their relationships?

Dialogue performs a number of functions in a text, such as revealing new information and adding variety to the narrative. However, its primary function is to develop the characters and bring them to life by enabling the reader or audience to hear their voices.

 Activity 4   Studying speech in your own exchanges and texts

In Chapter 2 Communication, you explored how we vary our language according to the roles and relationships that exist within any given communication. Begin by examining your own language in a variety of situations to see how it changes according to the social and situational context.

STEP 1   Work in pairs. Decide who is A and who is B. A will improvise three phone conversations with three different people while B listens and records the sort of language that is used in each conversation. B should listen for the following:
- The forms of address to the person being phoned
- The level of formality of the language
- The type of speech functions used.

The three calls should be made to:
- A friend to organize playing a game of sport (e.g. soccer or tennis)
- A friend's parent to ask permission to take a friend to an important social event (e.g. the prom or a party)
- A potential employer about a job interview.

Spend 3 to 5 minutes planning. A should think about what sort of things to say
them. B should predict the conversation and the type of language that will be u

A should first think about the person to ring and talk to. Outline the following:

- What is your relationship with the person you are phoning? How well do you
- What is the purpose of your call? What are you trying to get done?
- What are the context and circumstances of the phone call – at home, at the office, in the shops?
- How you will adjust your language depending on whom you are addressing and the purpose of your communication?

Use the following table to help you:

Phone call	Content of call – things to be addressed	Type of language used – ways to say them
Friend		
Friend's parent		
Potential employer		

Role-play the conversations with a partner. B should listen and write down types of language that seem interesting or important in helping achieve the desired goal of the conversation.

Conversation # Audience:		
Interesting / important language ▪ Vocabulary – any technical sounding language, jargon ▪ Formality ▪ Use of statements, questions, commands, exclamations ▪ Use of tentative language ("could I", "may I", "might", "perhaps", "possibly", "chance") ▪ Hesitations, pauses, restarts ▪ Verbal fillers ▪ Use of speech when expressing obligation, inclination		
▪ Tone of voice		
▪ Form of address		
Other observations (Posture, gestures, facial expressions)		
Notes on what helped achieve the purpose		

 Once the three conversations are improvised and written up, discuss the following questions as a group:

- How did A appear as a different person in each of the conversations?
- How did the language used change in each conversation – vocabulary, formality, number of statements, questions, exclamations, commands, use of speech/language etc.?
- How did the language help achieve the purpose of the conversation?
- How did A's body posture and position change depending on who they were addressing?
- How did A's tone of voice change according to whom they were talking to?
- How did the mode of communication (phone call as opposed to face to face or written down) affect the language A used?

STEP 3 Studying a character's speech, focusing on elements such as the type of language they use and how they address and interact with other characters can reveal much about their motivations and relationships and how they change.

Apply what you have learnt to texts you are reading and studying in class. Choose a key scene of dialogue from a fiction or non-fiction text you are reading and **analyse** a character's dialogue using the following prompt questions:

- Control: Who initiates the exchanges? Who dominates the conversation?
- How is their speech characterized? Do they use statements, questions, assertions, exclamations or commands?
- Turn-taking: Does anyone interrupt someone else? If so, do they do so to agree, complete their partner's sentences or show dominance over the other person?
- Are there any silences, gaps or pauses? What do they reveal about one or both characters?
- Does any one character appear more confident or more hesitant in the exchange?
- How does the pace and speed of the exchanges communicate the mood of the characters?
- Forms of address: How do they address each other and what does this reveal about their relationship?
- How are their thoughts revealed?
- Is the description of them sympathetic, negative or neutral?
- How do their speech and verbal interaction reveal their attitudes, motivations, and behaviour towards others?
- How do details of setting and characters' relationship with their surroundings reveal aspects of their personalities?
- Are any verbs or adverbs used to describe how characters speak (e.g. whispered, gasped, snapped, stammered, mumbled, softly, screaming) and convey their emotion and state of mind?

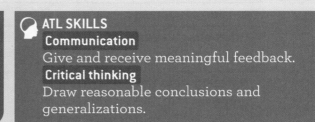

🌐 **GLOBAL CONTEXTS**
Personal and cultural expression

💭 **ATL SKILLS**
Communication
Give and receive meaningful feedback.
Critical thinking
Draw reasonable conclusions and generalizations.

Activity 5 | **Studying famous speeches**

We can learn a lot about the power and impact of spoken words by studying famous spee[...] different famous speeches by people in fiction or real life. Read and/or watch them, stud[...] which the speakers create an impact through both the choice of words they use and the ways in which they deliver them. Below are some suggestions:

WEB LINKS
You can find more speeches on the following website: www.famous-speeches-and-speech-topics.info.

- Martin Luther King: "I have a dream"
- Oprah Winfrey 54th Emmy Awards
- Lou Gherig: Farewell to baseball address
- Abraham Lincoln: the Gettysberg Address

You can use a framework (like the one shown in the following table) to help you analyse the speech:

Context	Where and when is the speech being delivered?
Purpose	What is the speaker's purpose in addressing his/her audience?
Audience	Whom are they addressing?
Mode of communication	Face to face, online etc.
Structure:	Opening How the speech builds to a climax Use of anecdote Shift between present reality and future expectations Concluding remarks
Language:	Vocabulary Rhetorical devices – rule of three (does any part come in threes? E.g. content or structure?), rhetorical questions (are questions asked that are answered by the speaker or questions asked where the answer is implied?) How emphasis is created though changes in pace, volume, tone Pauses and changes in pace Repetition rule of three Use of evidence – statistics and facts Use of emotional appeal Use of humour Emotive language
Delivery:	Pace, volume, eye contact, postures, gestures , movements

 **GLOBAL CONTEXTS**
Personal and cultural expression

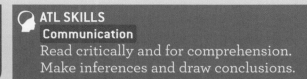 **ATL SKILLS**
Communication
Read critically and for comprehension.
Make inferences and draw conclusions.

Many researchers on communication agree that the majority of our communication is non-verbal and that the words we speak account for only a small part of the message we send. Now look at the role of non-verbal communication in dialogues and spoken exchanges.

 Activity 6 **Directing a scene**

On your own or with your teacher, select extracts of dialogue (approximately 15 to 30 lines) from any novel or play you have read. Imagine you are the director of the scene, giving instructions to an actor/actors performing the roles for a film or stage production. First, you will need to think about how you could use indirect techniques of characterisation to present your characters on film/stage.

To help you plan your directions consider the following questions:
- How can you create a dramatic impact at moments when characters deliver key lines?
- Which words and phrases will you give emphasis to and how?
  - Change in volume
  - A pause before or after the line
  - A gesture or movement when you deliver the line
- What symbols are associated with the character? How can you highlight these and the character connection to them?

> **WEB LINKS**
> The following site has some useful information on how to present monologues on stage using a range of theatrical devices: tedb.byu.edu.

- How can you draw out aspects of the character by using lighting (colours, light and shadow)?
- Body language: How should they stand, move and use their hands to communicate their emotions at different points in the exchange?
- Costume / dress: How will you dress your characters to reflect their states of mind? Where would you place your characters on stage/in the film at different points in the dialogue to show:
  - Their mental state?
  - Their relationship to the other characters?
- What props could be used to help communicate character? How should they interact with them to help further the audience's understanding of their characters?

In order to help you direct the scene, draw a map of the stage/film set and make notes on these questions. You could mark characters' movements on the stage/film set using letters and arrows and also illustrate the positioning of any key scene props. Write a brief description explaining your choices.

Physical space	
Costume / dress	
Props	
Backdrop	
Lighting	
Positioning on stage/film	

 GLOBAL CONTEXTS
Personal and cultural expression

 ATL SKILLS
Communication
Read critically and for comprehension.
Make inferences and draw conclusions.

Reflection

Use the following questions to reflect on what you have learnt:

- How has studying characters' speech in texts made you think about your own communication?

- How true is the saying, "It's not what you say, it's the way that you say it?"

- Write down three ways you can improve the way you communicate in different contexts using verbal and non-verbal cues.

TOPIC 3

Communicating character changes and development

Using a text you are studying, consider characters' roles and relationships and how they change. To help you do this, begin by thinking about some common character types and roles. Research and complete the table that follows and then apply these definitions to characters in your text. Use the web links box to help you.

⊂⊃ WEB LINKS
You can look up types of characters in fiction at: learn.lexiconic.net. Click on "Character Types" on the main screen.

Roles	Protagonist	
	Antagonist	
	Stock	
	Anti-hero	
	Foil	
	Outsider	
	Minor character	
Complexity	Round	
	Flat	
Development	Static	
	Dynamic	

Common character types and roles

Characters do not exist in isolation. Often writers use characters' relationships and interactions with other characters to help define and develop their character.

Use these prompts to consider different relationships between characters and the extent to which they unite and/or divide characters.

- Are some loners while others are sociable?
- Are some victims while others are predators?
- Are some leaders while others prefer to follow?
- Are some liberated while others are repressed?
- Are some introverts while others are extroverts?
- Are some thinkers while others take action?
- Are some motivated by greed while others are motivated by love?

Dynamic characters in a text undergo a change, for better or worse. In most texts the protagonist undergoes some sort of change. Many characters are also rarely consistent and may play different roles during a text.

 Activity 7   **Reflecting changes in characters through images and words**

In this activity you are going to explore creative ways to portray the ways in which characters in a text change.

STEP 1   Think about how you can communicate these changes graphically. You can choose from one of two visual options to do this activity:

Option 1: A character web
Create a character web to highlight roles, relationships, interactions and the effects of characters on one another and how they change during the course of a text:

1. List all the characters in the text – those who appear and those who are mentioned (if significant). Remember that even minor characters can teach you a lot about a main character through their interactions and relationships.
2. Group the characters according to their relationships with one another and the bonds that unite or separate them (financial, emotional, family, professional, friendships etc.).
3. Write a brief character description in each character box.
4. Draw lines showing relationships between characters and how they change and develop. Here are some suggestions for a key but you can develop it and create your own:
   - Thickness of line = strength of relationship (thicker = stronger).
   - Arrows show direction of love/affection. These may go only one way if characters do not return love/affection.

- Create a key of symbols to explain the basis of the relationship (e.g. $ = indicates relationship based on financial interests, heart indicates relationship based on emotional interests / love interest / professional interest).
- Family interests: lightning strike indicates stormy / aggressive relationship etc.
5. On / beside the lines, explain the relationship briefly in words and how it changes, if at all.

Example of a character web

The example that follows is a simple version of a character web, to help you visualise the task. Think of ways to develop its complexity to incorporate all of the aspects mentioned here.

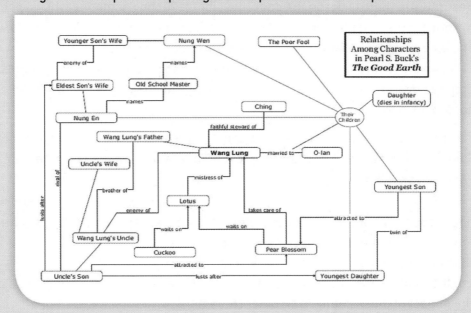

Option 2: A character's mind as a room

In Chapter 11, Setting, you explored how setting can be used to communicate aspects of character. This activity builds on that as a creative exploration of how images can be used to reflect changes in a character.

Take a dynamic character, one who undergoes a change, from a text you are studying and create a visual representation of the protagonist's mind as if it were a room. **Explore** the room and how it changes during the course of the text to reflect changes in the character's personality, motivations and behaviour. Produce three different images of the room and provide an explanation of each. Look at the Topic 1 activities in Chapter 11 for some ideas to get you started.

You could consider the following:
- Colours: How do different colours represent and reflect your character's mood and personality?
- Ornaments: They may be symbols reflecting the personality and behaviour of your character. A vase of red roses, for example, would reflect their romantic side.
- Pictures: The pictures on the wall may show important people or moments in your character's life. They may show family, loved ones or heroes.
- Furniture: The furniture will also reflect your character's personality. Are they minimalists (someone who enjoys a simple life with the minimum amount of material things)? Do they have expensive tastes? Are they environmentalists or people who like natural materials and textures?

- Structure: Is the room a small, compact place with narrow corridors (possibly reflecting someone who feels trapped, confined or frustrated in their life) or sharp angles (possibly reflecting a tense, aggressive personality)? If your character has a dual personality, the room might be split into two different sections reflecting each side of their personality.
- Lighting: Are there large windows (possibly reflecting a broad-minded person or someone who is observant and/or a happy person) or small ones (possibly reflecting someone who is shy or narrow-minded or refuses to see the truth)? Remember, darkness can symbolise evil, mystery, the unknown and the mysterious.
- Security: Are there locks on the door (possibly reflecting someone who is insecure, afraid, tries to shut out the outside world, or likes their privacy) or is the door left open (a warm friendly, sociable person who feels comfortable in the outside world)?
- Order: Is the room tidy (reflecting an organised and ordered individual) or messy with clothes dropped everywhere and the bed left unmade (reflecting someone with a lot of chaos and confusion in their life)?

These are merely suggestions. The important thing is that you are able to describe objects and explain their significance (what they represent or reveal about the character). Be as imaginative and detailed as you can.

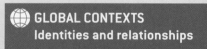 Having produced your visual representation of characters and relationships (either Option 1 or Option 2), present them to your class and explain:
a) the changes that occur in your characters
b) the techniques of characterisation that are involved in communicating these changes
c) the impact of these changes on other characters
d) the function of your characters and the way these changes are used by the writers to communicate the text's message.

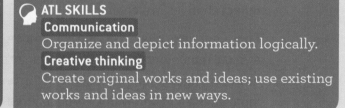

🌐 **GLOBAL CONTEXTS**
Identities and relationships

🧠 **ATL SKILLS**
Communication
Organize and depict information logically.
Creative thinking
Create original works and ideas; use existing works and ideas in new ways.

Reflection
- With a partner, explore other ways of representing changes in character (e.g. through their changing appearance). Design a series of costumes for the characters in your own text to highlight these changes.

- Consider the role and influence of other characters in your own life. Which characters have inspired you or defined choices you have made? Which minor characters and encounters have influenced key decisions you have made?

Summary

Other chapters have explored different methods of characterisation:

- Chapter 5, Perspectives, looked at different ways we interpret people's characters and behaviour and different ways we can represent them.

- Chapter 11, Setting, looked at how setting can be used to communicate characters and how they change.

- Chapter 2, Communication, looked at how our own language changes in different contexts when communicating with different people.

- Chapter 17, Self-expression, explored how a writer's choice of different narrative perspectives can influence the way a reader or audience interacts with a character.

From the activities in this and other chapters, and by reflecting on your own personality and how you appear to others you will see that human beings are complex and varied. Show your understanding of character and techniques of characterisation through one of the following creative explorations:

- Write and perform, in costume, a monologue for a fictional character of your own creation.

- Visually represent emotional shifts in character(s) in a text using a graph of your own design.

- Use hotseating, freeze-framing, thought-tracking or another drama activity to highlight your understanding of characters' thoughts and motivations at different moments in a text.

References

Deane, S. 1997. *Reading in the Dark*. Vintage. New edition.

Key, S. *Hands*. Spoken word poetry.

Owen, W. 1917-18. *Dulce et Decorum Est*. Extract from: http://www.warpoetry.co.uk/owen1.html.

INQUIRY QUESTIONS	**TOPIC 1** Theme in video
	▪ **What film techniques will convey the meaning we want to the viewers of our videos?**
	TOPIC 2 Theme in literature
	▪ **How can different readings in literature emphasize different themes?**
	TOPIC 3 Theme in propaganda
	▪ **As propaganda seeks to develop one idea and ignore others, how can we avoid being manipulated by it?**

SKILLS

ATL

✓ Create original works and ideas.

✓ Use critical-literacy skills.

✓ Present information in a variety of formats and platforms.

Language and literature

✓ Appreciate how a work of literature will have many different readings, each one emphasizing a different theme.

✓ Understand that to support a reading of a text, we must present evidence in order to demonstrate its validity.

✓ Be a critical reader, listener and viewer; essential if we wish to avoid being manipulated by texts.

✓ Understand texts have values within them that we may agree with, or may clash with our principles.

✓ Media/video. Appreciate the importance of camera angle in making effective videos.

✓ Media/video. Know other essential skills in video making.

OTHER RELATED CONCEPTS

Context	Point of view	Purpose	Style

GLOSSARY

Hyperbole exaggeration to create an effect.

Propaganda information designed to promote or criticize a political group, cause or leader.

Theme the topic or idea that is being raised or implied in discussion, art, literature, etc.

COMMAND TERMS

Analyse break down in order to bring out the essential elements or structure. To identify parts and relationships, and to interpret information to reach conclusions.

Comment give a judgment based on a given statement or result of a calculation.

Justify give valid reasons or evidence to support an answer or conclusion.

Introducing theme

A **theme** is a central idea, though texts can have more than one theme. Different interpretations of texts see different themes as dominant. In literature, critics give readings that focus on particular themes. In most texts the themes are embedded within them; however, in one field in particular, that of video games, some offerings allow the player to change the theme due to the choices that they make as they go.

This is a tremendously exciting development and will likely lead to new forms of self-expression.

Increasingly, video game manufacturers are offering free downloads as introductions to their games. Look to see what is available. You are looking for a game where you take on the role of the protagonist and make choices that have consequences. An example of the type we are talking about would be The Stanley Parable. Decide as a class which one you would like to download, download it and play it as far as it goes.

These new generation first-person role-playing games are different in many ways from the video game market before. Previous games had a set theme. You might have had to prevent the zombie apocalypse, defeat that extra-terrestrial invasion or set up a criminal empire, but the thing that they all had in common was that the theme was predetermined by the game designers.

What will be different in games of the future is that the players will increasingly be able to determine the theme of the game by the choices that they make. Is the game about what happens to a character who follows the rules, or is it about what happens to those who question the way things are? The work of art is becoming malleable, meaning that we can shape them; theme is becoming an interaction between the designer and the gamer.

CHAPTER LINKS
For more on self-expression see Chapter 17.

WEB LINKS
Go to http://www.stanleyparable.com/ to see an example of a free download.

TOPIC 1

Theme in video

In video making you start with a story, or a theme, to be told. How effectively that theme is told will depend on the techniques chosen to bring out that theme. The final test of this is to present the video to an audience and analyse the way they react to it. A possible activity that can get you started is analysing the videos of others who are filming on a similar theme to the one you are interested in.

CHAPTER LINKS
Some techniques for analysing the texts of others are included in Chapter 14.

The audience's reaction is key

For the first activity in this topic you will be making your own video, in other words, you will be in charge of deciding the theme. In the later activities, you will be analysing the work of others and deciding upon the themes within.

Activity 1   Making your own video

When you are making a video there are a number of things that you should pay careful attention to. Let's start with camera angles.

Theme and camera angles

The way you use a camera is extremely important as you can add or take away status depending on the relation of the camera to the subject. By putting the subject at a distance you may diminish its importance, while a low angle may make the subject seem stronger or imposing.

If your theme is something like "urban decay", for example, the way you shoot your city shots will still greatly affect the message you convey, and with care and thought you will emphasize the theme.

Camera position	What is seen and/or the effect
Establishing shot	Distant with lots of landscape or space
Long shot	Distant, but with recognizable figures
Full shot	The whole body can be seen so there is less background
Medium shot	Usually the figures from the waist up
Close up	Focusing on one face, or a key aspect of the subject
Extreme close up	Showing just one feature, no background
Point of view	As if looking through the eyes of one character, moving with them
Eye level	At the eye level of the characters, like normal vision
Undershot	From underneath characters, can suggest danger
Low angle	Looking up at something, often used to make something seem powerful
Panning	Moving round to take in background, but keeping subjects in view
Zoom in/out	Gets closer/ further away, with subject staying in focus
Overhead	Directly looking down, a "bird's eye" view
High angle	Not directly above, but makes the subject look small
Tilt	At an angle, perhaps emphasizing disorientation
Cutting	Changing from scene to scene
Slow/fast motion	Slowing/speeding up reality
Sharp/soft focus	Crisp or fuzzy/dreamy focus
Deep focus	Keeping different subjects at different distances in focus

Theme and audio

When considering audio remember that music is an emotional heightener and added sound can provide useful, or even essential, information for the viewer.

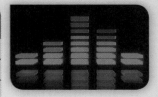

Sound	How it can add to your video
Musical score	Background music, possibly varied, possibly a recurring tune
Sound effects	Invented, altered or exaggerated that are added
Natural sounds	The normal sounds expected in this location
Dialogue	Conversation between your characters—each word counts
Voiceover	Adding a first or third person narrator and her or his perceptions

Theme, lighting and shadow

The amount of light can be altered; shadow can also be suggestive.

Lighting	The effect
High/low key lighting	Bright/dim, both change the mood
Front lighting	Little shadow, nothing is hidden
Underlighting	Catches the shadows around the eyes, creating a sinister mood
Toplighting	Bright with few shadows
Backlighting	Creates silhouettes and shadows, creating uncertainty
Symbolic lighting	A character moving from the light into dark, or dark into light
Lightning (and thunder)	Momentary light combined with loud noise, sinister and threatening
Coloured lighting	See below in colours

Theme, symbolism and colour

Codes and symbols can suggest meaning. The colour can be in the lighting, the costumes or the set.

Colour/symbol	The effect/possible meaning
Repeated images	These will create their own meaning depending on what you focus on
Symbols	Objects that suggest an idea
White	Innocence, childhood, purity, peace
Black	Evil, death
Red	Love, passion, anger, blood, danger
Blue	Sadness, cold
Yellow	Happiness, early in the day
Green	The natural world

Theme in composition and framing

The final thing that is essential is the composition or framing of all your shots. What is included and what gets left out? The things that are seen through the lens need to be carefully arranged. The space between characters, their closeness to the camera and their body language tell the viewer a huge amount about the relationships between them. Ask yourself the question, what do you want to convey?

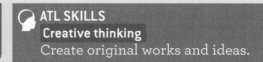
Interesting composition is vital in a good-quality video

Planning your video

Using the table below and all the information about the video techniques above, plan your video.

Video title	
The main theme you will focus on during the making of this video	
A brief description of what your video will be about	
Choose four camera effects you will use and explain how they will help to develop your theme	1) 2) 3) 4)
Choose two sound/music effects you will use and explain how they will help to develop your theme	1) 2)
Choose a lighting effect you will use and explain how it will help to develop your theme	1)
Choose a symbolic or colour effect you will use and explain how it will help to develop your theme	1)
What do you want to achieve in your video?	

Shooting your film

If you have been able to shoot the film, you will need to edit it with the appropriate software program. Show it to your peers and teacher after editing, get feedback and then make a final cut.

GLOBAL CONTEXTS
Personal and cultural expression

ATL SKILLS
Creative thinking
Create original works and ideas.

Reflection

Write a reflection explaining your film and why you chose the techniques that are in it:

- camera angles
- audio
- lighting
- other features.

🏃 TAKE ACTION

A video is a powerful way to take meaningful action, or can link to service work. With your classmates, discuss some ways in which a video could be used to make a difference.

TOPIC 2

Theme in literature

You will now turn to more traditional interpretations of theme as it appears in literature. The first thing to note is that the theme is not immediately apparent in a work. What you notice first are the characters and the setting. Then, as you continue, you appreciate the plot. The theme is something less obvious. You have to find it for yourself and as we all approach literature from our own unique mix of gender, race, class, culture and experience, that makes for a really interesting mix of interpretations that can come out of any text. Having said that, for many texts you are likely to come to a wide consensus on what is going on within them.

Consider the works of literature you have read before this point. Discuss with your classmates what the themes were in them.

When arguing for a particular theme in a text, it is necessary to provide evidence to support your views. This will usually be a combination of concise quotations and carefully laid out arguments.

👥 Activity 2   **Exploring theme in *Animal Farm***

For this activity we will be analysing extracts from the novel *Animal Farm* by George Orwell. The point of this activity is to see how three different interpretations/themes can be found in this text and to appreciate how each reading has its strengths and weaknesses.

Animal Farm—interpretation 1
After the end of World War Two, in 1945, the world rapidly entered into the period known as the Cold War. George Orwell's novel came out at this time and warned of the horrors of life in the Soviet Union (Russia), which, unlike the democratic nations of North America and Western Europe, was under the dictatorship of Stalin.

This interpretation of the novel is frequently taught in schools all over the world.

🔗 WEB LINKS
For this activity you will need some knowledge of the Cold War. You can find a lot of information about the events of this war online. Try searching "the Cold War" on the following websites:
www.bbc.co.uk/history
www.historylearningsite.co.uk
www.history.com.

Animal Farm—interpretation 2

A different interpretation of this work can be found by closely exploring parts of the character Old Major's speech in chapter one. We are told that Old Major "was so highly regarded on the farm that everyone was quite ready to lose an hour's sleep in order to hear what he had to say". This suggests that his words are crucial to understanding what develops in the novel.

Read this part of the novel carefully.

TIP

The character Old Major is the first character to be described in *Animal Farm*.

Animal Farm by George Orwell

Man is the only creature that consumes without producing. He does not give milk, he does not lay eggs, he is too weak to pull the plough, he cannot run fast enough to catch rabbits. Yet he is lord of all the animals. He sets them to work, he gives back to them the bare minimum that will prevent them from starving, and the rest he keeps for himself. Our labour tills the soil, our dung fertilises it, and yet there is not one of us that owns more than his bare skin...

Is it not crystal clear, then, comrades, that all the evils of this life of ours spring from the tyranny of human beings? Only get rid of Man, and the produce of our labour would be our own. Almost overnight we could become rich and free. What then must we do? Why, work night and day, body and soul, for the overthrow of the human race! That is my message to you, comrades: Rebellion! I do not know when that Rebellion will come, it might be in a week or in a hundred years, but I know, as surely as I see this straw beneath my feet, that sooner or later justice will be done. Fix your eyes on that, comrades, throughout the short remainder of your lives! And above all, pass on this message of mine to those who come after you, so that future generations shall carry on the struggle until it is victorious.

And remember, comrades, your resolution must never falter. No argument must lead you astray. Never listen when they tell you that Man and the animals have a common interest, that the prosperity of the one is the prosperity of the others. It is all lies. Man serves the interests of no creature except himself. And among us animals let there be perfect unity, perfect comradeship in the struggle. All men are enemies. All animals are comrades ...

I have little more to say. I merely repeat, remember always your duty of enmity towards Man and all his ways. Whatever goes upon two legs is an enemy. Whatever goes upon four legs, or has wings, is a friend. And remember also that in fighting against Man, we must not come to resemble him. Even when you have conquered him, do not adopt his vices. No animal must ever live in a house, or sleep in a bed, or wear clothes, or drink alcohol, or smoke tobacco, or touch money, or engage in trade. All the habits of Man are evil. And, above all, no animal must ever tyrannise over his own kind. Weak or strong, clever or simple, we are all brothers. No animal must ever kill any other animal. All animals are equal.

Questions:

a) According to Old Major, what are the failings of Man?

b) What would be the advantage of overthrowing him and putting the farm under animal control?

c) What does Old Major warn that animals should never do?

TIP

For this next interpretation, bear in mind that the neighbouring two farms represent Britain and Germany.

In this reading of the text, Animal Farm under Napoleon (the pig that represents the dictator Stalin) is a horrible exploitative place. What is continually measured, however, is how low Animal Farm has sunk when compared to the two human farms around it. Remember in 1946 many Western nations were democracies. Nevertheless, they ran colonial empires with widespread human rights abuses, racism, no democracy and continual economic exploitation. The author of this novel had seen this first hand as a police officer in colonial Burma/Myanmar.

TIP

Spoiler alert: don't read the next page if you are reading the whole novel in class.

When we reach the end of the novel, six human farmers, including Mr Pilkington, who represents the leaders of Britain, and Napoleon with five other pigs, who represent the Soviet Union's Communist party, get together for a drunken party. Unknown to them, the ordinary farm animals are secretly watching through the window. This is what happens.

Mr. Pilkington was about to spring some carefully prepared witticism on the company, but for a moment he was too overcome by amusement to be able to utter it. After much choking, during which his various chins turned purple, he managed to get it out: "If you have your lower animals to contend with," he said, "we have our lower classes!" ... Mr. Pilkington once again congratulated the pigs on the low rations, the long working hours, and the general absence of pampering which he had observed on Animal Farm.

And now, he said finally, he would ask the company to rise to their feet and make certain that their glasses were full. "Gentlemen," concluded Mr. Pilkington, "gentlemen, I give you a toast: To the prosperity of Animal Farm!"

There was enthusiastic cheering and stamping of feet. Napoleon was so gratified that he left his place and came round the table to clink his mug against Mr. Pilkington's before emptying it. When the cheering had died down, Napoleon, who had remained on his feet, intimated that he too had a few words to say.

Like all of Napoleon's speeches, it was short and to the point. He too, he said, was happy that the period of misunderstanding was at an end. For a long time there had been rumours — circulated, he had reason to think, by some malignant enemy — that there was something subversive and even revolutionary in the outlook of himself and his colleagues. They had been credited with attempting to stir up rebellion among the animals on neighbouring farms. Nothing could be further from the truth! Their sole wish, now and in the past, was to live at peace and in normal business relations with their neighbours. This farm which he had the honour to control, he added, was a co-operative enterprise. The title-deeds, which were in his own possession, were owned by the pigs jointly.

He did not believe, he said, that any of the old suspicions still lingered, but certain changes had been made recently in the routine of the farm which should have the effect of promoting confidence still further. Hitherto the animals on the farm had had a rather foolish custom of addressing one another as "Comrade." This was to be suppressed. There had also been a very strange custom, whose origin was unknown, of marching every Sunday morning past a boar's skull which was nailed to a post in the garden. This, too, would be suppressed, and the skull had already been buried. His visitors might have observed, too, the green flag which flew from the masthead. If so, they would perhaps have noted that the white hoof and horn with which it had previously been marked had now been removed. It would be a plain green flag from now onwards.

He had only one criticism, he said, to make of Mr. Pilkington's excellent and neighbourly speech. Mr. Pilkington had referred throughout to "Animal Farm." He could not of course know — for he, Napoleon, was only now for the first time announcing it — that the name "Animal Farm" had been abolished. Henceforward the farm was to be known as "The Manor Farm" — which, he believed, was its correct and original name.

"Gentlemen," concluded Napoleon, "I will give you the same toast as before, but in a different form. Fill your glasses to the brim. Gentlemen, here is my toast: To the prosperity of The Manor Farm!"

There was the same hearty cheering as before, and the mugs were emptied to the dregs. But as the animals outside gazed at the scene, it seemed to them that some strange thing was happening. What was it that had altered in the faces of the pigs? Clover's old dim eyes flitted from one face to another. Some of them had five chins, some had four, some had three. But what was it that seemed to be melting and changing? Then, the applause having come to an end, the company took up their cards and continued the game that had been interrupted, and the animals crept silently away.

But they had not gone twenty yards when they stopped short. An uproar of voices was coming from the farmhouse. They rushed back and looked through the window again. Yes, a violent quarrel was in progress. There were shoutings, bangings on the table, sharp suspicious glances, furious denials. The source of the trouble appeared to be that Napoleon and Mr. Pilkington had each played an ace of spades simultaneously.

Twelve voices were shouting in anger, and they were all alike. No question, now, what had happened to the faces of the pigs. The creatures outside looked from pig to man, and from man to pig, and from pig to man again; but already it was impossible to say which was which.

Questions:

a) Pilkington is given "various chins" by the author. What does this mean? What effect is created by this and by further giving the pigs and humans three to five chins?

b) Napoleon announces that he is changing the name of Animal Farm back to the previous name, Manor Farm. What do you think he means by doing this?

c) What is the symbolic effect of having both Mr Pilkington and Napoleon playing the ace of spades card at the same time?

d) What effect is created by having the pigs and humans look similar?

e) In what way could this be said to be an optimistic ending to the novel?

f) In what way does this ending contradict the first reading given of the novel?

Animal Farm—interpretation 3

For a third interpretation of the novel, read the second extract again. You will need to approach the reading a little differently. In the world of the 21st century, the Cold War and the Soviet Union are no more; therefore, this interpretation looks for the timeless theme in *Animal Farm* by asking the following question: How can we prevent power corrupting us? The theme here is a moral one. Though no angel at the start of the novel, power turned Napoleon into a self-obsessed murderer.

For us, the readers, to have a theme that relates to our own lives gives the novel added relevance beyond the historical issues in the previous two. We all have some form of power in our lives. It may be as a member of the student government for your school, or an organizer of a service programme. Outside school, it may be over younger brothers and sisters, over smaller children, or over pets. We can use that power to help, or we can abuse it.

What does the second extract say about corruption?

Corruption is as much with us today as in Orwell's time

REFLECTION

- Which of these three readings is most powerful to you? **Justify** your choice.
- Are these readings mutually exclusive? **Justify** your answer.
- To what extent do you think that themes are limitless and constantly changing?

GLOBAL CONTEXTS
Orientation in space and time

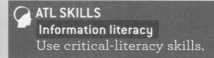
ATL SKILLS
Information literacy
Use critical-literacy skills.

TOPIC 3

Theme in propaganda

Propaganda is designed to influence us to be for or against a particular position. It involves the manipulation of facts, perhaps by presenting just the information that favours a position, or even by seeming to lie by leaving out information that is vital for a clear understanding of the issue. In propaganda the theme or message is distorted, so that the word propaganda is often used negatively; however, this is not altogether fair. Propaganda could, for example, be raising a health issue that is causing concern to the government, such as the warnings about smoking.

You may well have seen examples of wartime propaganda in your individuals and societies class. In the examples that follow the propaganda is mainly political in nature.

...mous examples of political statements that aim to ...me, or set up the limits in which the speaker ...wed.

First, here is a statement by former US President George W Bush on 20th September 2001 to the nation.

> *"Americans are asking 'Why do* [the terrorists] *hate us?' They hate what they see right here in this chamber: a democratically elected government. Their leaders are self-appointed. They hate our freedoms: our freedom of religion, our freedom of speech, our freedom to vote and assemble and disagree with each other."*

TIP

In order to appreciate this topic, go online and research the attacks on the Twin Towers on September 11th 2001 and the build up to the Iraqi War (2003).

STEP 1 **Comment** on the following statements.

Statement 1: The speech praises positive perceptions of the USA.

Statement 2: The speech avoids discussing other reasons behind the attacks such as US support for dictators in the Middle East, selling weapons to these dictators and training their police and military.

STEP 2 **Analyse** the following extract from the same speech. Look at how it establishes a theme and consider other ways of viewing the point that the President is making.

> *"Either you are with us or you are with the terrorists."*

And from the other main party in US politics, here is the Obama 2008 Presidential campaign slogan.

> *"Change we can believe in."* Followed by the chant: *"Yes we can!"*

a) **Analyse** these two phrases, including the word choice.

b) What do these phrases say and what don't they say?

GLOBAL CONTEXTS
Orientation in space and time

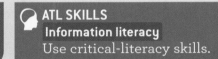
ATL SKILLS
Information literacy
Use critical-literacy skills.

The first interpretation of *Animal Farm* in Topic 2 became a powerful theme during the Cold War that may have helped defeat the Soviet Union. The West succeeded in portraying the Russians as a dangerous dictatorship. Though Western nations overthrew several democratically elected leaders during the Cold War through violent takeovers and supported many brutal dictatorships, the same Western nations have been successful in suppressing this theme of world history, so that even today many people are unaware of it.

Political propaganda seeks to impose a theme, or narrative, on the audience, leaving them unreceptive to alternative voices. Let's now look at the kind of techniques used in the creation of propaganda. The first few will be familiar to you. The later ones will be explained in more detail. Here we go:

- **Hyperbole** or "hype".

- Repetition.

- Symbols.

- Fear.

- Humour.

- Flattery.

- Vagueness: two of the political statements at the start of this topic fall into this category.

- Rhetorical questions: answering questions that you put forward yourself, thus maintaining complete control of the theme.

- The common touch: no matter how wealthy and privileged leaders are, it is desirable for them to be portrayed as being "just like us".

- Euphemism: using more pleasant language to cover an ugly reality. For example, instead of a leader saying that he or she killed innocent civilians, they may instead say that there was "collateral damage".

- Simple solutions: keep your theme understandable by a mass audience.

- Scapegoating: blaming a problem on a certain group. For example, if the "terrorists" are to blame for a problem then it avoids looking too closely at the injustices that caused those men and women to turn to violence.

- Testimonial: seeking the support of famous people to give credibility to your message.

- The straw man: creating a false, damaging message and then associating your opponents with it.

- Intentional fallacies: arguments that may appear to be logical, though they are calculated to manipulate or deceive. One of the political statements at the start of this topic falls into this category.

The sustained use of all these techniques is often called "spin". Spin is not a complimentary word in this context. These methods to control what an audience sees are clearly disagreeable in many ways; however, if we know what they are it is easier to recognize them in real life when they are used against us (which they undoubtedly will be).

Returning to *Animal Farm* for a moment, the sheep on the farm represented the ordinary people who uncritically believed what their leaders told them. In the novel, George Orwell consistently warns us what will happen if we are not critical about what we see and hear.

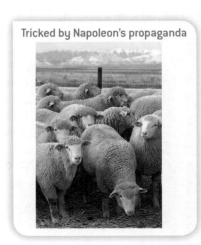
Tricked by Napoleon's propaganda

You have two choices for this activity:

Choice 1

Look back to Topic 2. Imagine the situation at the end of the novel when Napoleon has been exposed as a corrupt cheat. In the uproar that follows, he is forced to allow free and fair elections open to other animals that will be supervised by outside observers. Note: if you did not read the whole novel, find and read a summary of the novel. Design your political campaign to defeat Napoleon.

Choice 2

Consider political leaders you have studied in your individuals and societies classes. Create a campaign to run against one of them.

Whichever you choose you need to design the following:

- a logo, that then appears on/in:
  - a campaign poster
  - a political leaflet
- optional: a campaign video.

When you have finished your work, present it to the group for feedback then make any changes you consider appropriate before the final drafts.

REFLECTION

Reflect on the following idea: how principled am I?

- To what extent are these propaganda techniques distasteful?
- To what extent are they necessary?
- How can we know when they are being used on us?

Using the table below write a reflection explaining your campaign and why you chose the propaganda techniques that are in it.

Name of your leader	
Themes you have prioritized during the making of this campaign	
Take one propaganda technique you used and explain how it helped develop your theme	
Take a second propaganda technique you used and explain how it helped develop your theme	
Take a third propaganda technique you used and explain how it helped develop your theme	
Reflect on what you have achieved in your campaign. What were its strengths? What would you change for next time?	

GLOBAL CONTEXTS
Personal and cultural expression

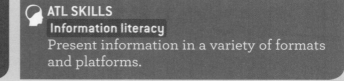

ATL SKILLS
Information literacy
Present information in a variety of formats and platforms.

Summary

This chapter has taken you through three activities. In the first, you had to choose the theme and then the techniques that brought it out. In the second, you were looking for different interpretations, or themes, that were hidden within the work of a famous writer. Finally, you explored texts where the theme was deliberately being obscured.

Some questions to consider:

a) When doing your own original work, is it better to start with the techniques you are going to use or the theme? Justify your response.

b) Take each of the following in turn: setting, characters, plot. How important is each in helping to work out what the theme is in the work of others? Justify your response.

Reference

Orwell, G. 1946. *Animal Farm*. Harcourt Brace and Company.

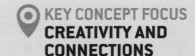

KEY CONCEPT FOCUS
CREATIVITY AND CONNECTIONS

INQUIRY QUESTIONS	**TOPIC 1** The role of setting in communicating character ■ How can setting help us better understand characters, their identity and how they change? **TOPIC 2** Exploring the role of setting in establishing context ■ To what extent do changes to the setting of a text impact our understanding of its purpose and message? **TOPIC 3** The function of setting in creating mood and atmosphere and communicating theme ■ How can we explore aspects of setting in our own creative writing?
SKILLS	**ATL** ✓ Give and receive meaningful feedback. ✓ Consider ideas from multiple perspectives. ✓ Interpret and use effectively modes of non-verbal communication. ✓ Read critically and for comprehension. ✓ Collaborate with peers and experts using a variety of digital environments and media. ✓ Use a variety of media to communicate with a range of audiences. ✓ Recognize unstated assumptions and bias. ✓ Write for different purposes. **Language and literature** ✓ Interpret and analyse visual texts. ✓ Speak and listen for a range of purposes. ✓ Analyse and produce creative and analytical responses to texts.
OTHER RELATED CONCEPTS	**Audience imperatives Context Theme** **Perspective**

GLOSSARY

Alliteration repetition of sounds and kinds of sounds at the beginning of words

Diorama a three-dimensional representation of a scene

Onomatopoeia words that make the sounds they describe or refer to e.g. plop, fizz, buzz

Pathetic fallacy attributing human emotions and behaviour to natural phenomena

Personification when human attributes or qualities are given to an inanimate object or abstract idea

Prop an object or piece of furniture used by actors in a play or film

COMMAND TERMS

Analyse break down in order to bring out the essential elements or structure. To identify parts and relationships, and to interpret information to reach conclusions.

Create to evolve from one's own thought or imagination, as a work or an invention.

Introducing setting

Setting is a central aspect to all our lives and influences, not only the shaping of our personality but also the perspectives we have on various people, ideas, beliefs and texts we read. Setting is not only restricted to the physical characteristics of the location, time of day or year and place but can also include broader aspects such as cultural setting, the historical point in time or geographical location. All these factors influence our own personality and outlook, as well those of characters, events, themes and ideas in texts that we read or view.

The setting of a text is comprised of a number of key elements:

- Time – many stories take place over a short time period

- Place – these include where you set individual scenes of your text

- Location – the geographic location

- Period – the historical period in which the text occurs.

Setting as a literary device performs a number of functions within literature, including:

- Establishing character – The location or time of day or year and a character's relationship with or reaction to their surroundings may suggest something about a character's mood, motivation or situation. Symbolic elements in the setting may also be used to reflect aspects of their personality or mental state.

- Establishing plot – The setting can cause events to occur, acting as an antagonist (creating conflict) or creating circumstances that force a character to take a certain course of action.

- Establishing cultural, historical or geographical context – External elements of time and place can add information and background against which we can judge events or characters.

- Communicating atmosphere and mood – Setting can be used to establish a general mood or atmosphere, sometimes foreshadowing (future) events or arousing a reader's expectations.

- Developing theme – The setting can reinforce certain ideas or aspects of a work, such as a character's alienation or isolation within society.

The role of setting in communicating character

The settings you inhabit, both public and private, affect your own attitudes, behaviours, the language you use, the things you discuss and messages and impressions you send to others. In different settings you may appear to be a very different person to those who do not know you. We are all more at ease in some settings than in others. Think of your own classes, for example. You may feel more comfortable being in an art studio or drama space than in a mathematics class or a science laboratory. You are a different person when:

- sitting at the dining room table with your grandparents
- being in different classrooms in school
- being with friends in the playground
- being online in a virtual setting.

QUICK THINK

Now focus on setting as a tool to communicate character. Reflect on your life and the impact these different aspects of settings and your surroundings have had on you.

Consider these questions:

- To what extent are we shaped by our physical surroundings?
- To what extent do our physical surroundings reflect our personality?

Think about your upbringing and what cultural, historical and geographical factors shaped you. Think of your life, the places and spaces where you spend your time. How do they reflect your interests, responsibilities, passions, aspirations, hopes and what you value in life? Share your thoughts with a partner.

Take a moment to consider some different settings in your life and how they affect how you feel, how you behave and the image of yourself that you project to others.

Feel free to add your own public and private settings.

Setting	How I feel	How I behave	How others see me
Online presence in social media networks			
In different classes			
With friends in playground			
At large family gatherings of relatives			
Other settings			

Questions

- How do you appear differently to different people in different settings?
- How are you different in a range of public settings?
- How are you different in a range of private settings?
- Are there settings your friends or teacher or relatives might be surprised to see you in (acting on stage in school, playing in the band)?

Share your findings with a partner you feel comfortable talking to.

 **GLOBAL CONTEXTS**
Identities and relationships

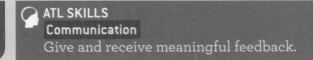 **ATL SKILLS**
Communication
Give and receive meaningful feedback.

Activity 2   A Room with a view

STEP 1   Let's start by thinking about a setting that many of you are most familiar with: your bedroom. This is possibly your most personal space and the one that reveals most about your personality. If you share a bedroom or live in a dormitory, you can think about somewhere else that's private to you, like your locker at school. What could the following aspects of your personal space reveal to someone about your interests, ambitions, character, personality and tastes?

- The pictures or photographs on the wall — What clues do they give as to your passions, dreams, things you value as important?
- The furniture — age, design, size and shape — How might it reflect your interests and tastes?
- The colour scheme — bright vibrant colours or darker, more restrained ones?
- The objects in your room — Which objects stand out or occupy a prominent position?
- The layout of your room — What areas are points of focus and importance?
- The cleanliness and order — How clean and tidy is it? Is it cluttered and busy or empty and spacious?
- The general appearance — Comfortable and cosy? Dark and dingy? Messy? Ordered and organized?

Using a camera, take five photographs of your room (or other personal space) which best display the type of person you are. The photographs should focus on aspects of your room that reflect your interests and personality. They can be pictures of important objects, furniture, pictures on your wall, or photos showing the colours and general organization of your space. All these aspects say something about your identity. Bring your photos to school.

STEP 2   Swap your five photos with someone in the class. Now swap the photos you got back from them with someone else. You should end up with five photos from an unknown member of your class. You do not need to know whose room you are looking at. Study the photographs and consider the following questions:

- What is the general appearance of the room — organized or messy, cluttered or bare?
- What objects or items appear prominent in the room?
- What objects appear to occupy a less important space?
- What pictures or posters are there on the wall?
- What colours stand out? Are they bright, vibrant colours or darker, more subdued ones?
- How much privacy is there?

- Which elements of this room appeal to you?
- What questions about the room do you have for the person who took the photographs? Write them down.

STEP 3   Using these observations, what general conclusions can you draw about the type of person who lives in this room?
- Their personality – outgoing, introverted (inward), organized
- Their passions, interests or dreams
- Their outlook and perspective
- Their behaviours and attitudes

See if you can guess whose room you were viewing. Share with a partner.

Questions

Use the prompt questions below to reflect on how changes in your own room have reflected changes in your life.
- How has your room changed over time? How similar or different would it have looked if you had photographed it (or a previous room) five years ago?
- What things have entered your room and what have now disappeared? How do these changes reflect changes in your own life— your priorities, responsibilities, hobbies, interests and dreams?
- How has your room reflected your growth, both physical and psychological?
- How can you use these notes to create a piece of creative writing about yourself?

GLOBAL CONTEXTS
Identities and relationships

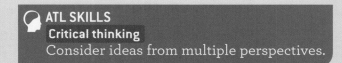
ATL SKILLS
Critical thinking
Consider ideas from multiple perspectives.

INTERDISCIPLINARY LINKS
Individuals and Societies
Research rooms from around the world, looking at different rooms of people from different cultures. Create a photo story of rooms around the world exploring how they communicate similarities and differences between cultures in terms of personality and lifestyles.

Present it to your peers.

CHAPTER LINKS
See Activity 7 in Chapter 9 Characterisation about representing a character's mind as a room.

STEP 1 Having explored what your own room says about you, consider some well-known texts where writers have used characters' rooms for a range of purposes, such as giving readers a clearer insight into the personality of their characters. Here are some classic examples from well-known texts:

- Crooks's room and the bunkhouse in *Of Mice and Men* by John Steinbeck
- The rooms inhabited by Torvald and in Henrik Ibsen's play *A Doll's House*
- Mrs Mallard's room in Kate Chopin's short story "The Story of an Hour"
- Miss Haversham's room in *Great Expectations* by Charles Dickens
- Gregor's room in Kafka's *Metamorphosis*
- Bilbo Baggins's room in *The Hobbit* by J.R.R. Tolkien
- *The Yellow Wallpaper* by Charlotte Perkins Gilman
- Frankenstein's laboratory in Mary Shelley's *Frankenstein*
- The poem *Mr Bleaney* by Phillip Larkin

Read one or more of these and apply the same questions you asked about your own room to the characters and settings in these stories. What do their rooms reveal about their characters and how they change, if at all?

STEP 2 Focus on Kate Chopin's *The Story of an Hour*. Follow the points below and then answer the questions about the text.

Before you read, what do you think the story is about?
- Where might it be set?
- What events might you expect to read about?
- At what time of day do you think the story will take place?
- What sort of hours or moments are important in people's lives?
- How might the title signal setting's importance in the story?
- The original title was "The Dream of an Hour". What further clues does this title give about the story's possible content?

WEB LINKS
You can find an extract from "The Story of an Hour" at: www.vcu.edu
Enter "The Story of an Hour" into the search box.

Now read the story either alone or as a group. It can be found in *The Awakening and Selected Stories of Kate Chopin,* or you can find and read the extract in the web link given.

While reading
- Identify as many aspects of setting as you can that are symbolic.
- What details give you clues as to the historical setting of the story?
- What details give you clues as to the cultural setting of the story?
- What aspects of setting relate to character? How do these details help convey the characters' internal mindscape – thoughts, feelings, motivations?
- How does the setting reflect or help establish the mood?

After reading

What is the significance of the following in terms of the possible message Kate Chopin is trying to communicate about women's role in marriage and within 19th century society?

- Mrs Mallard experiencing her epiphany behind closed doors inside the house
- The metaphorical phrase "the storm of grief"
- Her awakening taking place as she stands facing an open window
- The "comfortable, roomy armchair" in which she experiences her epiphany
- Only the women being upstairs in the house while the men remain downstairs below
- The patches of blue sky that are described
- The things she experiences outside her window

This story reveals how setting can do much more than establish character, mood and atmosphere. It also shows how the setting of events can help reinforce a writer's message. The fact that Mrs Mallard experiences her epiphany behind closed doors in her house reveals how such thoughts were seen as taboo or shocking in those days and had to be experienced in the privacy of one's room.

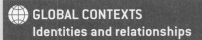 **GLOBAL CONTEXTS**
Identities and relationships

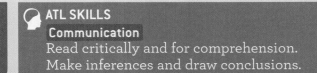 **ATL SKILLS**
Communication
Read critically and for comprehension.
Make inferences and draw conclusions.

Reflection

Consider these questions:

- How can I develop my explorations of setting in my own analytical responses to texts?

- How can aspects of setting in my own life be used to develop characters in my own creative writing?

- How can I apply my understanding of setting and its role in communicating someone's identity and apply it to the real world?

TAKE ACTION

Think about how you can apply your learning about setting to make a difference in the lives of others. As part of a service learning project, research low-cost housing initiatives in your area, investigate the needs of family and design a room/rooms for a low-cost house, using recycled materials, that meets the needs and reflects the tastes and interests of its inhabitants. You could work with a local organisation like Habitat for Humanity or apply your work to an existing challenge in your region.

Exploring the role of setting in establishing context

QUICK THINK

Consider the following quote:

"I think that any play does in fact exist in many time zones – any piece of work does. The chances are it exists in three time zones. There is the time in which it was written; there is the time which it refers to consciously; and there is the time in which it is being read or watched."

Ian McNeil (designer), *An Inspector Calls*

What does the quote say about the context of a text in terms of its production and reception?

In the previous topic, you considered changes in your room and how these reflected changes in you as a person. In the last activity you touched on the role of setting in communicating social, cultural and historical context. In reading Chopin's short story you also explored the role of setting in communicating context.

In this series of activities you will further explore setting's role in communicating context by asking the following key questions:

Factual:

- How does a text exist in a range of settings and contexts simultaneously?

Conceptual:

- How do setting and context provide a useful backdrop against which you can explore and analyze characters, ideas and events in texts?

- How does the setting and context of a text influence and/or reflect its content, production and reception?

- If a text exists simultaneously in a range of contexts and settings, how is its meaning affected?

 Activity 4   **Judging a book by its cover**

Choose any text you are studying and analyse its cover.

There are likely to be many editions of the text, especially if it is well-known. Research and find other examples of covers for your text. Try to find covers that contain either images or scenes from the text. If you cannot find a suitable cover, you can research and find other formats of the text like film covers/posters or theatre posters.

Once you have two or three covers, study the images on the cover and read the blurb on the back. Then answer the following questions:

- What details can you extract about the following:
  - the geographical location
  - the historical setting in time
  - the cultural setting?
- Do any details in the physical setting, weather, or colours reveal anything about the mood or atmosphere of the people, actions and events portrayed?

- If people are portrayed, how they relate to their surroundings? Do they seem at home, uncomfortable or at ease, are they interacting with their environment, do they seem to fit into to it?
- Do any details on the cover give clues about key themes or ideas in the text (e.g. power struggles, conflict, alienation, death etc.)? How do these link to the context and setting of the text?
- If the cover contains an image of a particular scene, locate the relevant passage in the text and consider whether the image reveals explicitly any aspects of the text and its setting and context which are not immediately apparent in the writing.

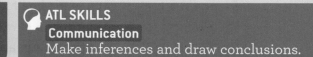

GLOBAL CONTEXTS
Orientation in space and time

ATL SKILLS
Communication
Make inferences and draw conclusions.

 Activity 5   Swapping settings – exploring setting through drama

One way to explore the impact a setting can have on a text is to set it in a different time and/or place. Many recent film versions of classic texts are doing this. You may well have watched recent productions of Shakespeare plays set in a modern context such as:

- *Macbeth on the Estate* (1997). Penny Woolcock's television adaption of the play set in a modern British council estate.
- *Romeo and Juliet* (1996) directed by Baz Luhrmann where Verona, Italy becomes Verona Beach in the USA.
- *Hamlet* (2000). Michael Almereyda's modern adaption of *Hamlet* set in modern day New York City.
- *Hamlet* (1996). Kenneth Branagh's film adaption of the play set in the 19th century.

Research or watch these films and consider the following questions:

- Did changes to the text's setting make it easier for you to understand? Give reasons why or why not.
- How, if at all, were the text's meaning and message affected by the change in setting and context?

Film and theatre directors and play producers often present texts in new cultural and historical settings to give the text a more meaningful context to a modern audience or more relevance to their cultural and historical settings. The themes and ideas of the texts are often timeless and universal, but by adapting their settings and contexts to a more contemporary context, producers are able to give the text a more relevant context for their audience or use the text as a an historical, social or political comment on contemporary society.

Taking a well-known scene from *Macbeth*, explore how changing the setting context of the play changes its meaning for a modern audience.

STEP 1 Organise yourself into groups of three and read act 1, scene 1 of the play.

Thunder and lightning. Enter three Witches

First Witch	When shall we three meet again?
	In thunder, lightning, or in rain?
Second Witch	When the hurlyburly's done,
	When the battle's lost and won.
Third Witch	That will be ere the set of sun.
First Witch	Where the place?
Second Witch	Upon the heath.
Third Witch	There to meet with Macbeth.
First Witch	I come, Graymalkin!
Second Witch	Paddock calls.
Third Witch	Anon.
ALL	Fair is foul, and foul is fair:
	Hover through the fog and filthy air. ***Exeunt***

10

> **TIP**
>
> Terms you need to know:
> **Hurly burly:** commotion, uproar, turmoil.
> **Paddock:** the second witch's familiar is a toad.
> **Graymalkin:** one of the witch's familiars.

STEP 2 Your task now is to create a new setting and context for the scene.

- The witches are no longer witches. Imagine what they could become.
- The setting is no longer a deserted heath in Scotland.

Be creative and think about how you can maintain the original essence of the scene. Below are some possible scenarios you could use. Imagine they are:

- gangsters meeting in a deserted building in a US city
- weird scientists planning to make a new creature in an isolated castle
- bank robbers in an abandoned warehouse planning a robbery
- generals in an underground bunker planning an attack.
- Alternatively, you could use a scenario of your own.

Spend 20 minutes thinking about how you will communicate the new setting and context for your setting to your audience. You will have to think about how you use gestures, postures, intonation and props to communicate this setting and context.

- Think also about how the meaning of some of the words will change. What new meanings could they take on? What, for example, could Graymalkin be?
- How will the physical characters change?
- How would Shakespeare's audience, who believed in witches and witchcraft, have reacted to the original scene? King James I was himself an expert in witchcraft and even wrote a treatise on witches, so it is likely Shakespeare included them in his play knowing they would have been a subject of interest to his king and patron. How would a modern audience respond similarly and differently to this scene?
- The three witches were original known in the first folio as "weyard" or weird sisters. The word "weird" has its origins in the Anglo Saxon word "wyrd", a concept relating to destiny and the role of past, present and future in shaping an individual's fate. How does this alter your reading of their characters and role in the play?
- How does changing the historical, geographical or social setting of a text alter its meaning for a reader or viewer?

GLOBAL CONTEXTS
Orientation in space and time

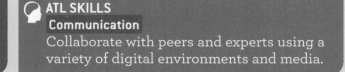

ATL SKILLS
Communication
Collaborate with peers and experts using a variety of digital environments and media.

Now look at the role of setting in communicating context in non-fiction texts that you may study.

 Activity 6   **Exploring settings in non–literary texts – advertisements**

Many advertisements rely on using setting to connect with a target audience and communicate a message about a product or brand. Aspects of setting help establish not only the cultural and historical context but also help communicate the image of product and the set of values and beliefs associated with it.

STEP 1 Research print advertisements for a common product. Choose a product which appeals to a range of target audiences (cars, perfumes, chocolate, clothes, sporting goods, drinks, confectionary etc.).

Select two or three print advertisements for your chosen product that appeal to different target audiences. For each advert/image complete the following information. If you are unsure, ask your teacher.

The advertisement	
Target audience	
Context: publication in which you found the advertisement and the sort of people who buy it	
Promises being made by the product. What is the primary appeal of the advertisement? What sort of thoughts/aspirations (e.g. fears, dreams, ambitions etc.) does the advertisement appeal to in the viewer?	

For example, you could explore print advertisements for different cars in different locations (city, wilderness, futuristic setting etc.). To help identify the target audience and the main appeal of the car, you may explore some of the following questions:

- In what publication was the advertisement located? What sort of people read this publication?
- What do advertisers promise will come with buying a car? Status? Freedom? Control? Power? Success? Independence?
- How is the viewer made to see the car as an emblem of himself/herself?
- What kind of people and relationships are shown in the advertisement (family, couples, business executive etc.)?
- Does the advertisement address the question of global warming? Is the target audience environmentally responsible?

Having identified these aspects of the advertisement, think about how its setting reinforces the message and image of the product.

 Swap your chosen adverts/images with a partner and answer the following questions:
- What is the setting of the advertisement and how can you tell? Look at elements such as:
  - the location including the backdrop, the physical landscape
  - the people in the advertisement – their clothing, relationships with others
  - the props – food, signs, objects being held and the relationship of people to these objects.
- What does the setting tell you about the target audience? Why is this appropriate for the product being sold?
- What image of the product is the advertisement trying to sell? How do the settings reinforce the image of the product the advertiser is trying to communicate (e.g. sophisticated, adventurous, professional, luxurious, futuristic etc.)? What concepts or lifestyle aspirations are they trying to promote (e.g. status, freedom, power)?
- How do the settings convey the mood and atmosphere that fits with the product image (calm, comfortable, relaxed, exhilarating, exciting, adventurous etc.)?
- Why did the advertiser choose this specific context for the advertisement?

TAKE ACTION

Focus on aspects of setting. Design an advertisement in print or other media for a campaign or appeal for action focused on a local environmental or humanitarian issue. Consider how a focus on aspects of setting will help you communicate the issue, problem or need and the ways to address it. Be sure to have a specific target audience in mind.

Present your advertisement to your class, explaining how aspects of setting highlight the issue's appeal to the target audience and emphasize solutions and change.

Reflection

Use the following questions and statements to guide your reflection:

- How might your chosen advertisements or book covers from the previous activities be interpreted in a different historical and cultural time and place?

- Changing the setting or context of a text forces you to consider different perspectives and readings.

- Up to what point can a text's meaning and message remain unaffected by changes to its setting and context?

The function of setting in creating mood and atmosphere and communicating theme

In this section you will explore how writers use setting as a tool to communicate themes, atmosphere and mood. You will explore the following questions:

- How can physical or described setting be used to communicate a text's message?

- How can the physical setting be used to communicate key ideas and themes in a text?

- What is pathetic fallacy and how is it used as a tool by writers?

- How can you create convincing and realistic settings in your own writing?

 Activity 7   **Staging a scene – drama diorama**

In this activity you will explore how setting can be used to communicate various aspects of a text, such as characters' mood and the atmosphere and how it can even highlight key ideas and themes.

Choose any scene from a play you have studied in class. With a partner construct a diorama of the scene in which you use elements of the setting to communicate the plot and action as well as aspects of character. Use the following questions to help you plan:

- What props will you include on stage? How will you position them in order to highlight their importance to the action and/or the character(s) on stage?
- Where will you set the scene?
- What aspects of lighting/sounds will you use to convey mood and atmosphere? How will changes in lighting affect the shifting mood of the characters and the scene in general? If the scene is set at night you need to think about how you can communicate this.
- What dominant colours will you use in your set (backdrop and lighting) to communicate mood and atmosphere?
- What props can be used to help communicate character and how should they interact with them to help further the audience's understanding of their character?
- How will you use shadows or dark spaces?
- What parts of the stage will your characters use? Where will they move and at what points in the dialogue?
- Think also about what your setting can communicate about the scene's historical and geographical location.

Complete the table to help you capture your plan:

Staging/backdrop	
Props	
Colours	
Lighting	
Actor's positioning on stage	

GLOBAL CONTEXTS
Personal and cultural expression

ATL SKILLS
Communication
Interpret and use effectively modes of non-verbal communication.

 Activity 8   Creative writing based on setting

Read the following extract from William Golding's novel *Lord of the Flies* and think about how the setting is used to help communicate events. Then answer the questions that follow:

Piggy touched Ralph's wrist.

"Come away. There's going to be trouble. And we've had our meat."

There was a blink of bright light beyond the forest and the thunder exploded again so that a littlun started to whine. Big drops of rain fell among them making individual sounds when they struck.

"Going to be a storm," said Ralph, "and you'll have rain like when we dropped here. Who's clever   5
now? Where are your shelters? What are you going to do about that?"

The hunters were looking uneasily at the sky, flinching from the stroke of the drops. A wave of restlessness set the boys swaying and moving aimlessly. The flickering light became brighter and the blows of the thunder were only just bearable. The littluns began to run about, screaming.

Jack leapt on to the sand.   10

"Do our dance! Come on! Dance!"

He ran stumbling through the thick sand to the open space of rock beyond the fire. Between the flashes of lightning the air was dark and terrible; and the boys followed him, clamorously. Roger became the pig, grunting and charging at Jack, who side-stepped. The hunters took their spears, the cooks took spits, and the rest clubs of firewood. A circling movement developed and a chant.   15
While Roger mimed the terror of the pig, the littluns ran and jumped on the outside of the

circle. Piggy and Ralph, under the threat of the sky, found themselves eager to take a place in this demented but partly secure society. They were glad to touch the brown backs of the fence that hemmed in the terror and made it governable.

"Kill the beast! Cut his throat! Spill his blood!"   20

The movement became regular while the chant lost its first superficial excitement and began to beat like a steady pulse. Roger ceased to be a pig and became a hunter, so that the center of the ring yawned emptily. Some of the littluns started a ring on their own; and the complementary circles went round and round as though repetition would achieve safety of itself. There was the throb and stamp of a single organism. 25

The dark sky was shattered by a blue-white scar. An instant later the noise was on them like the blow of a gigantic whip. The chant rose a tone in agony.

"Kill the beast! Cut his throat! Spill his blood!"

Now out of the terror rose another desire, thick, urgent, blind.

"Kill the beast! Cut his throat! Spill his blood!" 30

Again the blue-white scar jagged above them and the sulphurous explosion beat down. The littluns screamed and blundered about, fleeing from the edge of the forest, and one of them broke the ring of biguns in his terror.

"Him! Him!"

The circle became a horseshoe. A thing was crawling out of the forest. It came darkly, 35 uncertainly. The shrill screaming that rose before the beast was like a pain. The beast stumbled into the horseshoe.

"Kill the beast! Cut his throat! Spill his blood!"

The blue-white scar was constant, the noise unendurable. Simon was crying out something about a dead man on a hill. 40

"Kill the beast! Cut his throat! Spill his blood! Do him in!"

The sticks fell and the mouth of the new circle crunched and screamed. The beast was on its knees in the center, its arms folded over its face. It was crying out against the abominable noise something about a body on the hill. The beast struggled forward, broke the ring and fell over the steep edge of the rock to the sand by the water. At once the crowd surged after it, poured 45 down the rock, leapt on to the beast, screamed, struck, bit, tore. There were no words, and no movements but the tearing of teeth and claws.

Then the clouds opened and let down the rain like a waterfall. The water bounded from the mountain-top, tore leaves and branches from the trees, poured like a cold shower over the struggling heap on the sand. Presently the heap broke up and figures staggered away. Only the 50 beast lay still, a few yards from the sea. Even in the rain they could see how small a beast it was; and already its blood was staining the sand.

Now a great wind blew the rain sideways, cascading the water from the forest trees. On the mountain-top the parachute filled and moved; the figure slid, rose to its feet, spun, swayed down through a vastness of wet air and trod with ungainly feet the tops of the high trees; falling, still 55 falling, it sank toward the beach and the boys rushed screaming into the darkness. The parachute took the figure forward, furrowing the lagoon, and bumped it over the reef and out to sea.

Questions

- How does William Golding use pathetic fallacy to reflect the mounting tension and conflict in this scene?
- How do aspects of setting and weather help communicate rising tension in the scene?
- What does the storm symbolize in terms of the conflict between the boys?

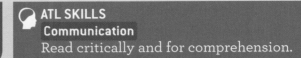

GLOBAL CONTEXTS
Personal and cultural expression

ATL SKILLS
Communication
Read critically and for comprehension.

 Activity 9   Planning a piece of writing based on setting

Having explored how Golding uses weather to communicate atmosphere in the previous activity, you are now going to step into the shoes of a writer and plan a piece of writing based on setting. The purpose of your writing is to consider how aspects of setting can communicate the mood and atmosphere as well as the themes and ideas of the piece.

Use the planning form that follows to help you think about the theme/idea you want to explore (e.g. love and loss) and the ways in which aspects of setting can help communicate the theme/idea, mood and atmosphere. In particular think about how setting can create tension. Ask your teacher to explain any terms you do not understand.

Theme/idea (emotion / mood / atmosphere):	
Possible situations:	
Lighting to convey atmosphere ■ intensity ■ colours ■ changes in light ■ shadow / sun	
Setting (time/place) **Weather**	

Sounds (effects) to create mood ■ alliteration ■ assonance ■ onomatopoeia ■ texture of words	
Speech / dialogue ■ tone of voice ■ vocabulary ■ punctuation marks ■ mode of address ■ volume	
Movements of people / objects to convey mood & attitude (Verbs)	
Images / symbols ■ similes ■ metaphors ■ symbols	
Point of view ■ close-up ■ aerial view ■ movement up/down	

Questions

Explain how the factors above combine to create an overall mood.

Describe how your piece builds to a climax and how the tension is reflected in your various elements above. This should then be followed by a denouement / resolution / falling action.

This plan can easily be used for a piece of prose writing.

TIP

In the earlier references to *The Story of an Hour* and *Lord of the Flies*, weather is used metaphorically to communicate characters' emotions and general tension. Use pathetic fallacy to transfer the emotions to your surroundings so that they convey your characters' mood. Use personification to bring the scene to life and make the setting become like one of the characters.

GLOBAL CONTEXTS
Personal and cultural expression

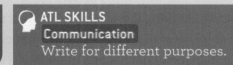

ATL SKILLS
Communication
Write for different purposes.

Creating a convincing piece of writing

Using realistic details

How can you convey a sense of place to someone who has never lived where you do? One way is to think of different aspects of the place that make it unique. These realistic details will make your setting convincing:

- food
- names of people and places
- animals
- plants and trees
- type of music played
- buildings and landmarks

Try this yourself. Write down names and examples local to you and create a sentence that describes a person moving through that landscape. Be as specific as you can. As an example, look at the following extracts. Think about the locations they describe and how through appealing to your senses they help transport you into the scene.

> Extract A
>
> *As Juan ambled across the dusty landscape, picking his way between cactus and mestize trees, his thoughts were interrupted by a coati scampering across the dusty path, a green mango in its mouth.*

And:

> Extract B
>
> *The sounds of mariachi drifted through the jacaranda trees, up up through the window of Guadelupe's kitchen and mingled with the rich smell of mole and frijoles emanating from her stove. A pair of chachalacas flew noisily past her window, chattering loudly like gossips in the plaza, no doubt mocking the lovers below, who sang boleros through tequila breath, their notes mingling with the smell of the frangipani trees.*

 Activity 10 **Appealing to the senses**

STEP 1 Re-read the lines from Wilfred Owen's poem *Dulce et decorum est* in Chapter 9 on characterisation and answer the questions that follow. The poem describes World War I soldiers as they return to their rest trenches from the front line.

Questions

- How does Owen bring the battlefield in France to life for his readers back in England and elsewhere? Consider his use of onomatopoeia, alliteration, and vivid images.
- What comparisons (similes and metaphors) does Owen use to create a clearer picture of the soldiers and their environment?

TIP

Creating tension

Tension can be created by varying the pace and rhythm of sentences. To vary pace and rhythm you need to use a variety of sentence types (simple, compound, complex compound-complex) and lengths. Ask your teacher for further information on different types of sentence.

In *Dulce et decorum est* for example, Owen conveys the slow trudging pace of the tired, injured men using punctuation to create a stilted, limping movement to the verse.

STEP 2 **Communicating emotion using verbs**

In his description Owen also pays close attention to the verbs he uses to describe the soldiers' movements and state of mind. Verbs are a powerful way to communicate character and convey emotions. Substitute a verb from the table into the space in the sentence that follows. Complete the table by considering the different moods and motivations suggested by each verb. Feel free to think of others

Samantha [… … … ….] into the classroom.

Verbs:	Possible moods and motivations implied
skipped	
ambled	
shuffled	
sprinted	
meandered	
marched	
stormed	
sneaked	

GLOBAL CONTEXTS
Personal and cultural expression

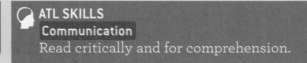

ATL SKILLS
Communication
Read critically and for comprehension.

Reflection

- How successful was your piece of creative writing?

- What improvements could you make to your planning and writing next time?

- What advice would you give to someone else to improve their writing?

Summary

In this chapter you have explored some of the key functions of setting in communicating character, context, theme, mood and atmosphere. Can you think of any other functions?

To demonstrate your learning of the concept of setting, choose one of the following activities:

1. Develop a service learning project to improve an aspect of the physical setting of your school or local community. Investigate how your project can address a true need and make a positive impact on the setting and community. Monitor the impact of these changes on the community through questionnaires and surveys.

2. Change setting: Spend time in an unfamiliar environment or change settings in a familiar environment (e.g. eat lunch somewhere differently, visit somewhere new in your local community, move seats in your classroom). Reflect on how the change affects you—your outlook, mood, perspective, attitudes and/ or values.

3. Design a new book cover: For a text you are studying, design a new book cover which uses setting to communicate one or more aspects of the text: character, theme, mood, atmosphere. Consider the key elements to incorporate in order to communicate as much as you can about your text.

References

Golding, W. 2012. *Lord of the Flies*. Faber and Faber.

Shakespeare, W. 2007. *Macbeth*. Penguin Classics. New Edition.

INQUIRY QUESTIONS	**TOPIC 1** Exploring elements of style ■ **What is the reason behind an author's choice of style?** **TOPIC 2** Writing in the same style ■ **What forms a certain style?** **TOPIC 3** Building your own style ■ **How can you build your own style?**
SKILLS	**ATL** ✓ Analyse complex concepts and projects into their constituent parts and synthesize them to create new understanding. ✓ Use critical-literacy skills to analyse and interpret media communications. ✓ Apply existing knowledge to generate new ideas, products or processes. ✓ Draw reasonable conclusions and generalizations. **Language and literature** ✓ Analyse the content, context, language, structure, technique and style of text(s) and the relationships among texts. ✓ Evaluate similarities and differences by connecting features across and within genres and texts. ✓ Make stylistic choices in terms of linguistic and literary devices, demonstrating awareness of impact on an audience. ✓ Select relevant details and examples to develop ideas. ✓ Write and speak in a register and style that serve the context and intention.
OTHER RELATED CONCEPTS	**Setting** **Self-expression** **Context**

GLOSSARY

Denotative meaning the literal, dictionary meaning of a word.

Diction the author's choice of words and their effects on the total work.

Imagery the evocation of a sensory experience through words.

Syntax sentence structure and punctuation. e.g.: complex, simple, compound, dialogue.

COMMAND TERMS

Analyse break down in order to bring out the essential elements or structure. To identify parts and relationships, and to interpret information to reach conclusions.

Compare give an account of the similarities between two (or more) items or situations, referring to both (all) of them throughout.

Discuss offer a considered and balanced review that includes a range of arguments, factors or hypotheses.

Explore undertake a systematic process of discovery.

Interpret use knowledge and understanding to recognize trends and draw conclusions from given information.

Introducing style

Style is the author's way of communicating their message. All authors have a style, but not all authors' styles are the same. Style is the author's choice of words, their arrangements in sentences and paragraphs to express themselves. The style of a text shows how the author perceives something—an experience or an event—and how they want the reader to experience this perception.

There are three elements of style that we will focus on in this chapter: diction, imagery and syntax.

Diction can be explained as the author's choice of words and their effect on the writing. There are different ways that any particular word can be read in a text. There is the literal meaning of a word—the one that you would read in the dictionary definition if you looked it up. This is called the **denotative meaning**. Then there are the suggestions and associations that you might make when you read a word or group of words. This is called connotative meaning. Several words may have the same literal meaning while differing significantly in their connotation.

Imagery is the use of language by the author to evoke a sensory experience for the reader. This can help a reader visualize a place in a text, or imagine smells, tastes and sounds.

Syntax is the sentence structure and punctuation used in the text.

TOPIC 1

Exploring elements of style

Authors can influence your interpretations about the facts presented by their choice of wordings and phrases. The stylistic choices that a writer selects give you certain impressions about the situation, the speaker and the person spoken to (the audience). The following activities will show you how authors of literary works use elements of style to make readers see what they see. You will explore the elements of style and analyze famous authors' use of stylistic devices. You will recognize how the choice of a certain style can deliver a message.

 Activity 1   Exploring elements of style

Read the following excerpt from *Animal Farm* by George Orwell.

"Now, comrades, what is the nature of this life of ours? Let us face it: our lives are miserable, laborious, and short. We are born, we are given just so much food as will keep the breath in our bodies, and those of us who are capable of it are forced to work to the last atom of our strength;

and the very instant that our usefulness has come to an end we are slaughtered with hideous cruelty. No animal in England knows the meaning of happiness or leisure after he is a year old. No animal in England is free. The life of an animal is misery and slavery: that is the plain truth. But is this simply part of the order of nature? Is it because this land of ours is so poor that it cannot afford a decent life to those who dwell upon it? No, comrades, a thousand times no! The soil of England is fertile, its climate is good, it is capable of affording food in abundance to an enormously greater number of animals than now inhabit it. This single farm of ours would support a dozen horses, twenty cows, hundreds of sheep—and all of them living in a comfort and a dignity that are now almost beyond our imagining. Why then do we continue in this miserable condition? Because nearly the whole of the produce of our labour is stolen from us by human beings. There, comrades, is the answer to all our problems. It is summed up in a single word—Man. Man is the only real enemy we have. Remove Man from the scene, and the root cause of hunger and overwork is abolished for ever. "

In the following table you will find a list of examples and prompt questions that help you to determine a text's style. (For example, this could be a lyrical, flippant, comic, fussy, serious, scientific, plain, formal, vivid, comic, or imaginative style.)

Area of communication	Is it for a mass audience, is it poetic, is it professional or academic?
Type of text (genre)	Is it a news article, letter, poem, speech, etc.?
Topic	What subject the text is about?
Theme	What message is the text is trying to convey? This is usually written as a statement.
Purpose of the text	Is it to entertain, persuade or inform?
Context	Where and when does the text take place?
Audience	Who is the text addressing?
Tone	Is there an attitude to the voice used? For example, is the voice affectionate/ flat/secure/confused?
Mood	What atmosphere is created by the writer? E.g.: gloomy, dull.
Diction	What words are used in the text? For example, short words/ slang words/ formal language?
Imagery	What imagery is created in the text? Are there any metaphors or similes that contribute to the imagery in the text?
Syntax	Is there anything unusual about the grammar and punctuation in the text? For example, are the sentences complex or simple? Are there questions in the text? Is there dialogue?

Using the table, analyse the extract and interpret how the writer uses different aspects of style (diction, syntax, tone, mood, figures of speech, descriptive details etc.) to get his message through to the reader and reach his aim (purpose).

GLOBAL CONTEXTS
Personal and cultural expression

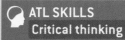

ATL SKILLS
Critical thinking
Analyse complex concepts and projects into their constituent parts and synthesize them to create new understanding.

 Activity 2 Comparing styles

Read the excerpts from two novels describing difficult journeys and answer the questions that follow:

Text One: *Touching the Void* by Joe Simpson

I stumbled through the chaotic maze of boulders and scree*. I sagged wearily against a boulder, letting my mind run haphazardly over my pain and sorrow. The thirst had become unbearable. My mouth was dry and I swallowed. What little saliva it produced failed to ease the discomfort. The descent had become a confused blur of endless boulder fields, burning midday sun, and the thirst. My legs felt weighted down and so weakened I fell repeatedly among the rocks. When loose rocks slipped suddenly under my feet, I found that I had no strength to prevent myself falling. I used the axe to steady myself, and occasionally flung a hand out for support. Fingers slapped unfeeling against sharp boulders. The sun had failed to revive any sensation in them and they remained numb and cold. After an hour I saw the rounded boulder, with water glistening as it ran over its flank. I quickened my pace, feeling a burst of energy come through me at the thought of water.

When I reached the hollow at the base of the boulder, and dropped my rucksack on the wet scree, I saw that there was not enough water to satisfy my craving thirst. Carefully I built a catchment area in the gravel at the base of the rock. It filled with tantalizing slowness and, after sucking a gritty mouthful, was empty again. I crouched at the rock drinking and waiting, and drinking again. There seemed no end to the amount I could drink.

Text Two: *The Last Ride* by Thomas Eidson

They had been riding without a break since morning. The afternoon rays of the desert sun burned into them with a fierceness, but it seemed that nothing would stop the old man and his little horse. Dot followed on Alice. The mule kept her head tucked in close behind the old mare's rump. Further back rode Maggie. Clouds of thin dust kicked up, billowing over her, coating her in a muddy film of perspiration.

> **TIP**
>
> Difference between descriptive features and stylistic features:
>
> Descriptive features are the concrete language elements writers use to capture a particular event, experience or time.
>
> Stylistic features are the choices of language to capture the impression of a particular event, experience or time.

> **TIP**
>
> Term you need to know:
> **Scree:** small loose stones.

The land was dry, mostly sand, a place of flash floods and little more. Forbidding dunes rose like ocean waves in the distance; cactus and creosote were closer by. There were lizards and lots of colinia warblers in the brush1. The terrain was sparse pickings and thirsty. In the distance, in all directions, were tall, barren-looking mountains.

TIP

Terms you need to know:
Brush: undergrowth, small trees and shrubs.
Gray: the horse.

The gray pony was beginning to fade badly, stumbling over small things; the heat, the fatigue and lack of water were taking their toll on her. Dot kicked Alice into a canter and moved alongside the old man, slowing the mule to a bone-jarring halt. She looked worried.

At 118 degrees Fahrenheit, Mannito had told her, a man exposed to the desert sun could last a day without water. One day. She didn't know how long it was for horses and mules. Maybe more, maybe less. She gazed off into the distance, watching the air dance in the harsh sunlight, and guessed the temperature to be 115 degrees. She and her mother had a little water left, but the animals hadn't drunk since the previous night.

'We need water, grandpa. And we need to let the gray rest.'

Answer the following questions using the table above to help you analyse the style of the two texts.

- What descriptive features do the two texts have in common and what descriptive features are different?
- What stylistic features make the first text more factual and the second text fictional?
- Write a comparison of the two styles. How are they the same? How are they different?

GLOBAL CONTEXTS
Personal and cultural expression

ATL SKILLS
Information literacy
Use critical-literacy skills to analyse and interpret media communications.

 Activity 3  Assess your understanding

Analyse and compare the following two texts. Discuss the similarities and differences between the texts. Include comments on the ways the authors use elements such as structure, tone, images and other stylistic devices to communicate their purposes.

Text One: The Wave

We sensed it was coming and the others just dropped to the floor to protect themselves. I was steering and the white water just threw me forward into the wheel. It was just an unbelievable wave. It picked us up and the boat took off across the face of the wave like it was a surfboard. We were absolutely charging across this wave, like I'm talking about literally thumping across the water.

But we're in a 43-foot, nine-tonne yacht. It's going whack, whack, whack across the wave doing 15 maybe 20 knots, and I'm hanging onto the wheel, crouched down, waiting for the wave to break over us. I'm thinking in a split second, what do I do? Do I try and pull the boat away? Do I let it go straight ahead and try to steady it? Do I try and pull up through the back of it or what? Then I realized the yacht was just hanging in there. I decided I'd just steer her straight and let her go the way she wanted. This is all happening in a split second. I'm crouched down waiting for the water to literally engulf us and then suddenly I'm thinking, God, I've got no water around. I've got my eyes and my mouth closed and there's no water around. What's going on?

I opened my eyes and looked up and could see the wave curling over us. We were literally in the tube of the wave. It was just a phenomenal, unbelievable situation. You could see it breaking over us, and we were just staying out of the break. Next thing, of course, it caught up with us and whumphh, it broke all over us. Equally quickly it was all gone.

Text Two: Helmsmanship

Steering is one of the seaman's most responsible tasks. A helmsman is not only required to be familiar with the steering qualities of his ship and have a complete knowledge of the compass, but is also required to be absolutely reliable, trustworthy and capable of concentration. A good, intelligent helmsman is highly regarded in every ship by the master and the officers, and every young sailor should aspire to become a helmsman upon whom officers and pilots can rely implicitly. A mistake on the helmsman's part which is not at once detected, and corrected, can lead, and often has done, to disaster.

The successful helmsman is one who maintains a steady course with the least possible movement of the wheel. To this end his undivided attention is essential. If, through inattentiveness or inexperience on the helm's part, a ship yaws from side to side of her course, the steering engine is continually on the move. Naturally it is better for him if he turns the wheel a little than if he turns it a lot.

A conscientious helmsman will only hand over to a relief when a manoeuvre has been completed and the ship has been steadied on her course. An indication of how the vessel is steering, that is, carrying port or starboard helm, steering well or steering badly, should always be given by the man-at-the-wheel to his relief. If the wheel is handed over in a proper manner, it will make things easier for the new helmsman.

TIP

Term you need to know:
Helmsman: the person responsible for steering a boat.

REFLECTION

Consider the following:
- How did you feel when you were doing this activity?
- Have you mastered any skills?
- What are the skills you feel you need to work on?
- What are you going to do next to improve you performance?

 **GLOBAL CONTEXTS**
Personal and cultural expression

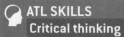 **ATL SKILLS**
Critical thinking
Analyse complex concepts and projects into their constituent parts and synthesize them to create new understanding.

TOPIC 2

Writing in the same style

Now that you have explored the features and components that form a style, you will imitate a style after analyzing it. You will be exposed to different literary genre with their unique styles. You will explore descriptive prose highlighting the process of thinking, then look at creating suspense and investigate the styles of different poetry genres.

When analyzing style there are certain expressions and language to be used. The following table gives you some examples of literary language to use when answering questions about style. You may want to consult with your teacher for further explanation of the terms and language used in this table.

Stylistic feature	Examples
The general style of the text	■ simple – the author chooses to portray his characters or ideas candidly with few chances for misunderstanding ■ complex – the subject is many-faceted, so the author's style must try to capture these aspects, perhaps with figures of speech, longer sentences, use of analogies, etc. ■ literal – the author means to communicate on one level, i.e. he is referring to the primary meaning of the words he chooses; he is concerned with the facts; he exaggerates or embellishes very little ■ figurative – style which makes use of figures of speech, metaphorical or rhetorical writing. direct – a straightforward, candid, frank form of writing which does not deviate ■ involved – style which tries to take an in-depth look at the subject, exploring feelings and behaviours ■ abstract – the author intentionally stays away from specifics concentrating on the theoretical rather than the practical ■ concrete – the author relies heavily on specific facts and instances to flesh out his ideas ■ ponderous – heavy and dull ■ epigrammatic – containing wise sayings smartly expressed ■ didactic – instructive (teaching)

	- dogmatic – positive, assertive - colloquial – using the vernacular (common speech) - pompous – pretentious, affecting a false dignity - gushing – without reserve, usually without reflection - coy – a pretense of bashfulness - other …..
Mood of the text	- ironic – the use of words to convey the opposite of their literal meaning - humorous – funny, laughable, comical - gay – merry, cheerful, jolly - solemn – deeply earnest, serious, grave - wistful – pensive, wishful - romantic – extravagantly ideal - religious – conscientious devotion to topic - serious – sober, earnest, sincere - melancholy – thoughtfully sad - sad – sorrowful, unhappy, dispirited - whimsical – oddly funny - reminiscent – things remembered - sentimental – cloying or sickening - pensive – musing, thoughtful - reverent – showing respect - sportive – mischievous - reflective – thoughtful - somber – gloomy - sinister – boding evil - nostalgic – longing for home or country, or for something that is absent - other …….
Paragraph development	- sequential – organized by steps or through time - spatial – organized through distance or space - logical – reasoning from one supposition to another - systematic – according to a method - haphazard – to convey a sense of confusion - other …….
Sentence structure	- short – giving an effect for excitement or speed - long – characterizes formal styles, especially discussions of ideas, also common in fiction (i.e., descriptive passages) - varied in length – figures of speech may be used in order to exaggerate ideas - loose – makes sense if brought to a close at one or more points before the end - periodic – makes complete sense only when one reaches the end (or period). This may add to suspense or variety

	- parallel – two or more parts of a sentence follow the same grammatical construction. Use for emphasis - balance, antithesis, inversion, repetition and subordinate construction adds emphasis to ideas discussed in the passage - simple and compound sentences lend simplistic tone and style; subject is not meant to be portrayed in a complex manner - complex sentences may help to convey a conflict of ideas - logical connectives between sentences solidify the argument - rhetorical questions – used to make the reader supply additional material for the passage, and to motivate reader to consider implications of passage - other...
Diction	- monosyllabic – one syllable – this style may be used to effect simplicity or it may be used for the purposes of austerity - polysyllabic – two or more syllables – a more formal, serious style which may make use of any of the constructions mentioned previously - archaic – belonging to ancient times – in this case, the style is obviously meant to transport the reader into a different era - connotative – suggesting more than the plain meaning – a figurative style meant to be emotive or reflective - rare words – the intent may be lofty, lighthearted, informative or comparative - technical and scientific words – serious writing with a referential intent - slang and colloquialisms – may be used for humour or for realism - abstractions – intended to make reader reflect or accept alternate ideas - dialect words – used to portray a definite group of people, to convey realistic flavour - allusions – formal writing; the author supposes readers can make comparative judgements - onomatopoeic words – to convey realism, a sense of presence, a re-enactment of the original - vivid verbs – convey a sense of action - alliteration – helps bind phrases and thus thoughts together; lends completeness to passage - vivid imagery – takes reader away from commonplace; suggests alternatives

Table 12.1 Using literary analysis language

Activity 4   Using the same stylistic features

The following excerpt is from James Joyce's *Ulysses*. It describes part of the inner conversation of Leopold Bloom, the main character, as he walks through Dublin in 1904. The novel is considered one of the most important works of 20th century literature. Before Joyce, no writer of fiction had highlighted the process of thinking.

> *He crossed at Nassau street corner and stood before the window of Yeates and Son, pricing the field grasses. Or will I drop into old Harris's and have a chat with Young Sinclair? Well mannered fellow. Probably at his lunch. Must get those old glasses of mine set right. Goerz lenses, six guineas. Germans making their way everywhere. Sell on easy terms to capture trade. Undercutting. Might chance on a pair in the railway lost property office. Astonishing the things people leave behind them in trains and cloak rooms. What do they be thinking about! Women too. Incredible. Last year trvelling to Ennis had to pick up that farmer's daughter's bag and hand it to her at Limerick junction. Unclaimed money too. There's a little watch up there on the roof of the bank to test these glasses by.*

STEP 1   Read the excerpt. Using the literary analysis language table to help you, answer the following questions:

1. What is the general style of the text?
2. What is the mood of the text?
3. Describe the paragraph development in the text.
4. Describe the sentence structure in the text.
5. Describe the use of diction in the text.

STEP 2   Now that you are aware of the stylistic features used in the text, write your own passage about your thoughts as you walk through your hometown. In your passage, use as many of Joyce's stylistic features as possible.

GLOBAL CONTEXTS
Orientation in space and time

ATL SKILLS
Creative thinking
Apply existing knowledge to generate new ideas, products or processes.

Activity 5   Creating suspense

STEP 1   Write a 100-word passage which describes an action that takes ten seconds to do. For example, the action could be "opening a door". Add descriptions of the moment and create a full image of what happens in the ten seconds. Describe who is there, where the action takes place, how it happens, and the feelings you have when doing the action.

Share it with others and discuss how it can be refined to make it more exciting or give more impact.

Read the following excerpt from the short story *Contents of the Dead Man's Pocket* by Jack Finney, describing a scene where the narrator is trying to rescue a piece of paper from drifting through the window.

Analyse the style Finney uses to describe this moment in his passage. You can use the literary analysis language table to help you.

Turning, he saw a sheet of white paper drifting to the floor in a series of arcs, and another sheet, yellow, moving towards the window, caught in the dying current flowing through the narrow opening. As he watched, the paper struck the bottom edge of the window and hung there for an instant, plastered against the glass and wood. Then as the moving air stilled completely, the curtains swinging back from the wall to hang free again, he saw the yellow sheet drop to the window ledge and slide over out of sight.

He ran across the room, grasped the bottom of the window and tugged, staring through the glass. He saw the yellow sheet, dimly now in the darkness outside, lying on the ornamental ledge a yard below the window. Even as he watched, it was moving, scraping slowly along the ledge, pushed by the breeze that pressed steadily against the building wall. He heaved on the window with all his strength, and it shot open with a bang, the window weight rattling in the casing. But the paper was past his reach and, leaning out into the night, he watched it scud steadily along the ledge to the south, half plastered against the building wall. Above the muffled sound of the street traffic far below, he could hear the dry scrape of its movement, like a leaf on the pavement.

STEP 3 Write a passage about the next ten seconds in this description using the same style.

🌐 **GLOBAL CONTEXTS**
Orientation in space and time

🧠 **ATL SKILLS**
Creative thinking
Apply existing knowledge to generate new ideas, products or processes.

Activity 6   Exploring poetry genres

STEP 1 Read and **explore** the five genres of poetry that follow.

Sonnet
Excerpt from **Sonnet Number 18 by William Shakespeare**

Shall I compare thee to a summer's day?

Thou art more lovely and more temperate.

Rough winds do shake the darling buds of May,

And summer's lease hath all too short a date.

Sometime too hot the eye of heaven shines,

Emily Dickinson wrote renowned narrative poetry.

And often is his gold complexion dimmed,

And every fair from fair sometime declines,

By chance, or nature's changing course untrimmed.

Narrative poetry

I Felt a Funeral in my Brain by Emily Dickinson

I felt a Funeral, in my Brain,

And Mourners to and fro

Kept treading – treading – till it seemed

That Sense was breaking through –

And when they all were seated,

A Service, like a

Drum – Kept beating – beating – till I thought

My Mind was going numb –

And then I heard them lift a Box

And creak across my Soul

With those same Boots of Lead, again,

Then Space – began to toll,

As all the Heavens were a Bell,

And Being, but an Ear,

And I, and Silence, some strange

Race Wrecked, solitary, here –

And then a Plank in Reason, broke,

And I dropped down, and down -

And hit a World, at every plunge,

And Finished knowing – then –

Sure to taste sweetly, — is that poison too?

Haiku

Haiku by Matsu Basho

In the cicada's cry
No sign can tell
How soon it must die.

First day of Spring-
I keep thinking about-
the end of autmn.

Moonless night...
a powerful wind embraces
the ancient cedars.

Don't imitate me;
it's as boring
as the two halves of a melon.

The moon so pure
a wandering monk carries it
across the sand.

Haiku by Issa

Written in Hoshina village on a spring Kannon festival day:

Wind-strewn blossoms—
Buddha gathers secret coins
In a shady nook

The gentle willow,
Pliant as a woman, tempts me
Into the garden

Belly full of rice cake,
To digest, I go out and
Graft another tree

Edward Lear wrote well known limericks and nonsense poems.

Limerick

By Edward Lear

There was an Old man with a beard,

Who said, "It is just as I feared!—

Two Owls and a Hen,

Four Larks and a Wren,

Have all built their nests in my beard!

There was an Old Man of Dundee,

Who frequented the top of a tree;

When disturbed by the crows, he abruptly arose,

And exclaimed, I'll return to Dundee.'

Ballade

Heart not so heavy as mine by Emily Dickinson

Heart, not so heavy as mine

Wending late home —

As it passed my window

Whistled itself a tune —

A careless snatch — a ballad — A ditty of the street —

Yet to my irritated Ear

An Anodyne so sweet —

It was as if a Bobolink

Sauntering this way

Carolled, and paused, and carolled —

Then bubbled slow away!

It was as if a chirping brook

Upon a dusty way —

Set bleeding feet to minuets

Without the knowing why!

Tomorrow, night will come again —

Perhaps, weary and sore —

Ah Bugle! By my window

I pray you pass once more.

STEP 2 Now that you have read these poems from different genres, copy the table and fill it out. A few sections have been started for you.

Features	Types of poems				
	Narrative poetry	Sonnets	Haiku	Limerick	Ballade
Rhyme scheme		**A strict rhyme scheme.** The rhyme scheme of a Shakespearean sonnet is ABAB / CDCD / EFEF / GG			

Rhythms					
Alliteration (repeating letter or sound at the beginning of words)			Standard syllabic pattern of five syllables in the first line, seven in the second, and five in the last.		
History & origin			Japan Seventeenth century		
Length		14 lines, can be broken down into four sections called quatrains.	Short from three to 17 lines		
Special features					Uses simple language and tells a story
Famous poets			Basho first poet, then Buson and Issa.		

STEP 3 Choose one of the poems and analyse its style, considering the following:
- **Genre** → Structure
- **Tone/narrative tone** → Chronological order of events; describes an event and follows it with an argument; does not emphasize specific events, etc.
- **Setting**
- **Speaker** → Diversity of moods → syntax and diction
- **Purpose/theme**
- **Mood** → Thoughtful, confused, puzzled, competitive, etc.
- **Imagery**
- **Figures of speech** → personification, metaphor or extended metaphor, etc.
- **Sound** → Repetition, confirmation, assurance, declaration
- **Rhyme scheme**
- **Symbols and ambiguities**
- **Syntax and diction related to mood**

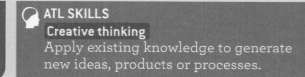

GLOBAL CONTEXTS
Personal and cultural expression

ATL SKILLS
Creative thinking
Apply existing knowledge to generate new ideas, products or processes.

Reflection

Consider the following:

- What can you do to become a more efficient and effective learner?

- How can you become more flexible in your choice of learning strategies?

- What factors are important for helping you learn well?

TOPIC 3

Building your own style

The context of a text can affect its level of formality. Different situations call for different ways of putting words together. The way you write in academic and scientific settings differs greatly from the way you write to a friend or someone close to you. The tone, vocabulary, and syntax all change as the occasion changes. This difference in styles of writing is the difference between formal and informal writing.

Vocabulary in formal settings:	Formal writing uses advanced vocabulary with full words (for example, "advertisement") instead of contractions or abbreviations (for example, "ad" or "advert").
Vocabulary in informal settings:	Informal writing uses simple words using abbreviations and contractions.
Tone in formal settings:	Formal writing uses an impersonal tone and discusses topics stating main points confidently and offers fully supported arguments.

Tone in informal settings:	Informal writing uses an emotional tone, first or second person point-of-view, and often discusses topics with humour.
Sentences in formal settings:	Formal writing favors longer, more detailed sentences to thoroughly convey a thought. Sentences are usually in the third person.
Sentences in informal settings:	Informal writing favors short, simple sentences.
Punctuation in formal settings:	Formal writing uses conservative punctuation (e.g., periods, commas, etc.).
Punctuation in informal settings:	Informal writing is generous with abrupt and dramatic punctuation (e.g., exclamation marks, the ellipses, the dash, etc.).

Activity 7   Level of formality

STEP 1 The following is an excerpt from a short story. Complete the missing parts in the most descriptive way you can.

A .... woman with ....came in the room, her .... and her .... was .... like a .... that ....

She .... When she .... she reminds me of .... You could not resist ....

She .... and said ....

STEP 2 The following is an excerpt from a police investigation witness report of the same woman from the first excerpt. Fill the missing parts in the most descriptive way you can.

Sue Thomason, a freelance journalist, testified that the terrorist witnessed in the crime scene was a woman. She was wearing ....

She was described as a .... with .... and ....
Her .... was .... that ....

She was standing .... when suddenly she .... her ....
from her .... In two seconds exactly she .... her ....
.... and .... her .... and stated ....

STEP 3 **Compare** your two descriptions. How are they the same? How are they different? How much did the given context change your style?

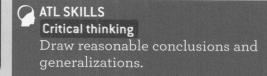

🌐 **GLOBAL CONTEXTS**
Personal and cultural expression

ATL SKILLS
Critical thinking
Draw reasonable conclusions and generalizations.

  **Activity 8** Writing with style

STEP 1 The following are two excerpts from the first chapter of *The Great Gatsby* describing the character of Daisy. Read the extracts and note how the narrative style is used—the use of words (diction), sentences (syntax) and imagery (figures of speech)—to deliver the message.

STEP 2 Read the first excerpt and answer the questions that follow.

The only <u>completely stationary</u> object in the room was an enormous couch on which two young women were <u>buoyed up as though upon an anchored balloon</u>. They were both in <u>white</u>, and their dresses were <u>rippling and fluttering as if they had just been blown back in after a short flight around the house</u>. I must have stood for a few moments listening to the <u>whip and snap</u> of the curtains and the <u>groan</u> of a picture on the wall.

The other girl, Daisy, made an attempt to rise — she leaned <u>slightly</u> forward with a <u>conscientious</u> expression — then she laughed, <u>an absurd, charming little</u> laugh, and I laughed too and came forward into the room. "I'm p-paralyzed with happiness." She laughed again, as if she said something very <u>witty</u>, and held my hand for a moment, looking up into my face, promising that there was no one in the world she <u>so much</u> wanted to see. That was a way she had. She hinted in <u>a murmur</u> that the surname of the balancing girl was Baker. (I've heard it said that Daisy's murmur was only to make people lean toward her; an irrelevant criticism that made it <u>no less charming</u>.)

Answer the following questions.
- How are figures of speech used?
- How are the underlined sections used to show Daisy in Nick's eyes?

STEP 3 Read the second excerpt from the same novel and answer the questions that follow.

I looked back at my cousin, who began to ask me questions in her low, thrilling voice. It was the kind of voice that the ear follows up and down, as if each speech is an arrangement of notes that will never be played again. Her face was sad and lovely with bright things in it, bright eyes and a bright passionate mouth, but there was an excitement in her voice that men who had cared for her found difficult to forget: a singing compulsion, a whispered "Listen," a promise that she had done gay, exciting things just a while since and that there were gay, exciting things hovering in the next hour.

- How are sentences (structure and punctuation) used in the extract to describe Daisy's voice?
- How did Scott Fitzgerald create his style? Is it effective? How?

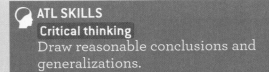

WEB LINKS

There are many free handouts available on the Writing Center website from the University of North Carolina (writingcenter.unc.edu). Click on the tab "Handouts" and select "Style" under the category "Citation, Style, and Sentence Level Concerns".

GLOBAL CONTEXTS
Personal and cultural expression

ATL SKILLS
Critical thinking
Draw reasonable conclusions and generalizations.

Activity 9 — Assess your understanding: reshaping a piece of work

In this activity you will reshape a piece of work. Your task is to adapt and reshape the following short story to modify its style. Make the piece of work more vivid by using better stylistic elements. Add, delete, adapt or keep any elements of style that would refine this short story.

And Here We Go Again

The swift train went along. Looking outside the window, I felt as if no years have passed; same everything. The same time of year with those golden short wheat stems alongside the horizon. It was always in April when I had to travel to Manhattan to see my family. First, with the tragedy of my father's sickness, then death. Repeated after two years, by my mother's suffering and receiving the same destiny.

I took a deep sigh and couldn't help memories crawling down my mind. Out of my control, they brought tears to my eyes.

"Am I going there again?" I asked myself.

This time, it's my brother. A young man with three little kids and a wife. That's a heavy load to leave behind. Being at the same school and university we grew up mostly together. We shared lots of events with all what childhood and youth times hold. Even at the age of 40, there is still a part in me that longs for his presence.

The long loud horn of an opposite train stroke my thoughts, to hear someone saying; "it's five minutes to Manhattan". The distressing scenes faded away, and I took shape to step at the station.

Opening the door at his house, his three kids stood there; not beyond the height of the table at the entrance hall.

"Hi aunty" the youngest joyfully said. "Is this for us?" He took the pack of chocolates I got them and showed me the way in.

Just the sight of his tired smile and his deep hollow look, I couldn't help rolling back to my gloomy reminiscence. I hid my feelings and gave him a smile back. We talked, we ate, we laughed, and we spoke about all walks of life except his case and what the doctors said.
I was curious to know, but I thought I didn't need to ask. It was clear in the atmosphere of the place around us; and I could tell, that something was very much wrong.

When the time came for me to leave, I stood and leaned to put a kiss on his forehead. Two tears shone on his face; and I felt my life time had shriveled in that exact moment. As if all blessings I had vanished and were replaced by that painful sorrow that is still growing everyday.

I gave him my back walking to the door. One question forced itself and kept ringing in my head; "Will I ever get to see him again?"

Consider the following:

- How well do you think you approached the piece of writing *And Here We Go Again*?
- What was the best amendment you made to it? Why you think it is the best?
- What was the amendment that did not make much difference? Why do you think so?
- What aspect of style analysis do you think you still need to learn more about?

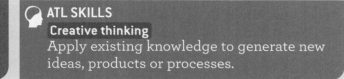

🌐 **GLOBAL CONTEXTS**
Personal and cultural expression

🧠 **ATL SKILLS**
Creative thinking
Apply existing knowledge to generate new ideas, products or processes.

Summary

The concept of style is central to the subject of language and literature as it strengthens your understanding of how language affects literature, and how literature affects language. Exploring the concept of style offers you the key to unlocking the mysteries of the talent of an author in a piece of work. By analyzing the manner of how the author uses words and phrases (language) to convey a view, portray sensations or deliver a message (literature), you realize and appreciate the author's style in vividly revealing their thoughts and feelings.

Figure 12.2 Have you tried this thinking routine?

Use the following thinking routine to reflect on the chapter:

Compass Points

E = Excited: What excites you about the concept of style? What's the upside?

W = Worrisome: What do you find worrisome about this concept ? What's the downside?

N = Need to Know: What else do you need to know or find out about it? What additional information would help you evaluate things?

S = Stance or Suggestion for Moving Forward: What is your current stance or opinion on the concept of style? How might you move forward in your evaluation of this concept?

References

Basho, M. *Haiku by Matsu Basho. From: Basho's Narrow Road: Spring and Autumn Passages*. Rock Spring Collection of Japanese Literature. Stone Bridge Press. 1996.

Bonwick, G. 1958. *Seamanship Handbook*. 2nd ed. G. Philip.

Dickenson, E. (author), Johnson, T. (Editor). 1976. *The Complete Poems of Emily Dickinson*. Back Bay Books.

Dickinson, E. *I Felt a Funeral in My Brain*. From: *The Pocket Emily Dickinson*. Shambhala Pocket Classics. 2009 edition.

Eidson, T. 1995. *The Last Ride*. UK. Penguin.

Finney, J. 1956. *Contents of the Dead Man's Pocket*. Colliers.

Fitzgerald, F. 1974. *The Great Gatsby*. Penguin Classics, 2001.

Issa, K. (author), Hamill (translator). 1997. *The Spring of My Life: And Selected Haiku*. Published by Shambhala; 1st edition.

Joyce, J. 1922. *Ulysses*. Published by Create Space Independent Publishing Platform. 2011.

Lear, E (author), Jackson, H. (introduction). 1951. *The Complete Nonsense of Edward Lear*. Dover Publications.

Mundle, R. 2000. *Fatal Storm, the Inside Story of the Sydney-Hobart Race*. TAB books Inc.

Orwell, G. 2003. *Animal Farm*. Houghton Mifflin Harcourt; 1st edition.

Shakespeare, W. *Shakespeare's Sonnets*. Penguin Classics. New edition 1999.

Simpson, J. 1997. *Touching the Void*. UK. Vintage.

CHAPTER 13 Intertextuality

KEY CONCEPT FOCUS
CREATIVITY, CONNECTIONS

INQUIRY QUESTIONS	**TOPIC 1** Using intertextuality to inspire creativity	

- How can intertextuality be used to inspire creativity?

TOPIC 2 Using intertextuality to create humor or a larger message

- How can intertextuality be used to create humor or a larger message?

TOPIC 3 Creating credibility through literary allusion

- How can intertextuality be used for greater credibility?

SKILLS

ATL

✓ Make connections between various sources of information.

✓ Access information to be informed and inform others.

✓ Develop contrary or opposing arguments.

✓ Make unexpected or unusual connections between objects and/or ideas.

✓ Propose and evaluate a variety of solutions.

✓ Use and interpret a range of discipline-specific terms and symbols.

✓ Write for different purposes.

✓ Demonstrate awareness of media interpretations of events and ideas.

✓ Read critically and for comprehension.

Language and literature

✓ Utilize and imitate the tools of another creator.

✓ Persuade an audience through propaganda and advertisements.

✓ Use sources from recognized conventions.

OTHER RELATED CONCEPTS

Style   Character   Genre/conventions

GLOSSARY

Literary allusion when a creator/writer/poet/etc. intentionally refers to another literary work in order to add depth of meaning to their own.

Parody an imitative work modifying or mocking an original work in order to create humor.

Pastiche a work of visual art, literature, or music that imitates the style or character of the work of one or more other artists. Unlike parody, pastiche celebrates, rather than mocks, the work it imitates.

Plagiarism using someone else's ideas or words within your own writing/speaking/multimedia without giving that person credit, thus representing it as your own in an unprincipled manner.

COMMAND TERMS

Evaluate make an appraisal by weighing up the strengths and limitations.

Synthesize combine different ideas in order to create new understanding.

Introducing intertextuality

The language and literature guide defines intertextuality as;

> The connections between one text and other texts, the ways in which texts are interrelated, and the meanings that arise out of their interrelationship. An overt reference to another text (as in a direct quote from another text) is also an example of intertextuality.

The first sentence of the definition is often more subtle, though an entire work often would not be possible without this intertextual connection. For example, James Joyce may not have developed his own style of writing without examples from the modernist movement. Or transcendentalists like Ralph Waldo Emerson would have not had anything to transcend without the philosophies of John Locke and 18th century Calvinists. In other words, no one creates in a vacuum and all creators become inspired by experiencing other artistic works.

This chapter will focus on the many ingenious ways that modern writers, artists, cinematographers, marketers, etc. are using the ideas of others with transparency and achieving extraordinary results. Intertextual devices that you will focus on include using stock characters and plot lines, allusion, quotations, plagiarism, pastiche and parody.

Though the term *intertextuality* has been used in many ways since its modern naming by Julia Kristeva in 1966, the concept is definitely not a new one. Figures 13.1 and 13.2 are simple illustrations of how intertextuality has been used openly by artists for centuries:

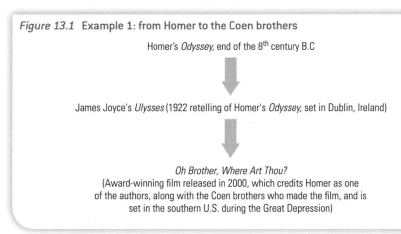

Figure 13.1 **Example 1: from Homer to the Coen brothers**

Homer's *Odyssey,* end of the 8th century B.C

James Joyce's *Ulysses* (1922 retelling of Homer's *Odyssey,* set in Dublin, Ireland)

Oh Brother, Where Art Thou?
(Award-winning film released in 2000, which credits Homer as one of the authors, along with the Coen brothers who made the film, and is set in the southern U.S. during the Great Depression)

Figure 13.2 **Example 2: from John Donne to Metallica**

John Donne poem 'Meditation 17' in 1624: " Therefore, send
not to know for whom the bell tolls, it tolls for thee."

Ernest Hemingway 1940 novel set in the Spanish Civil War, *For Whom the Bell Tolls*

Metallica song "For Whom the Bell Tolls" on the *Ride the Lightning* album in 1984

Be aware of the link between intertextuality and plagiarism. **Plagiarism** means using someone else's ideas or words within your own work (whether this is writing, speaking, or multimedia) without giving that person credit, attempting to represent their work as your own.

While this can be seen as being intertextual—your words mixed with someone else's—you will focus upon the command term synthesize— as great artistic ideas merge into something unique and often quite entertaining.

TOPIC 1

Using intertexuality to inspire creativity

In this topic you will learn about intertexuality in rap music as a way to create and inspire music and lyrics. Artists in rock and roll, jazz, blues, Irish music, bluegrass—virtually any type of music—learn and take inspiration from each other. Rap music, perhaps more than any other, has long been a genre defined by using a large variety of samples of other artists' work within rap songs as well as making many lyrical allusions.

At the time this book was printed, the most sampled song was by a band called Beside. Their song "Change the Beat (Female Version)" written in 1982 has been sampled in over 1,000 other songs. In the list of most influential artists there are well-known names like the Beatles, Jay Z, James Brown and Led Zeppelin. As a more recent example, Robin Thicke and Pharrell used an old Motown song to create their hit song "Blurred Lines".

Understanding musical history is one the best ways of understanding music's future. Take a look at the web links to further understand how one musical genre contributed to the development of another.

Those who have an in-depth knowledge about the roots of songs are a valuable resource to artists trying to create a new sound. It is said that "mimicry is the highest form of flattery". Rap music, therefore, could be said to constantly flatter older artists through allusion, exact quotations and sampling.

WEB LINKS
You can go to the website www.whosampled.com to see exactly which songs sampled which beats, loops, or lyrics. Take a look at the Charts tab to find out the most influential artists and songs.

Activity 1 — Allusions and sampling in music

Look at the examples below, taken from the song "Intergalactic"—a song performed by the Beastie Boys on their *Hello Nasty* album in 1998. Listen to the song if you have access to it and think about the lyrics. Then answer the questions that follow

Examples of intertextuality:

"Also known for the Flintstone Flop"
"The Flintstone Flop" refers to an episode of *The Flintstones* in which Fred and the gang end up at a teen dance hall. Fred jumps from a table and flops belly first onto the floor. A group of teens sees this happening and start imitating Fred, promptly starting a dance craze called the Flintstone Flop.

"Tammy D getting biz on the crop"
Tamra Davis is the wife of Mike D and an accomplished film director in her own right (*Guncrazy, CB4, Billy Madison*). "Crop" could refer to the act of "cropping" which is an editing technique. It also calls to mind the popular 1960s device of the "big-time Hollywood director" caricature. This stereotype often wore a beret, carried a megaphone or bullhorn, and often carried a riding crop. This type of "shout-out" is a very frequently used intertextual trick within rap music, giving credit to other inspirational artists.

"Beastie Boys known to let the beat… mmm… drop…"

This intertextual reference actually refers to the group's own lyrics, using an exact quote said in the same manner on the Beastie Boys first album, *Licensed to Ill*, in the song "The New Style". In this way the band references their own place in musical history while creating a similar effect in a new song.

Questions:
1. Take one of your favourite songs (not necessarily rap), do some research, and label as many instances of intertextuality as you can find.
2. Label any musical riffs, beats, or samples that have been utilized as well as any lyrical allusions or quotes.
3. Explain what the larger effect of having so many "shout-outs" to other artists might be.

> **TIP**
>
> This song is also a great example for anyone studying rhyme scheme in terms of the structure of the song. This song uses the same scheme in each verse in a playful manner—A × 16, B × 16, C × 16—using a wide range of rhyme and side rhyme.

> **WEB LINKS**
>
> You can see many more examples of intertextuality in Beastie Boys albums/ songs on the website www. beastieboysannotated.com.

> **GLOBAL CONTEXTS**
> Personal and cultural expression

> **ATL SKILLS**
> Information literacy
> Make connections between various sources of information.
> Access information to be informed and inform others.

Read this quote from Jason Stephens, professor of the University of Connecticut, and answer the questions with a partner.

Scholarship is like bringing your little rock to the mountain and putting it on the top of the heap.

Questions

- What do you think Stephens means by this statement?
- What implications does this have for how you view new or original ideas?
- Global context question: Is the concept of sampling just a major part of U.S. rap expression or is this borrowing and crediting from the ideas of others more global?

 **GLOBAL CONTEXTS**
Personal and cultural expression

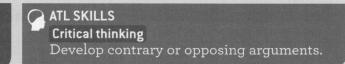 **ATL SKILLS**
Critical thinking
Develop contrary or opposing arguments.

Inspiring creativity: using intertextuality to create plot elements

When stories were first passed down through the oral (spoken) tradition instead of being written, there was still a lot of intertextuality—particularly in the creation of certain plot elements (setting, conflict, characters).

One of the most common was in the creation of archetypal characters: character types that occur across cultures and historical periods. Here are some examples:

- heroes
- tricksters
- damsels in distress
- underdogs
- a shaman or witch doctor
- femme fatales (a woman who seduces men to their demise)
- the male charmer (Don Juan is a famous example)
- a martyr
- the dreamer/artist/poet, or a hermit.

 **Activity 3**   Archetype team brainstorm

The table that follows has been filled with examples of the trickster archetype. In teams, choose two archetypes of your own and write down as many examples as you can for each, drawing from fairy tales, music, television, films, novels, etc. Think across music, film, literature, or cartoons and across cultures.

You can also add more examples to the trickster archetype below if you would like. See which group can think of the most examples. More importantly, think of who can come up with the most creative examples and offer the best reasoning behind their choices.

Archetype # 1: The trickster

Folk	Popular culture	Literary
Loki, Norse god of mischief	Bart Simpson	Puck in *A Midsummer Night's Dream*
African American Brer Rabbit	Bugs Bunny	Odysseus in *The Odyssey*
Hindu Baby Krishna	Daffy Duck	Tom Sawyer
Chinese Monkey King	The Joker from Batman	Robin Hood
Muslim folktales—Nasreddin	Captain Jack Sparrow	The Weasley Twins in *Harry Potter*
West African Anansi the spider	Charlie Chaplin	Lazaro the Spanish picaro

Your turn! Choose two archetypal characters and see how many examples your group can brainstorm.

Archetype # 2:

Folk	Popular culture	Literary

Archetype # 3:

Folk	Popular culture	Literary

🌐 **GLOBAL CONTEXTS**
Personal and cultural expression

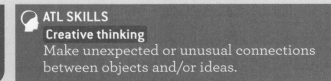 **ATL SKILLS**
Creative thinking
Make unexpected or unusual connections between objects and/or ideas.

Inspiring creativity: recontextualizing

Many stories have been recontextualized to demonstrate similar themes to a new audience. A good example is William Shakespeare, whose works have been modified to suit many audiences over the last 500 years of performance.

William Shakespeare allegedly adapted the story of *Romeo and Juliet* from an Italian tragedy that was initially written down in 1530 by Luigi da Porto and translated into an English poem in 1562 by Arthur Brooke. Therefore, the *Romeo and Juliet* that we are all familiar with was recontextualized for an English audience from its earliest beginning.

Centuries later the play was converted to a musical in *West Side Story*. In 1968, in one of the many film versions of *Romeo and Juliet,* Franco Zeffirelli set the play in its original setting of Renaissance Verona, Italy. Though there are more modern versions, the 1996 Baz Luhrmann version of the play was set in Verona Beach, USA, changing the setting, costuming, and some of the action of the play without changing any of Shakespeare's language or message. And these are just a few of the many movie re-enactments of the play that have occurred in the history of cinema.

The photos below show the famous balcony scene in four of its different settings, each depicted by the set and clothing of the characters.

And the list goes on, with online video performances raising the number of versions every day.

TIP

Look up the different film productions of Romeo and Juliet to see how the same scenes have been set in different contexts.

Figure 13.3 The balcony scene from *Romeo and Juliet* has been recontextualized many times.

Inspiring creativity: utilizing a writer's style

 Activity 4   Writing 2 mini-pastiches

The following activity focuses on the process of writing a **pastiche**, which is one common way of learning and practicing an author's style and structure of writing, and therefore improves your own ability to create. If you have not tried this, it can be an excellent exercise to see if you really understand what an author or poet has done within their work and to see if you can apply the tools they used. The art of pastiche writing also takes you completely through the levels of Bloom's Taxonomy and several important command terms in three different stages:

Stages for Writing a Pastiche

- **Reading:** You must first read the piece, understanding what has been written then analyse the decisions the author made, the structure they chose, and the literary devices/techniques they employed.
- **Planning:** You need to think of a similar creation that you would like to write yourself. Evaluate which tools and literary devices you will use from the original piece and must plan out your creation to emulate (imitate) the style of the original author. A well-planned pastiche will outline the exact structural choices and literary devices you will use prior to beginning as well as brainstorming possible stories you could tell.
- **Create and synthesize :** This process is at the top of Bloom's taxonomy, as you move back and forth between mimicking another author's style and employing your own ideas. Then, evaluate how well you have done and reflect on your struggles and successes.

STEP 1 Look at the styles of two authors (who shared some aspects in common in what they were trying to convey) and analyse how a story can be written using two very different styles. Comparing and contrasting are thinking skills that often help to show a concept more clearly.

Style #1: Ernest Hemingway's "iceberg theory", as shown in the short story *Hills Like White Elephants*

Influenced by his journalistic background, Hemingway uses the "fly on the wall" narration, telling the story from an objective point of view without entering into the thoughts or internal emotions of his characters. He felt that a good writer should not have to explicitly communicate a character's underlying thoughts or emotions. If the writer was telling the story well through dialogue, action, and imagery there might be a lot going on below the surface (hence the iceberg metaphor), but additional detail would be unnecessary for an attentive reader. He also prided himself on his precise use of language, using short sentences and minimal description. The lines between personal experience and fictional writing are often a little blurred in Hemingway's writing and he was reluctant to admit that anything was biographical.

Excerpt from *Hills Like White Elephants* by Earnest Hemingway

The hills across the valley of the Ebro were long and white. On this side there was no shade and no trees and the station was between two lines of rails in the sun. Close against the side of the station there was the warm shadow of the building and a curtain, made of strings of bamboo beads, hung across the open door into the bar, to keep out flies. The American and the girl with him sat at a table in the shade, outside the building. It was very hot and the express from Barcelona would come in forty minutes. It stopped at this junction for two minutes and went to Madrid.

'What should we drink?' the girl asked. She had taken off her hat and put it on the table.

'It's pretty hot,' the man said.

'Let's drink beer.'

'Dos cervezas,' the man said into the curtain.

'Big ones?' a woman asked from the doorway.

'Yes. Two big ones.'

The woman brought two glasses of beer and two felt pads. She put the felt pads and the beer glass on the table and looked at the man and the girl. The girl was looking off at the line of hills.

They were white in the sun and the country was brown and dry.

'They look like white elephants,' she said.

'I've never seen one,' the man drank his beer.

'No, you wouldn't have.'

'I might have,' the man said. 'Just because you say I wouldn't have doesn't prove anything.'

The girl looked at the bead curtain. 'They've painted something on it,' she said. 'What does it say?'

'Anis del Toro. It's a drink.'

'Could we try it?'

The man called 'Listen' through the curtain. The woman came out from the bar.

'Four reales.' 'We want two Anis del Toro.'

'With water?'

'Do you want it with water?'

'I don't know,' the girl said. 'Is it good with water?'

'It's all right.'

'You want them with water?' asked the woman.

'Yes, with water.'

'It tastes like liquorice,' the girl said and put the glass down.

'That's the way with everything.'

'Yes,' said the girl. 'Everything tastes of liquorice. Especially all the things you've waited so long for, like absinthe.'

'Oh, cut it out.'

'You started it,' the girl said. 'I was being amused. I was having a fine time.'

'Well, let's try and have a fine time.'

'All right. I was trying. I said the mountains looked like white elephants. Wasn't that bright?'

'That was bright.'

'I wanted to try this new drink. That's all we do, isn't it – look at things and try new drinks?'

'I guess so.'

The girl looked across at the hills. 'They're lovely hills,' she said. 'They don't really look like white elephants. I just meant the colouring of their skin through the trees.'

'Should we have another drink?'

'All right.'

The warm wind blew the bead curtain against the table.

'The beer's nice and cool,' the man said.

'It's lovely,' the girl said.

'It's really an awfully simple operation, Jig,' the man said. 'It's not really an operation at all.'

The girl looked at the ground the table legs rested on.

'I know you wouldn't mind it, Jig. It's really not anything. It's just to let the air in.'

The girl did not say anything.

'I'll go with you and I'll stay with you all the time. They just let the air in and then it's all perfectly natural.'

'Then what will we do afterwards?'

'We'll be fine afterwards. Just like we were before.'

'What makes you think so?'

'That's the only thing that bothers us. It's the only thing that's made us unhappy.'

Use the following questions to make sure you really understand this example of Hemingway's style.

- What do you think is the underlying conflict that the couple is facing?
- What does imagery like the hills, the landscape, the weather or the rail lines provided tell you about the relationship of the two speakers and the situation they are facing?
- What can be interpreted from the dialogue and the actions of the two characters?

Style #2: Spontaneous prose as shown in Jack Kerouac's *On the Road*

Jack Kerouac dubbed his style "spontaneous prose", a style that drew upon the stream-of consciousness style of writing, trying to emulate the human thought process, combined with an absolute disregard for the usual grammatical, sentencing, and paragraphing structures. The goal was to recreate the often high-powered emotions of the experience being described. Kerouac writes in the first person point of view through the autobiographical character of Sal Paradise. Quite the opposite of Hemingway's attempt to distance his emotions from the writing, Kerouac seasons all of his events with his own mood, writing in an autobiographical style (though pseudonyms or fictional names were used to make the novel less autobiographical in the originally published version).

The *On the Road* manuscript, showing how Kerouac's spontaneous prose was written as a continuous scroll in just 3 weeks.

From *On the Road*

But then they danced down the streets like dingledodies and I shambled after as I've been doing all my life after people who interest me, because the only people for me are the mad ones, the ones who are mad to live, mad to talk, mad to be saved, desirous of everything at the same time, the ones who never yawn or say a commonplace thing but burn, burn like fabulous yellow roman candles exploding like spiders across the stars and in the middle you see the blue centerlight and everybody goes "Aww!"

Trying the styles of Hemingway and Kerouac

STEP 2 Understanding: Make some notes about the style of each author:

Major features of Hemingway's style	Major features of Kerouac's style

STEP 3 **a)** Brainstorm possible writing topics: What stories can you tell? See if you can quickly write down 4–5 life experiences that would be worth retelling. This is practice, though this could lead you towards a larger piece of writing.

b) **Evaluate** which story would be the best to retell. You will only initially write half a page so think about which story would help you to focus on the style of writing as well as which one would be the most personally interesting.

 Planning your story: Write down some key points about how you will write in each author's style:

Telling my story using Hemingway's style	Telling my story using Kerouac's style
Narrator and point of view:	Narrator and point of view:
Major part of your story being focused upon:	Major part of your story being focused upon:
Literary features you will use:	Literary features you will use:

Are you ready to start writing? Give it a try!

GLOBAL CONTEXTS
Personal and cultural expression

ATL SKILLS
Critical thinking
Propose and evaluate a variety of solutions.
Communication
Use and interpret a range of discipline-specific terms and symbols.

Reflection

1. Where is the line between using another's creativity to inspire your own and just using another person's ideas?

2. How can a writer use someone else's ideas in a principled manner? At what point does using someone else's ideas become plagiarism or academic dishonesty?

3. Are there truly any original ideas that have not been derived from someone else?

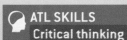 TOPIC 2

Using intertextuality to create humor or a larger message

As shown in the previous section, many forms of media replay original stories by recontextualizing and changing some plot elements. Another take on this recontextualizing is to create a **parody**, which has a very different goal than simply changing the setting or telling roughly the same story with different characters. A parody takes key components of the original work and uses the audience's familiarity with it to create humor.

Magazines have made a profit from creating parodies of famous books, movies, politicians and pop culture for many years.

 **Activity 5**   Parody in magazines

Part 1

Find a magazine (such as Mad magazine) which displays parodies of well known films or characters on its' cover and think about the following questions.

1. What are the common elements included in each parody?
2. What is the goal of each of the magazine covers?
3. Which one of these parodies do you think is most effective? Why?

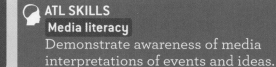 **WEB LINKS**
For some sample MAD magazine covers go to www.madcoversite.com

Part 2

Take a TV show or film of your choice and sketch or describe a magazine cover that you would design. Or create your own parody, possibly changing the name of the movie in the way that famous film parodies have done. These include **Space Balls** (a **Star Wars** parody), the **Scary Movie** series, **Monty Python and the Holy Grail,** and **Shaun of the Dead**.

🌐 **GLOBAL CONTEXTS**
Personal and cultural expression

🧠 **ATL SKILLS**
Media literacy
Demonstrate awareness of media interpretations of events and ideas.

Satire

Satire goes beyond mocking a text or idea for the sake of humor. Satire takes a philosophy, a literary work, or an art form to try and make a change in the way that people think or act.

George Orwell's *Animal Farm* is one of the more famous examples of satire. Orwell utilized Russian historical figures and events as a backdrop for a satirist statement about Joseph Stalin and Soviet communism, using a farm as a setting with allegorical farm animals used to represent his political views.

Plays upon words and images, particularly in video, have become more common in the information age, where many people have the tools, knowledge, and audience for these kinds of statements.

Recontextualizing in modern cartoons

Many modern cartoons have drawn ideas from popular culture, works of literature, films, other television shows, etc. While the intentions of the cartoons are not usually to preserve the original message or story, the characters, conflict, setting, and themes are borrowed in order to entertain a well-read or well-viewed modern audience.

Activity 6 — Group presentations of intertextuality

See below for a list of some of the modern television cartoon takes on classic works of literature. As a warm-up with a partner, write down what original work or works inspired each cartoon.

Cartoon takes:

- *The Simpsons*: "Four Regrettings and a Funeral", "The Tell-Tale Head"
- *Family Guy*: "Chitty Chitty Death Bang"
- *South Park*: "The Hobbit", "World War Zimmerman"
- *Futurama*: "Stench and Stenchability"
- *Veggie Tales*: "A League of Extraordinary Vegetables"

STEP 1 **a)** Form groups based upon your knowledge of one of the examples below.

- *Romeo and Juliet*
- The horror movie genre
- *Star Wars*
- *Lord of the Flies*
- The historical witch trials

It is important that everyone in your group should be familiar with your chosen example. If you do not have any experience with any of the above, a new group should be formed around something you do have in common.

b) As a group, think of a work, clip, television episode or film made based on the example you have chosen from Step 1 a. You need to look for something that represents intertextuality. To give you some inspiration, look at the web links box for suggestions. For example, if your group is looking at *Lord of the Flies*, you might want to use the Simpsons clip given, which references the novel.

WEB LINKS

- For the *Romeo and Juliet* group: Enter "(RSC) Romeo and Juliet Part 1" at www.youtube.com.
- For the horror movie group: Look up the script of the film *Scream*. Whole script available at www.imsdb.com; enter "Scream" in the search box.
- For the *Star Wars* group: Enter "Spaceballs Schwartz scene" at www.youtube.com.
- For the *Lord of the Flies* group: Enter "Simpsons: Das Bus" at www.youtube.com.
- For the historical witch trials group: Enter "Monty Python and the Holy Grail Witch Trial" at www.youtube.com.

STEP 2 Answer the questions below to help you better understand the example you are looking at.

1. What type(s) of intertextuality does it show? For example, is it a parody, a satire, a recontextualisation, a pastiche or an archetype?
2. How much does familiarity with the original work/genre help you to appreciate what you are analysing? Compare those in the group who have read or studied the original works/genres and those that have not.
3. If appropriate, what are some lines and literary elements that have been included from the original?
4. If appropriate, what are the biggest differences from the original?
5. What are some of the specific choices that were used to create humor?
6. Think of some of your group's own parody ideas that you would use in a reproduction.

STEP 3 Prepare a presentation for the other groups, analysing the choices that were made and presenting the intertextuality in the example that your group chose.

The rules for the presentation are below.

- Create a logical order to your presentation, being mindful of organization. Use the provided questions as a starting point, but do not stop there.
- All members of the group must take a topic or section or at least present and explain an example during the presentation.
- No visuals should be used other than excerpts from the text/script you are using.

 **GLOBAL CONTEXTS**
Personal and cultural expression

 **ATL SKILLS**
Media literacy
Demonstrate awareness of media interpretations of events and ideas.

Reflection

1. What is the value of using intertextuality to create humor? A political or social message?

2. Can you think of any examples not demonstrated in this section that use intertextuality to create a new message with a previous idea?

3. How could you use intertextuality in this way in your daily life?

TOPIC 3

Creating credibility through literary allusion

Another way that authors and speakers use intertextuality is to create greater credibility for themselves by using direct quotations and subtle allusions to the words, ideas, and structures of other authors or speakers. For example, no awards ceremony or graduation speech seems complete without a quotation from a famous coach, athlete, philosopher, activist, writer, leader etc.

In many of his early novels, author Stephen King began each chapter he wrote with a quote from pop culture or literature, often from musical lyrics or poetry. These quotes would hint at the content of the chapter and create a mood or setting. At the same time, they also showed the reader the range of King's literacy. For example, in the novel *Christine* he foreshadows his protagonist's first introduction to a car that would later possess him (well beyond the normal teenage obsession) by quoting from Eddie Cochran's song *Somethin' Else*, shown here. It is probably not a coincidence that Eddie Cochran died tragically in a car accident at a young age.

> "Hey, looky there!
>
> Across the street!
>
> There's a car made just for me,
>
> To own that car would be a luxury...
>
> That car's fine-lookin, man,
>
> That's something else."

Authors do this frequently. Once a reader is aware of it, the device is recognizable across all genres. As another example, Robert Frost's poem "Out, Out—" alludes to Macbeth's famous soliloquy. Numerous novels and short stories use allusions to classical mythology to highlight their message. Two common ones are the reference to a very strong person as being "Herculean" or describing someone who got carried away with fame as "flying too close to the sun" (this refers to the story of Icarus and Daedalus). Finally, the entire *Percy Jackson* book series is based upon the mythological character of Perseus, son of Poseidon.

Literary allusions are even more common in every day speech. Have you ever heard "Big Brother is watching you?" or "That is a Catch-22 situation"? These quotes refer to George Orwell's novel *1984* and Joseph Heller's novel *Catch-22*.

Political speeches are a wonderful genre for studying just how emotionally and logically powerful literary allusion and intertextuality can be.

Figure 13.4 U.S. President Barack Obama speaks at the Nelson Mandela funeral on December 10, 2013.

When U.S. President Barack Obama spoke at Nelson Mandela's memorial on December 13, 2013, he included allusions to other world leaders that had helped to conquer systems of racism or oppression, placing Mandela alongside some of the greatest leaders in history. He also ensured that he used the leader's ancestral title of *Madiba* to honor what he was often called in his home country. He also used other words that would have been spoken by the people of South Africa, like the word *Ubuntu*—a word used to express the oneness of humanity. Most importantly, he used a great many quotations from the lifetime of the deceased leader. This speech and others like it show the power of literary allusion and intertextuality. Without these elements, the speech would have lacked the necessary credibility for such an important historical moment.

 **Activity 7**   **Speech analysis**

Many speeches could be evaluated for their use of literary allusion, but the *I Have a Dream* speech by Dr Martin Luther King is an excellent example because of its extensive use of literary allusions, as well as rhetorical and poetic techniques. Once you have understood this example as a class, you will be able to apply this understanding to other cultural contexts and speeches and even create your own. Read the speech as a class and answer the questions below.

WEB LINKS
You can find the *I Have a Dream* speech online at: www.archives.gov or view it on www.youtube.com.

An analysis of the speech can be found at sixminutes.dlugan.com. Enter "I Have a Dream analysis" into the search box.

1. How many literary allusions can you find in the speech?
2. Try to determine where the allusions came from.
3. Analyse and discuss what the effects of these literary allusions were to King's audience. Also analyse some of the other literary devices he employed for their effect.
4. Read the Six Minutes *I Have a Dream analysis* online to see how your analysis compares with someone else's. Pay particular attention to Lesson #3.

 **GLOBAL CONTEXTS**
Personal and cultural expression

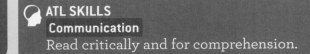 **ATL SKILLS**
Communication
Read critically and for comprehension.

Reflection

1. What is your own definition of intertextuality?
2. Which literary techniques associated with intertextuality do you feel most comfortable with at the conclusion of this topic and chapter? Which ones have you struggled with?
3. What artists are your greatest influences and how are they reflected in your own personal or cultural expression?

CHAPTER LINKS
See chapter 9 for more analysis of famous speeches.

Summary

The related concept of intertextuality holds a wealth of opportunity for young writers and readers. Though the interconnected online world is rife with temptations for academic dishonesty, it is also filled with wonderful learning opportunities. This chapter shows that you do not need to avoid the ideas of others—you should in fact expose yourself to as many great artists and thinkers as you can, utilizing the ATL tools of information literacy, research, media literacy, and critical thinking to ensure that you can utilize this information for empowerment, not shortcuts.

References

Hemingway, E. *The Essential Hemingway*. Arrow; New Ed. 1995.

Kerouac, J. *On the Road*. Penguin Classics; Film tie-in edition 2012.

Stephens, Jason. Quoted in Daniloff, C. *Unoriginal Sins: (Re) defining Plagiarism in the Digital age*. An article in BU Today (online publication): http://www.bu.edu/today/2010/unoriginal-sins.

KEY CONCEPT FOCUS
COMMUNICATION

INQUIRY QUESTIONS

TOPIC 1 Preparing for commentaries/textual analysis

- How can I make a mnemonic of literary and linguistic terms work successfully for me when doing this type of work?

TOPIC 2 Doing commentaries/textual analysis successfully

- How can I develop a systematic approach to commentaries/textual analysis and combine it with practice and careful reflection?

TOPIC 3 Selecting elements to fit your purpose

- How can I successfully combine a variety of oral and dramatic elements in order to communicate clearly?

SKILLS

ATL

✓ Make effective summary notes for studying.

✓ Read critically and for comprehension.

✓ Give and receive meaningful feedback.

✓ Organize and depict information logically.

Language and literature

✓ Analyse written texts.

✓ Analyse visual texts.

✓ Practise close observation.

✓ Appreciate denotation and connotation (literal meaning and implied "reading between the lines" meaning).

RELATED CONCEPTS

Setting   **Structure**   **Style**

GLOSSARY

Annotate to make notes on an existing text. In this case they explore the original critically.

Macro level large scale.

Micro level small scale.

Mnemonic a device or code to help you remember something.

Non-literary not having the features or characteristics associated with literature – often, but not always, factual writing

Paradox statement that seems contradictory, though on closer examination is true.

COMMAND TERMS

Analyse break down in order to bring out the essential elements or structure. To identify parts and relationships, and to interpret information to reach conclusions.

Comment give a judgment based on a given statement or result of a calculation.

Introducing purpose

If someone said to you, "The King is dead; long live the King!" you might be confused. That is because the statement is actually a **paradox**.

In fact, the statement was one of critical importance and had the following purposes:

- to demonstrate continuity of government from the dead king to his successor

- to transfer power instantaneously

- to prevent civil war, disorder or rival claimants to the throne.

In this chapter you will start by learning the skills necessary to understand and appreciate purpose in the writing of others.

- This is at the **macro level**: what is the purpose of this text?

- And the **micro level**: what is the purpose of this choice of words?

Understanding the purpose of a text is essential in language and literature.

QUICK THINK

Figure 14.1 The Last Sleep of Arthur by Edward Burne-Jones (1833–1898)

Study the image and imagine that you are at the royal court in the late Medieval/early Renaissance era. Think again about why the statement "The King is dead; long live the King" could not only be true, but a statement that would be vitally important to make.

Preparing for commentaries or textual analysis

One way to consider writers is to think of them as artists with pen and paper (or laptop). A perfectly produced piece of writing has the right amount of words; nothing is missing and there is no unnecessary clutter. In other words, the literature exactly fits its purpose. That might be seeking to entertain or to describe the wonders of falling in love or the horrors that prejudice can lead to. Literature is not real life. It is an artificial creation and a good writer has to keep the purpose of that writing in mind at all times.

If the text is **non-literary**, such as a newspaper or magazine article, a review or an advertisement, its purpose is equally important. The words are working to create meaning too, though perhaps in different ways.

In this topic you will learn how to explore the purpose in a text. Whether the whole text or just a single word within it, the skills used to find meaning are broadly the same.

In this topic you will look at what is happening on a page or two of text. Above all, you will analyse the language. Before you start, there's another important thing to remember: a text can be one of many different things. It could be a film clip, or a web page. Think of texts as widely as possible.

General comments

The key to doing well on a commentary or textual analysis is the amount of planning you do. In other words, take time to organize your thoughts, so your response has structure to it

A good written response will usually have a structure almost identical to a formal essay. Your teacher may make some small changes to this, but essentially you should have:

- hook/beginning to catch the reader's attention
- thesis statement where you explain what the document is essentially about (its purpose)
- body paragraphs that develop the thesis statement's idea
- topic sentences to introduce each body paragraph
- quotes and references within the body paragraphs that illustrate your points
- comments on each quote and reference
- transitions linking your ideas and further developing them
- concluding paragraph that restates your thesis strongly, yet avoids introducing new points.

INTERDISCIPLINARY LINKS
The skills that you use in this chapter are very useful for analysing primary sources in individuals and societies. The analysis of the language and choices in these documents will reveal the purposes of the people who wrote them.

Treat a commentary or textual analysis with respect. They are not easy and can't be rushed.

Below is a **mnemonic** to help you to understand commentary and textual analysis. Knowing the mnemonics is a way of having key language and literature terms in your head.

The mnemonics contain a range of literary and linguistic terms that you may find in a text. Ask your teacher to explain these to you if you are unsure about any of them.

The commentary and textual analysis mnemonic

For the purpose of the mnemonics, we have broken the terms below into linguistic and literary features. In reality, they might not fit so neatly into these categories.

Analysing the overall work	Analysing the creator's style/technique	
CONTEXT	LINGUISTIC FEATURES	LITERARY FEATURES
G enre *	C acophonic	S ymbolism
E ffects (on the viewer)	E uphonic	H yperbole
T hemes *	C olloquial	I rony
S etting *	I dioms	P ersonification
		S atire
S tructure *	I magery *	
T one / (Mood) *	S imile	R hyme (all types of)
A udience		O xymoron
N arrator/point of view *	H umor	A llusion
	O nomatopoeia	R hythm
	M etaphor	
	E uphemism	
GETS STAN	CECI IS HOME	SHIPS ROAR

Table 14.2 Mnemonics learn this mnemonic and the words within it

Writing a commentary or textual analysis

Look at each of the columns in the mnemonics table above more closely. You can use the prompts below to help you write commentary or textual analysis.

Context (the macro)

- What is the relationship between the title of the text and content?

- Describe the content, main ideas and themes.

- Determine who the intended audience is (don't just say "everyone").

- What is the point of view/narrator?

- Is the writing descriptive, persuasive (arguments, editorials, advertisements, propaganda) or expository (facts and information)?

- Is the writing subjective (opinions) and/or objective (facts) comments?

- Are there stated or implied comments?

- What is the register, tone or mood of the piece? Which words and punctuation help create this tone? Why does the author use this tone?

- Describe the structure. To help you:

  - Short sentences or paragraphs are usually there to make a passage easier to read or to change the pace.

  - Longer sentences and paragraphs may suggest a greater amount of sophistication.

  - Other points of presentation may need a comment, for example, sub-headings. Any images within the text will need analyzing in detail.

  - Any unusual punctuation to show emotion. This could be an exclamation mark or question mark or even ellipses (...).

Style and technique (the "micro"): linguistic and literary devices

In your commentary or textual analysis, look for the following:

- Does the writer use symbols or literary terms? If so what are the effects of each?

- What imagery is used? Think of sensory details. We all remember seeing, but what about hearing, touching, smelling and tasting?

- Is there satire, humour or irony? Make sure you explain these points in sufficient detail.

- Is the language formal or informal?

- What is the level of vocabulary—complex or simple?

- Comment in detail on the effects of similes and metaphors you find.

- Describe the imagery and its impact.

- Does the writer use colloquialisms, slang, or idioms? Why?

- Can you see any plays on words, puns, or double meanings?

- Is there any biased language? Comment on this and use it to develop your answer. Example: freedom fighters (positive), insurgents (neutral), terrorists (hostile).

 Activity 1   **How to annotate a text**

In order to write a commentary or textual analysis, you need to **annotate** the text you are analysing.

For this activity you need to choose a text. This may be something you are reading in class, or your teacher may already have one planned.

You will need a selection of different coloured pens, a pencil, and a highlighting pen.

Having a range of different pens and highlighting pens makes annotating easier.

Read the text paragraph by paragraph. Think before you annotate.

- Only annotate words and phrases. Avoid colouring in whole blocks of text as this will not help you.
- Develop your own code; for example, circling a word means one thing, underlining means something else.
- Have the mnemonic in mind as you go, noting down any terms you may wish to use later.
- You can ask yourself questions to reflect on and make a decision later, such as, "Is this ironic?"
- Keep asking yourself, "Why did the writer/creator of the text do that... why did they do this?" as you go.

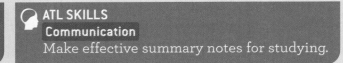 **WEB LINKS**
There are many systems for annotation. For example, go to www.youtube.com, then search for annotating text.

🌐 **GLOBAL CONTEXTS**
Personal and cultural expression

ATL SKILLS
Communication
Make effective summary notes for studying.

 **Activity 2**   **Using mnemonics**

In this activity you will plan and write a commentary or textual analysis based on a text you are using in class. Your teacher will tell you beforehand which text to use.

To help you complete this activity, you will need to use the commentary/textual analysis mnemonic above and the information about writing a commentary or textual analysis.

TIP

If you are doing a commentary/textual analysis under exam conditions, make sure you write out the mnemonics out on lined paper, before you even look at the question.

STEP 1   Using your mnemonics, read the text very carefully a few times.

STEP 2   Annotate the text using the skills you used in the previous activity. Underline or highlight interesting sections or key words. You can do this whether you are working on paper or on a screen.

STEP 3   Remember that the text(s) chosen will have much material for comment. If you have gaps then you might have missed something. Re-read the text and check again.

STEP 4   When you have all your notes, start planning your commentary or textual analysis essay. Once you have a plan in place, try to write a strong thesis statement that includes your informed opinions about the text. If you cannot do this yet, you are not ready to leave the planning stage yet.

STEP 5   Now you are ready to write your commentary/textual analysis.

By as you write, cross out the annotations you have made on the text, one at a time. This way you will ensure you include all of your ideas in your answer.

Proofread your work for clarity. Correct careless errors by reading again.

Make sure you have used a mature vocabulary and the correct structure.

Lists, like mnemonics, can never be complete. There are more literary terms out there and there is always something else to comment on. Keep your eyes open as a commentary or textual analysis is also about your powers of observation.

Ultimately, the commentary/textual analysis tests your ability to think independently.

TIP

Can you make useful references to other texts you know?

TIP

Commentaries/textual analysis are difficult and can seem frustrating; it is easy to miss things. We therefore recommend:
- practice frequently
- be persistent
- After your work is returned to you, review it carefully; reflect carefully on your teacher's comments. Learn from your errors, make adjustments and keep doing what is already going right.

GLOBAL CONTEXTS
Personal and cultural expression

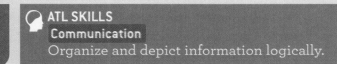
ATL SKILLS
Communication
Organize and depict information logically.

Reflection

1. Explain how clear you are on the difference between reacting to the text as a whole and reacting to a tiny part of it, such as just one word or phrase (the micro and the macro).

2. How long did it take you to learn the mnemonic?

3. Explain what advantages you gain by having the mnemonic in your head.

TOPIC 2

Successful commentaries or textual analyses

Now that you have considered how to open up a text, there is no substitute for creating one. In this topic you will work as a class, analysing the text individually then coming together to discuss it carefully, line by line, section by section.

Activity 3 Writing commentaries

The reading room in the British Museum

Write a commentary or textual analysis on the following extract from the novel *Three Men in a Boat* (1889) by Jerome K Jerome:

I remember going to the British Museum one day to read up the treatment for some slight ailment of which I had a touch – hay fever, I fancy it was. I got down the book, and read all I came to read; and then, in an unthinking moment, I idly turned the leaves, and began to indolently study diseases, generally. I forget which was the first distemper I plunged into – some fearful, devastating scourge, I know – and, before I had glanced half down the list of "premonitory symptoms," it was borne in upon me that I had fairly got it.

I sat for awhile, frozen with horror; and then, in the listlessness of despair, I again turned over the pages. I came to typhoid fever – read the symptoms – discovered that I had typhoid fever, must have had it for months without knowing it – wondered what else I had got; turned up St. Vitus's Dance – found, as I expected, that I had that too, – began to get interested in my case, and determined to sift it to the bottom, and so started alphabetically – read up ague, and learnt that I was sickening for it, and that the acute stage would commence in about another fortnight. Bright's disease, I was relieved to find, I had only in a modified form, and, so far as that was concerned, I might live for years. Cholera I had, with severe complications; and diphtheria I seemed to have been born with. I plodded conscientiously through the twenty-six letters, and the only malady I could conclude I had not got was housemaid's knee.

I felt rather hurt about this at first; it seemed somehow to be a sort of slight. Why hadn't I got housemaid's knee? Why this invidious reservation? After a while, however, less grasping feelings prevailed. I reflected that I had every other known malady in the pharmacology, and I grew less selfish, and determined to do without housemaid's knee. Gout, in its most malignant stage, it would appear, had seized me without my being aware of it; and zymosis I had evidently been suffering with from boyhood. There were no more diseases after zymosis, so I concluded there was nothing else the matter with me.

I sat and pondered. I thought what an interesting case I must be from a medical point of view, what an acquisition I should be to a class! Students would have no need to "walk the hospitals," if they had me. I was a hospital in myself. All they need do would be to walk round me, and, after that, take their diploma.

Then I wondered how long I had to live. I tried to examine myself. I felt my pulse. I could not at first feel any pulse at all. Then, all of a sudden, it seemed to start off. I pulled out my watch and timed it. I made it a hundred and forty-seven to the minute. I tried to feel my heart. I could not feel my heart. It had stopped beating. I have since been induced to come to the opinion that it must have been there all the time, and must have been beating, but I cannot account for it. I patted myself all over my front, from what I call my waist up to my head, and I went a bit round each side, and a little way up the back. But I could not feel or hear anything. I tried to look at my tongue. I stuck it out as far as ever it would go, and I shut one eye, and tried to examine it with the other. I could only see the tip, and the only thing that I could gain from that was to feel more certain than before that I had scarlet fever.

I had walked into that reading-room a happy, healthy man. I crawled out a decrepit wreck.

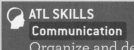

TIP

Terms you need to know:
Indolently: lazily.
Ailment, distemper, malady, scourge: different words used her to describe sicknesses and diseases.
St Vitus's dance... zymosis: a long list of diseases.
a slight: a snub, an insult
Invidious: causing anger or resentment in someone.

Here are some guiding questions to help you frame your answer:
- What is the **purpose** of this type of writing?
- Explore the narrator's character fully.
- Explain how the humour works.
- Comment on the importance of social class in this extract.

TIP

A normal pulse for adults is 60 to 100 beats per minute.

GLOBAL CONTEXTS
Identities and relationships

ATL SKILLS
Communication
Organize and depict information logically.

  **Activity 4**   **Globalization**

In this activity, you'll try a different type of commentary/textual analysis.

Compare and contrast the following two texts. These are differing views on globalisation, both from the USA. Note that the first text gives a definition of globalisation at the beginning.

Text 1

The simple definition of globalization is the interweaving of markets, technology, information systems, and telecommunications networks in a way that is shrinking the world from a size medium to a size small. It began decades ago, but accelerated dramatically over the past 10 years, as the price of computing power fell and the world became an ever-more densely interconnected place. People resist this shift — see, for example, the G8 protests of 2001 (one of the bloodiest uprisings in recent European history) or the recent rioting in Pittsburgh at this year's G20 conference—because they think it primarily benefits big business elites to the detriment of everyone else. But globalization didn't ruin the world—it just flattened it. And on balance that can benefit everyone, especially the poor. Globalization has pulled millions of people out of poverty in India and China, and multiplied the size of the global middle class. It has raised the global standard of living faster than that at any other time in the history of the world, and it is supporting astounding growth. All world economic activity was valued at $7 trillion in 1950. That's equal to how much growth took place over just the past decade, even including the recent downturn. Whatever people's fears of change, globalization is here to stay—and, if properly managed, it will be a good thing.

TIP

Terms you need to know:
The G8 protests of 2001 or the recent rioting in Pittsburgh at this year's G20 conference: protests seeking to change the current model of globalization.
Flattened it: made communication easier/made distance less of a problem for communication.

Text 2

Listen to the track *Globalisation (Scene of the Crime)* by dead prez. Study their lyrics on globalisation at the web link given.

Some lyrics explained:

Uncle Sam: a way of referring to the USA

Halliburton... Chevron: large multi-national business corporations

covert: secret

"Pop the hammer...": fire a gun

gentrification: when wealthy people gradually move into an area and the poorer people move out

WEB LINKS

Go to www.azlyrics.com and enter "Globalisation (Scene of the Crime)" into the search box.

You will find the track on www.youtube.com if you enter the same title into the search box.

Here are some guiding questions to help you frame your answer:
- What are the purposes of both these texts?
- Fully explore the language used in both texts.
- Analyse the song using poetic terms.
- Discuss the tone of both extracts.

A commentary or textual analysis of this type also needs the use of transitions of comparison and transitions of contrast such as:

Comparison	Contrast
■ similarly	■ however
■ likewise	■ yet
■ in the same way	■ on the other hand
■ by the same token	■ nevertheless
	■ nonetheless
	■ at the same time
	■ after all
	■ though
	■ on the contrary
	■ in contrast
	■ notwithstanding

GLOBAL CONTEXTS
Globalization and sustainability

ATL SKILLS
Communication
Read critically and for comprehension.

The last of these texts shows that commentary/textual analysis is not just about exploring "classic" literature texts. Once you have the analytical skills that come from the mnemonic you have already covered, you can explore any text. Here are two visual texts to explore. For these activities, not every term in the mnemonics is relevant.

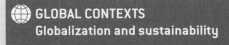 **Activity 5**   **Visual texts**

Choose the image or the video below to analyse.

Image

Here are some questions to help you frame your answer:

- What is the purpose of this text?
- Explore the postures of both soldiers fully.
- Analyse the colours used.
- Discuss the way the symbol is presented.

WEB LINKS
Analyse the following image: http://www.pixel77.com then search for "Banksy peace". The image is called War and Peace.

Analyse the following video: www.youtube.com/ then search for "Photoshop by Adobe".

Video

Here are some guiding questions to help you frame your answer:

- What is the purpose of this text?
- How is the sense of a beauty/fashion video created at first?
- Analyse the language used in the voice over and the music.
- Discuss the way the way 'Adobe' is pronounced.

TIP

Adobe (from the video in this activity) is a graphics editing program.

🌐 **GLOBAL CONTEXTS**
Identities and relationships

🗣 **ATL SKILLS**
Communication
Read critically and for comprehension.

Reflection

1. Why is continual practice important when doing a commentary or textual analysis?

2. What is the difference between a commentary or textual analysis on one text and a commentary or textual analysis on two texts?

3. How does analysing a text help you discover its purpose?

Now it's time for some creative work about purpose.

TOPIC 3

Selecting elements to fit your purpose

Hundreds of years ago, storytelling was one of the main forms of entertainment. Storytelling with music was considered even better. A good storyteller, just like a good writer, chose their words carefully and their characters smoothly fitted the role assigned to them.

👥 **Activity 6**   **Storytelling warm-up**

In this activity, you will pick up this semi-forgotten art of storytelling and present it to an audience to entertain them.

Start this activity with an improvisation icebreaker. Your teacher will divide you into groups and assign you a theme. It may be based on something you have been working on recently, as this will allow you to use prior knowledge to give your improvisation greater depth.

When you have your improvisation ready, present it to the class. Explain your improvisation in as much detail as you can:

- Why did you put those characters in that context/setting?
- Why did they do what they did?
- Why did they say what they said?
- What was the purpose of your piece?

Now invite feedback from the class on what they got out of your improvisation.

- Was your purpose clear to them? If not, why not?
- Was everything they needed as an audience there for them to understand your presentation clearly?
- Was there any unnecessary material or clutter?

After this activity, reflect on your feedback as a group. Now present your work again. How does it improve? How are the purpose and the techniques you used to get there better?

That was a warm-up. Now for the real thing!

GLOBAL CONTEXTS
Personal and cultural expression

ATL SKILLS
Communication
Give and receive meaningful feedback.

 **Activity 7**   Your story

Just as in Chapter 17, about self-expression, where creativity will be defined in more detail, your story needs to have certain structural and creative elements:

- A gripping opening – hook the reader from the start
- A setting – this must be convincing or intriguing
- A plot – the story should have a logic to it; a plot with a twist is great too
- Conflict of some kind – to add excitement
- Characters – they should act like real people, have appropriate names; the audience should believe in them, and even more importantly, care about them
- The purpose – what message are you trying to convey to your reader beyond entertaining them?
- The ending/resolution – everything should combine at the finish of your work, as it should have been working to this point all the way through. Again, no clutter, or vital information left out.

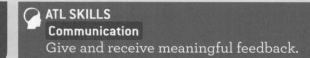 **INTERDISCIPLINARY LINKS**
There are two elements that you should consider that could heighten the quality of your story:

- Music – will adding certain instruments at certain moments give your story added emotional depth? If so, where?
- Theatre – how can costumes, sound effects and/or changes in lighting make your presentation more effective?

As noted before, your teacher will decide who your audience is.

Present your story at least once to your class and receive constructive feedback from your peers before you present to your target group.

TAKE ACTION

What if your audience has no one from your school? Can you tailor this activity to become part of a service activity, where you are linking to children or adults as part of a service learning project?

GLOBAL CONTEXTS
Personal and cultural expression

ATL SKILLS
Communication
Give and receive meaningful feedback.

Reflection

1. What is the difference between doing something purely within the class group and having an external audience to perform for?

2. How can focusing on your own creative work allow you to get a greater appreciation of purpose?

Summary

In everyday English, the purpose is the reason for which something is done. In language and literature, purpose is defined as the "intent" or "author's choices". Through this chapter you have analysed the choices of others and made your own decisions about them in your own creative work. Now consider the following:

- How and why would your storytelling piece change if you were presenting it to people from a completely different culture?

- How and why would your storytelling piece change if you were presenting it to elementary school children?

References

Friedman, Thomas. 2010. *Globalization*. Retrieved from: http://2010.newsweek.com/top-10/most-overblown-fears/globalization.html.

Jerome, K. 1889. *Three Men in a Boat*. Bristol: Arrowsmith, 1889.

INQUIRY QUESTIONS

TOPIC 1 Context and its effect on style

- ■ **How can we interpret a text, using the three levels; the text level, the sentence level and the word level?**

TOPIC 2 Context and literature

- ■ **Does literature always deal with feelings? Can literature live in a materialistic world? Why? Why not?**

TOPIC 3 Context clues

- ■ **How can reading between the lines increase our understanding of a text and help us reach conceptual ideas?**

SKILLS

ATL

- ✓ Analyse complex concepts and projects into their constituent parts and synthesize them to create new understanding.
- ✓ Use appropriate strategies for organizing complex information.
- ✓ Demonstrate awareness of media interpretations of events and ideas.
- ✓ Make connections between various sources of information.
- ✓ Gather and organize relevant information to formulate an argument.
- ✓ Make inferences and draw conclusions.

Language and literature

- ✓ Analyse the effects of the creator's choices on an audience.
- ✓ Evaluate similarities and differences by connecting features across and within genres and texts.
- ✓ Organize opinions and ideas in a sustained, coherent and logical manner.
- ✓ Make stylistic choices in terms of linguistic, literary and visual devices, demonstrating awareness of impact on an audience.

OTHER RELATED CONCEPTS

Setting   **Self-expression**

GLOSSARY

Context clues a method by which the meanings of unknown words may be obtained by examining the parts of a sentence surrounding the word.

Editorial article that presents a newspaper's opinion on an issue.

Idiomatic expressions words that bring the writing context closer to the reader, they magnify the feelings, clarify the ideas. They differ according to purpose, audience, tone and type of writing.

COMMAND TERMS

Explain give a detailed account including reasons or causes.

Interpret use knowledge and understanding to recognize trends and draw conclusions from given information.

Introducing context

In a book called *How to Get a 2:1 in Media Communication and Cultural Studies*, Noel Williams writes:

> *Context* is one of those words you will encounter again and again, without anyone offering anything like a useful definition. It is something of a catch-all word usually used to mean "all those things in the situation which are relevant to meaning in some sense, but which I haven't identified."

He goes on to say that *context* is typically used to refer to one or more of the following:

- the context (other words used recently; the kind of language in use, such as questions or answers, or greeting, or insult)

- the physical situation (time, place, speaker, setting, etc)

- the knowledge and beliefs of the participants in the communication (such as whether one person thinks the other is lacking in knowledge, or when both participants think they are working towards an agreement)

- the historical circumstances leading up to the communication.

TOPIC 1

Context and its effect on style

The style used in a text cannot be seen in isolation from the context it is used in. This means that the language used is directed by the context it is used in.

In this topic you will look at how style is affected by context, in particular when comparing editorials and formal essays. Although editorials and formal essays can share the same purpose, the different context they are used in changes the style used in each.

Editorials

An **editorial** is an article that presents a newspaper's opinion on an issue. Editorials are meant to influence public opinion, promote critical thinking and sometimes cause people to take action on an issue.

Editorials can have four main aims:

1. To *explain or interpret*: To explain the way the newspaper covered a sensitive or controversial subject. School newspapers may explain new school rules or a particular student-body effort like a food drive.

2. To *criticise*: These editorials constructively criticise actions, decisions or situations while providing solutions to the problem identified. The immediate purpose is to get readers to see the problem, not the solution.

3. To *persuade*: Editorials of persuasion aim to immediately see the solution, not the problem. From the first paragraph, readers will be encouraged to take a specific, positive action. Political endorsements are good examples of editorials of persuasion.

4. To *praise*: These editorials commend people and organizations for something done well. They are not as common as the other three.

Structure

Editorials can be organized in three paragraphs framed by an introduction and a conclusion. Each paragraph addresses a point connected to the thesis statement in the introduction.

The introduction usually contains an attention grabber and the thesis statement at the end, middle or beginning of the introduction.

Editorials can be organized in different ways, with short paragraphs each addressing a point, then two lines after each paragraph stressing the point or concluding ideas.

Grammar and style

- Usually semi-formal, having a clear tone of sarcasm, seriousness, humor, aggression, etc.

- This tone is clearly marked by the use of **idiomatic expressions** that are usually heavy.

- Most of the time the language is emotive; the piece is trying to win over the reader.

- Sentences are a mix of all types, but the sequence of sentences again clarifies the point the author wants to make.

For example, you may find a rhetorical question or questions, then short sentences, then a long simple sentence followed by a complex sentence and so on, to bring the point through.

Read the following editorial and answer the questions that follow.

Graduation Dreams, a New York Times article by Carey Mulligan

We were <u>caught between</u> **exhilaration (excitement)** and **despair (misery)** on Tuesday as we watched more than 500 young people <u>in caps and gowns</u> gather in a park a few steps from the United States Capitol. <u>It was a graduation, but it wasn't.</u> There were <u>awards, but no diplomas</u>. And while there was talk of bright futures, the speeches were threaded with notes of **impatience (annoyance)** and defiance (rebelliousness) and made clear that those hopes were in no way assured.

That is because all of the students are in this country illegally. They were **rallying (gathering)** to support the Dream Act, a bill in Congress that would open a path to citizenship for undocumented high school graduates who complete two years of college or military service. These students came here as minors, **hitched (clichéd)** to their parents' **aspirations (ambition)** for a better life. But once they graduated from high school, they found their choices **restricted (limited)** to the same dead-end jobs and <u>shadowed lives</u> that their parents live.

The Dream Act, their best hope, has languished since it was first introduced in 2001, **welded (connected)** in recent years to comprehensive immigration **reform (development) bills (lists)** that have <u>gone nowhere</u>. The all-or-nothing comprehensive strategy holds that if a **bipartisan (follower)** immigration bill doesn't <u>contain the right mix of sweeteners</u> like the Dream Act to **offset (make up for) hard-line (forceful)** enforcement measures, it won't attract enough votes to pass.

That strategy hasn't worked but **backers (supporters)** are hoping that President Obama will lead the way. The youthful **grass-roots (working class) advocates (supporters)** from more than a dozen states who **rallied (gathered)** on Tuesday share that hope, but they also know they are <u>running out of time</u>. They are getting older, and their <u>window of eligibility (suitability) for relief is closing</u>. One speaker, Walter Lara, 23, who graduated from college with honors, was caught by immigration in Miami. He is scheduled to be **deported (transported)** to Buenos Aires on July 6.

Just to talk with him and his fellow advocates who came up with him from Florida is to see an inspiring wealth of potential — with no place to go. They are from Argentina, Brazil, Colombia, Peru. They all went to community college. But because they are here illegally, they got no financial aid or in-state tuition (they paid $800 per class, instead of $250) or loans or work-study jobs. They want to go into international relations, psychology, chemistry, engineering, mass communications, political science. But one is a handyman; the others work in restaurants and as church volunteers.

The drive to Washington took them 18 hours. They looked tired, solemn, defiant, hopeful in the way young people have that **banishes (threw out) cynicism (suspicion)**. They seemed **incredulous (disbelieving)** that a message they grew up with — work hard, stay in school, study and you will succeed — does not apply to them.

Questions

1. What do you think makes this type of writing an editorial? Support with evidence from the text.
2. What is its purpose? Support with evidence from the text.
3. What is the tone? Support with evidence from the text.
4. What is the function of the shaded sentences?

5. The underlined words are idiomatic expressions. Divide them in the category they belong to using the following table:

Similes/Metaphors	Repetitions	Opposites	Strong, colorful words

6. The words in bold in the editorial are formal words. Their less formal synonym has been put in brackets beside them. The following table contains those words in the synonyms column. Fill the antonym column by finding antonyms (opposites) of both the formal and the less formal words:

Synonyms		Antonyms	
More formal	**Less formal**	**More formal**	**Less formal**
exhilaration	excitement		
despair	misery		
impatience	annoyance		
rallying	gathered		
hitched	clichéd		
aspirations	ambition		
restricted	limited		
welded	connected		
reform	development		
bills	lists		
bipartisan	follower		
offset	make up for		
hard-line	forceful		
grass-roots	working class		
advocates	supporters		
incredulous	disbelieving		
banishes	threw out		
cynicism	suspicion		
deported	transported		

7. A text (written or spoken) is explored at three levels:
   - The text level: where you identify its purpose, author, audience, situation, and/or genre that specifies the text outline (structure) and its tone.
   - The sentence level: where you specify the type of sentences used to serve the text's context: passive or active, complex or simple, use of questions, imperative, reported speech, etc.
   - The word level: where you think about the idiomatic expressions that fit your text: type of adjectives, verbs, level of formality, figures of speech, etc.

   You can use a table like this one with any text to help you analyse a text. Use it to analyse the editorial.

Text level	Sentence level	Word level
Type of text:	Type of sentences:	Adjectives:
Context:		
Purpose:		Verbs used:
Audience:	Type of connectors:	
Outline:		Idiomatic expressions:
Tone:		

 **GLOBAL CONTEXTS**
Personal and cultural expression

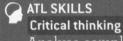 **ATL SKILLS**
Critical thinking
Analyse complex concepts and projects into their constituent parts and synthesize them to create new understanding.

Formal essays

The social purpose of a formal essay is to express opinion, discuss an issue, analyse an issue or find solutions for a problem.

Structure

Introduction

- Attract the reader's attention
- Thesis statement

Main body

- Paragraph 1:
  - Idea One in a topic sentence
  - Rest of the paragraph sentences to develop the idea:
  - Giving examples, giving reasons, facts, etc.
- Paragraph 2:
  - Idea Two in a topic sentence
  - Rest of the paragraph sentences to develop the idea:
  - Giving examples, giving reasons, facts etc.
- Paragraph 3:
  - Idea Three in a topic sentence
  - Rest of the paragraph sentences to develop the idea:
  - Giving examples, giving reasons, facts etc.

Conclusion

- Restate opinion
- Future projection

Grammar and style

It is a formal piece of writing with impersonal language with the following: passive, advanced vocabulary, formal connectors, no abbreviations, complex and compound sentences, and no phrasal verbs.

 Activity 2   **Exploring formal essays**

Read the essay and **interpret** the text to answer the questions that follow.

The Real Me by Rebecca Huss-Ashmore

Each year an <u>increasing</u> number of Americans make this a trip to an operating room or surgical suite for cosmetic surgery. Figures <u>vary</u>, depending on the types of surgery included, but the number of procedures per year now <u>exceeds</u> 1 million, and may be as high as 2 million. Do these increasing figures make sense in the American cultural context?

Americans have contradicting ideas about cosmetic surgery. Media coverage reflects the fascination and the unease at the same time, with articles in just the past two years in The Chronicle of Higher Education, Newsweek, National Geographic, Vogue, and Parade magazines, as well as newspapers ranging from The New York Times and The Philadelphia Inquirer to free neighborhood weeklies and supermarket tabloids. While these articles record the increasing number of surgeries <u>performed</u>, they also advise carefulness, including examples of failed or fatal surgery and warning about unqualified practitioners.

*In spite of the dangers, cosmetic surgery is more acceptable than it was a decade ago. In today's
society, as our children grow up, they face many <u>obstacles</u> in life. One obstacle for many females is
to be tall, thin, and beautiful; for men, the obstacle is to be muscular and good looking. The reality
is, in rare cases is that even true. To most, in order to achieve this image, they must <u>undergo</u> plastic
surgery. The improvement of self esteem and self worth that these surgery create, pass them as
accepted procedures in the American society. the correlation of beauty with health and individual
happiness encourages Americans to choose to <u>alter</u> their appearance through surgery. Thus the
surgeon, by altering physical features that mark the patient as different, allows the patient to "pass"
as a member of the desired group.*

*Due to the fact that the American culture values technological and medical advances, cosmetic
surgery found a good vehicle to the market. America has always been the land embracing, <u>aiding</u>
and supporting new technologies. These technologies helped <u>constructing</u> different medical
equipment enabling sergeants to perform complicated operations with desirable outcomes that were
<u>unattainable</u> before. Since the results were mostly positive more Americans started <u>acknowledging</u> the
idea. Moreover, these advances decreased the expenses of cosmetic surgery in general. For example
the price of a nose job that cost a fortune twenty years ago, is available today for an affordable price
for many.*

*In conclusion, beauty, however defined, affects one's status as a person in a society. In American
culture, the emphasis on individuality and self-definition makes "self" perception especially
important. Add to this the American admiration for all things medical makes cosmetic surgery
appropriate mean for finding or creating the authentic self. It provides a culturally meaningful setting
in which self-transformation can be performed.*

Questions

1. Substitute the formal words underlined with more informal ones:

   increasing   ....

   vary   ....

   exceeds   ....

   alter   ....

   obstacle   ....

   undergo   ....

   performed   ....

   aiding   ....

   acknowledging   ....

   unattainable   ....

   constructing   ....

2. What makes this a formal essay? Support with evidence from the text.
3. How is it structured? Support with evidence from the text.
4. How formal is the text? Support with evidence from the text.

5. What is the function of the shaded sentences?
6. **Interpret** the essay using the table. Refer to Activity 1, Question 7 for an explanation of exploring text at three levels.

Text level	Sentence level	Word level
Type of text: Context: Purpose: Audience: Outline: Tone:	Type of sentences: Type of connectors:	Adjectives: Verbs used: Idiomatic expressions:

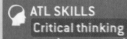 GLOBAL CONTEXTS
Personal and cultural expression

ATL SKILLS
Critical thinking
Analyse complex concepts and projects into their constituent parts and synthesize them to create new understanding.

  **Activity 3**   Assess your understanding

This activity will help you to practise the skills you have developed in this topic.

STEP 1   Scenario: You are concerned about something that is going on at your school (such as bullying or an environmental issue). You feel strongly that you should do something about it. Write an editorial about the issue for your school newspaper, trying to persuade the other students of your point of view.

STEP 2   Reflect on your editorial by filling out the following post-writing table. Answer the reflective questions and reconsider your piece of writing.

Text level	Sentence level	Word level

Who is your audience? ....
 	
 What is the purpose? (entertaining/informative/ persuasive) ....
 	
 What is the context? (who are you/ where is it published?) ....
 	
 What tone is used? (your attitude towards the topic) ....
 	
 How do you know? (words used to stress it) ....
 	
 How did you outline (organize) your text?
 	
 ■ Highlight your thesis statement and the topic sentences of each paragraph in the editorial.
 	
 ■ How are the ideas developed in each paragraph? (chronological, cause & effect, examples, facts, etc.)
 	
    P.1:..............................
    P.2:..............................
    P.3:..............................
 	
 What is the level of formality in general?
 ....
 	
 To what extent is your editorial authentic?
 ....
 	
 How can you make it more authentic?
 ....
	Highlight on the editorial your attention grabber (sentence).
	
	 What types of sentences are used?
	
	 (questions, short, long, complex & compound, short simple, dialogue etc.)
	
	 1. ....
	 Why? ....
	 2. ....
	 Why? ....
	 3. ....
	 Why? ....
	 4. ....
	 Why? ....
	
	 Check if you have any run-on sentences, and write them again correctly.
	
	 How varied are your sentence structures? (Are all sentences starting with a subject?)
	 ....
	 ....
	 ....
	
	 Type of connectors:
	 ....
	 ....
	 ....
		What are the type of adjectives used? (positive, negative) Why?
		 ....
		 ....
		
		 Anything you want to express about verbs?
		 ....
		 ....
		
		 How about nouns?
		 ....
		 ....
		
		 Idiomatic expressions (figures of speech, idioms, phrasal verbs, etc.):
		 ....
		 ....
		 ....
		 ....
		 ....
		
		 Is your tone consistent?
		 ....
		
		 Is your level of formality consistent?
		 ....

- Where is the weakest part in your editorial?
- How can you improve it?
- Do you think you would get a good mark for your editorial? Explain why.

GLOBAL CONTEXTS
Personal and cultural expression

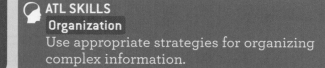
ATL SKILLS
Organization
Use appropriate strategies for organizing complex information.

Reflection

Consider your personal learning strategies:

- What can you do to become a more efficient and effective learner?

- How can you become more flexible in your choice of learning strategies?

- What factors are important for helping you learn well?

TOPIC 2

Context and literature

The concept of context in literature can be clarified through the study of different literary works, investigating how their contexts shaped their ideas. This topic explores the concept of context by studying a number of different kinds of literary works from the United States at the beginning of the 20th century and examining how this era shaped the reflection of the "American Dream" in literature.

QUICK THINK

Translating product names and advertising slogans between languages is difficult: For example, the brief dynamic feel of Nike's slogan *"Just Do It!"* does not translate well into different languages. "Just do it!" reflects a particular attitude in US culture, the "can-do" attitude. This is also seen in the US President Obama's slogan "Yes we can!" In Japan, a very different kind of message is more appropriate, for example, "hesitation makes waste."

"Nothing makes meaning unless it is put in a context."

How true can this statement be?

The following article was written about the BYU Museum of Art's *American Dreams* exhibit. The article is divided into two sections for this activity; each section has questions.

TIP

What is the "American Dream"? It is a set of ideals of freedom, equality, opportunities and success. Chances are open for everyone based on hard work, regardless of social class or circumstances at birth.

SECTION 1 Read the first part of the article and answer the question that follows.

American Dreams by Ryan B. McIlvain ('07)

The Museum of Art's new exhibit explores ever-evolving ideas about America and its people.

ON JAN. 20, 1961, John F. Kennedy uttered his now-famous line "Ask not what your country can do for you—ask what you can do for your country." Less famous is what the poet Robert Frost said next. After concluding, the president introduced Frost, who was to read a poem he had written for the occasion.

WEB LINKS

You can search for more about the American Dream on the Library of Congress website: www.loc.gov.

Taking the podium, the 87-year-old poet squinted into the glare from new-fallen snow on the Capitol grounds, unable to make out the poem in front of him. Improvising, Frost recited from memory "The Gift Outright," a poem he had written some 20 years earlier.

The land was ours before we were the land's.

She was our land more than a hundred years

Before we were her people. She was ours

In Massachusetts, in Virginia,

But we were England's, still colonials,

Possessing what we still were unpossessed by,

Possessed by what we now no more possessed.

Something we were withholding made us weak

Until we found out that it was ourselves

We were withholding from our land of living,

And forthwith found salvation in surrender.

Such as we were we gave ourselves outright

(The deed of gift was many deeds of war)

To the land vaguely realizing westward,

But still unstoried, artless, unenhanced,

Such as she was, such as she would become.

The sweep of Frost's poem is the sweep of American history—promises giving rise to boldness, violence, westward expansion and new beginnings. It contains elements that, together, give us our sense of the "American Dream," however vague or evolving that notion may be.

Question

Do you agree with the author of this article? Why? Why not?

SECTION 2 Read the rest of the same article by Ryan B. McIlvain and answer the questions that follow.

American Dreams, the BYU Museum of Art's new exhibit from its permanent collection of American art, tracks variations on this theme. Through the visual expressions of 18th-, 19th-, and 20th-century artists, the exhibit demonstrates the changing, and at times conflicting, ideas of America and what it is to be American. Exploring broad themes, the exhibit is split into three parts: the Dream of Eden, American Aspirations, and Envisioning America. With 115 pieces on display at a time, works will rotate in and out of the exhibit during its five-year run. More than 200 works will be part of the presentation.

This article presents a sampling of the paintings and sculptures in the exhibit, coupled with the words of leaders, writers, and poets about America, "such as she was, such as she would become."

Envisioning America

Perceptions of American identity derive in part from its founding stories, which are at times confirmed and at times challenged by the realities of American life. In their works, American artists suggest various roles for the nation—from the inheritor of classical Western ideals to a bastion of freedom to a crucible of unresolved tensions.

I always consider the settlement of America with reverence and wonder, as the opening of a grand scene and design in providence, for the illumination of the ignorant and the emancipation of the slavish part of mankind all over the earth.

—John Adams (1735–1826)

The gap between ideals and actualities, between dreams and achievements . . . is the most conspicuous, continuous landmark in American history . . . not because Americans achieve little, but because they dream grandly. The gap is a standing reproach to Americans; but it marks them off as a special and singularly admirable community among the world's peoples.

—George F. Will (b. 1941)

American Aspirations

Long tied to attainment—of refinement, comfort, leisure, beauty—the American Dream has been a motivating force throughout the nation's social strata. That dream has been perpetuated through artists' depictions of the fashions, material goods, and entertainment enjoyed by the upper classes of society.

Conspicuous consumption of valuable goods is a means of reputability to the gentleman of leisure.

—Thorstein Veblen (1857–1929)

The Dream of Eden

For many settlers of America, the land seemed an endless frontier, a pristine wilderness of pastoral simplicity and limitless opportunity. As that frontier diminished and the land's native peoples were displaced, however, the longing for a lost Eden became a broad theme in American consciousness and art.

For this is what America is all about. It is the uncrossed desert and the unclimbed ridge. It is the star that is not reached and the harvest that is sleeping in the unplowed ground.

—Lyndon B. Johnson (1908–73)

We know that the white man does not understand our ways. One portion of land is the same to him as the next, for he is a stranger who comes in the night and takes from the land whatever he needs. The earth is not his brother, but his enemy, and when he has conquered it, he moves on.

—Chief Seattle (1786–1866)

Questions

When and how do you think the "American Dream" started?

What helps the American dream revive? How did the context of the 1920s revive it?

GLOBAL CONTEXTS
Orientation in time and space

ATL SKILLS
Media literacy
Demonstrate awareness of media interpretations of events and ideas.

  **Activity 5**   The setting of *The Great Gatsby*

Examine the advertisements from the summer of 1922 and read the quotes from *The Great Gatsby* that follow (written in 1922). Then answer the questions that follow.

Advertisements:

Oak Grove Beach offered more to visitors than just swimming. For example, New Year's Eve in 1923 was advertised with the promise of "lots of noise, good music". The Pavilion and cottages were constructed to draw visitors all year round.

Oak Grove Beach advertisement.

1922 American Rolls-Royce automobile advertisement.

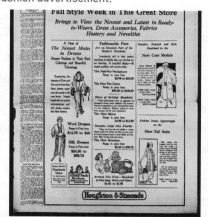

Fashionable dresses in 1922 women's fashion advertisement.

Jazz violinist Herman Curtis and his band were providing entertainment at the Chinese Temple in Grand Rapids. The Chinese Temple was under public scrutiny as early as January of 1921, as police arrested and imposed heavy fines on young dancers for "improper and indecent" dancing.

Advertisement for jazz violinist Herman Curtis and his band.

Quotes from *The Great Gatsby*:

- Nick: Gatsby believed in the green light, the orgastic future that year by year recedes before us. It eluded us then, but that's no matter — tomorrow we will run faster, stretch out our arms farther... And one fine morning — So we beat on, boats against the current, borne back ceaselessly into the past. P.188
- Daisy: I hope she'll be a fool — that's the best thing a girl can be in this world, a beautiful little fool. P.24
- Jordan: Well, I don't care. He gives large parties, and I like large parties — they're so intimate. Small parties, there isn't any privacy. P.56
- Daisy: Open another window. It is too hot.
  Nick: There aren't any more.
  Daisy: Then telephone for an axe. P.132
- Nick: They were careless people, Tom and Daisy. They smashed up things and people, and then retreat back into their money and their vast carelessness. P.186

Questions

- What are the most stand-out or unusual ideas of this era?
- What reasons can there be for presenting these ideas this way? Why did they start?
- How does this era seem to us looking back from the present day?
- To what extent does the surrounding culture and environment drive people's actions and behaviours?

GLOBAL CONTEXTS
Personal and cultural expression

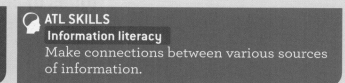

ATL SKILLS
Information literacy
Make connections between various sources of information.

Write a literary analysis essay supporting the following statement. You will need to concentrate on the main features of literary works in US between the years 1920 and 1922. Support your ideas with reasons and examples.

Statement:

"Literary works can see what people cannot see. They are a magnified reflection of life."

⚭ INTERDISCIPLINARY LINKS

Context is also a related concept in Individuals and Societies. If you have been studying, for example, post-World War 1 in history, then you can make a conceptual connection between this task and your history lesson.

🌐 GLOBAL CONTEXTS
Personal and cultural expression

🧠 ATL SKILLS
Critical thinking
Gather and organize relevant information to formulate an argument.

Reflection

Consider what you learned in this topic by asking yourself the following questions:

- What did you understand about the topic?

- What don't you yet understand?

- What questions do you still have?

Context clues

Our understanding of most of what we read depends on our ability to use the context to decode both explicit (clear) and implicit (suggested) messages. Sometimes authors do not make their ideas explicit: we have to read between the lines to get what they mean. Other times the word is there, but it is too difficult to understand. In these cases, you use the context to understand. You can use the words and phrases around the word in question to make sense of a text.

Types of context clues

There are different types of **context clues**. Some words are explicitly defined in the same sentence or the sentence after, while others are implicitly understood from the holistic (overall) meaning. The following are some of those types with examples:

- Synonym: A word that gives the same meaning is used in the sentence.
  Example: David is fond of tedious, boring films.

- Antonym: A word (or more) that has the opposite meaning is used to clarify the meaning.
  Example: Although some men are loquacious, *others hardly talk at all.*

- Explanation: The explanation of the unknown words is explained either in the same sentence or in the sentence after.
  Example: The natives were hostile when the settlers approached their village. They lined up across the road and drew their weapons.

- Examples: specific examples to define the word
  Example: The bird's appetite is voracious. In one day he ate plenty.

- Cause and effect: Through the implicit meaning of the sentence the word is clarified.
  Example: Since no one came to the first voluntary work session, attendance for the second one is *mandatory* for all the members.

How you infer meanings of words in literature can make all the difference in the interpretation of the significance of events and ideas. Context clues can be synonyms, comparison and contrast, definition or description, association, series, setting, cause and effect, mood or tone, or just an inference. The following activities will help you understand how context clues work.

TIP

Context clues are hints that the author gives to help define a difficult or unusual word. The clue may appear within the same sentence as the word to which it refers, or it may follow in a preceding sentence. Context clues are also used to help readers get a general meaning from the text.

 Activity 7   **Using context clues to read between the lines**

The following excerpt has some implicit meanings and messages. Read the text, then answer the questions to practice reading between the lines.

The Real Thing? by Alan Hacksman

One of the most successful commercial products ever launched is said to have come about as the result of a mistake. In 1896, Jacob's Pharmacy in Atlanta, Georgia, was selling a nerve tonic known as "French Wine Cola - Ideal Nerve Tonic". By accidentally adding fizzy water instead of still water to the recipe, a pharmacist called John S. Pemberton invented what has today become the most popular soft drink in the world: Coca-Cola. Along with its closest rival – Pepsi – which appeared on the market three years later, Coke has enjoyed phenomenal success worldwide, particularly in the past fifty years. Indeed, old Coke bottles and "limited edition" cans can often fetch considerable sums from collectors, and there are even stores which deal exclusively in Coke products and memorabilia.

What could possibly account for the amazing success of Coca-Cola? How has this combination of carbonated water, sugar, acid and flavourings come to symbolize the American way of life for most of the world? After all, even the manufacturers could hardly describe Coke as a healthy product since it contains relatively high amounts of sugar (admittedly not the case with Diet Coke which contains artificial sweeteners instead of sugar) and phosphoric acid, both of which are known to damage teeth.

One explanation may be found in the name. The original recipe included a flavouring from the coca plant and probably included small amounts of cocaine (an addictive substance), but since the early part of this century all traces of cocaine have been removed. However, Coke (like all cola drinks) also includes a flavouring from the cola tree; cola extract contains caffeine, which is a stimulant, and the Coca-Cola company adds extra caffeine for good measure. While caffeine is not thought to be an addictive substance in itself, there is considerable evidence that over a period of time the consumption of caffeine has to be increased in order for its stimulating effect to be maintained, and so sales of Coke perhaps benefit as a result.

A more likely reason for the enduring popularity of Coke may, however, be found in the company's enviable marketing strategies. Over the years it has come up with some of the most memorable commercials, tunes, slogans and sponsorship in the world of advertising, variously emphasizing international harmony, youthfulness and a carefree lifestyle. Few other companies (arguably including Pepsi) have been able to match such marketing tricks so consistently or effectively. As suggested earlier, the influences of American culture are evident just about everywhere, and Coca-Cola has somehow come to represent a vision of the United States that much of the rest of the world dreams about and lookup to. Perhaps drinking Coke brings people that little bit closer to the dream.

Questions

1. In paragraph 1, "cans can often fetch considerable sums" has the same meaning as:
   a) Coke is quite expensive in some parts of the world
   b) collectors consider carefully how much they are paying for a can of Coke
   c) some collectors will only drink Coke in exclusive stores
   d) certain Coke cans are worth a lot of money as collectible items

2. "Coke has enjoyed phenomenal success", paragraph 1, suggests the writer:
   a) thinks that the success of Coke is very strange
   b) believes that the success of Coke has been impressive
   c) rather disapproves of the success of Coke
   d) considers the success of Coke to be undeserved

3. In the last sentence of the passage the writer meant that:
   a) most people would like to live in America
   b) many people wish for a lifestyle like they imagine most Americans have
   c) drinking Coke reminds a lot of people of visiting America
   d) living in the United States is a bit like living in a dream

4. In paragraph 1, the writer points out that:
    a) Coke is so popular that some shops sell nothing else
    b) only certain people are allowed to enter the most popular Coke stores
    c) some stores can successfully sell Coke at higher prices
    d) Coke is so popular that some shops only sell goods with the Coke label

5. The sentence "Few other companies (arguably including Pepsi) have been able to match such marketing tricks" means that:
    a) Pepsi and a few other companies have had better marketing than Coca-Cola
    b) the Coke company has been more successful in marketing than most others
    c) some companies have copied Coca-Cola's marketing strategies very effectively
    d) no other company has been as successful as Coca-Cola in marketing its products

6 . "Just about everywhere" in paragraph 4 is closest in meaning to:
    a) in a lot of countries
    b) in every part of the world
    c) in a majority of places
    d) in almost every part of the world

7. In the last sentence of paragraph 2, the writer implies that:
    a) it is easy for the company to argue that Coke is a healthy drink
    b) he/she considers Coke to be unhealthy as a drink
    c) the company believes Coke is not an unhealthy product
    d) Coke is, in fact, quite a healthy drink

8. "Along with its closest rival – Pepsi" paragraph 1 refers to the fact that:
    a) Coke and Pepsi work very closely together
    b) Pepsi is Coke's only competitor
    c) Coke and Pepsi are competitors in the same market
    d) Coke and Pepsi between them keep rivals out of the market

9. In the second sentence of paragraph 2, the writer seems surprised that:
    a) something so normal could have such importance
    b) all the ingredients can be found in most countries
    c) most of the ingredients are not very healthy
    d) Coke must be so easy to produce

10. Which of the following statements about the passage is true?
    a) Cocaine and caffeine are addictive substances.
    b) At least one of the ingredients of Coke is addictive.
    c) The stimulating effect of caffeine is reduced over time unless consumption of it is increased.
    d) The Coca-Cola company has gradually increased the amount of caffeine it puts in Coke.

🌐 **GLOBAL CONTEXTS**
Personal and cultural expression

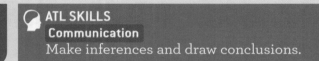

ATL SKILLS
Communication
Make inferences and draw conclusions.

Macbeth's soliloquy

After Macbeth discussed his crime with Lady Macbeth, he was sitting alone when an invisible dagger appeared to him. In the famous excerpt that follows he speaks to himself, questioning whether it is real. Read the passage, paying special attention to the words in bold, then complete the table.

> Is this a dagger which I see before me,
>
> The handle toward my hand? Come, let me clutch thee.
>
> I have thee not, and yet I see thee still.
>
> **Art thou** not, **fatal** vision, **sensible**
>
> To feeling as to sight? or art thou but
>
> A dagger of the mind, a false creation,
>
> Proceeding from the heat-oppressed brain?
>
> I see thee yet, in form as **palpable**
>
> As this which now I draw.
>
> Thou **marshall'st** me the way that I was going;
>
> And such an instrument I was to use.
>
> Mine eyes are made the fools o' the other senses,
>
> Or else worth all the rest; I see thee still,
>
> And on thy blade and dudgeon **gouts** of blood,
>
> Which was not so before.

Now complete the table.

Word	Part of speech	What do you think it means?	What were your clues?
art thou			
fatal			
sensible			
palpable			
marshall'st			
gouts			

GLOBAL CONTEXTS
Personal and cultural expression

ATL SKILLS
Communication
Make inferences and draw conclusions.

Reflection

Consider your learning by asking yourself the following questions:

- Can you identify strengths and weaknesses of your personal learning strategies?

- Do you demonstrate flexibility in the selection and use of learning strategies?

- What new skills, techniques and strategies of effective learning did you develop?

Summary

The concept of context can be explored from different angles. In this chapter you examined how context can give meaning by shaping the style of a text and defining its genre. When viewing the concept of context through literature you studied historical background and how it structures the themes and ideas of literary works. Context also was identified as giving clues to discover implicit and explicit meanings in a text.

Reflect on the chapter by considering the following:

What did I GANE?

G   Generate and write down all the ideas and thoughts that you learned in this chapter.

A   Circle ideas that appeal to you.

N   Form a nest by connecting those ideas.

E   Elaborate on how you see those connections.

References

Hacksman, Alan. *The real thing?* Article published in Good Housekeeping Magazine.

Huss-Ashmore, R. Spring 1999. "The Real Me: Therapeutic Narrative in Cosmetic Surgery." *Expedition Magazine.* Vol 41, number 1.

McIlvain, R. Fall 2006. "American Dreams." *Bringham Young University Magazine.*

Mulligan, C. 2009. Extract from an editorial *Graduation Dreams,* The New York Times. Retrieved from: http://www.nytimes.com/2009/06/24/opinion/24wed2.html.

Shakespeare, W. *Macbeth.* 2000. Extract taken from: http://www.shakespeare-online.com/plays/macbeth/soliloquies/isthisadagger.html.

Williams, N. 2004. *How to get a 2:1 in Media, Communication and Cultural Studies.* Sage Publications; 1st ed.

INQUIRY QUESTIONS

TOPIC 1	How audience members respond

■ **How do we respond as members of an audience?**

TOPIC 2	How creators reach different audiences

■ **How do creators reach different audiences?**

TOPIC 3	Reaching the intended audience

■ **How do we identify the tools used to reach audiences?**

SKILLS

ATL

✓ Use intercultural understanding to interpret communication.

✓ Use a variety of speaking techniques to communicate with a variety of audiences.

✓ Use critical-literacy skills to analyse and interpret media communications.

✓ Analyse complex concepts and projects into their constituent parts and synthesize them to create new understanding.

✓ Identify trends and forecast possibilities.

✓ Use a variety of media to communicate with a range of audiences.

✓ Compare, contrast and draw connections among (multi) media resources.

Language and literature

✓ Analyse the effects of the creator's choices on an audience.

✓ Make stylistic choices in terms of linguistic, literary and visual devices, demonstrating awareness of impact on an audience.

OTHER RELATED CONCEPTS

Purpose   Character   Structure

GLOSSARY

Documentary a film or piece of writing with a goal of factually representing an issue, topic, or situation.

Propaganda information, especially of a biased or misleading nature, used to promote or publicize a particular political cause or point of view.

Register a form of language associated with a certain social situation.

Reputable trustworthy.

COMMAND TERMS

Create to evolve from one's own thought or imagination, as a work or an invention.

Discuss offer a considered and balanced review that includes a range of arguments, factors or hypotheses. Opinions or conclusions should be presented clearly and supported by appropriate evidence.

Introduction to audience imperatives

The IB MYP curriculum guide for language and literature defines audience imperatives as;

> an umbrella concept to refer to whomever (the reader, the listener, the viewer) a text or performance is aimed at, and the characteristics, impact or desired responses created.

The following experiment will test your awareness of audience imperatives.

 Activity 1   **Spontaneous conversations**

Follow the steps and answer the questions that follow.

STEP 1   Find a partner.

STEP 2   Take turns responding to each of these conversational situations. These are spontaneous conversations so you will have no time to prepare—just respond to the best of your abilities. Each section will last roughly 60 seconds.

- Student 1: Speak as if to a younger student at your school about challenges they will face when they're your age.
- Student 2: Speak as if to a large audience of adults about a major world issue.
- Student 1: Speak as if in a job interview responding to the question: "What are your biggest strengths?"
- Student 2: Speak as if with one of your friends about what you are going to do this weekend.
- Student 1: Speak as if to your mother or father about what you did at a friend's house last weekend.
- Student 2: Speak as if with a senior member of your community about what things were like when he/she was your age.

Questions:

1. What are some other situations you face in your daily life that could have been included in this activity?
2. Do you feel that your responses were representative of how most people would respond, or are there unique ways that someone in your family, your culture, or your school would need to respond that others might not be aware of?
3. How did your audience change the way that you responded? What specifically changed?
4. Thinking about question 3, did you use any of these language features?
   a. **Register** (a form of language associated with a certain social situation):
      i. Colloquial language/slang
      ii. Polite phrases or grammatical structures.

b. Any different vocabulary (the body of word options in a language)

c. Non-verbal communication: body language, shown through arm or hand position, facial expression, eye contact, gestures, and posture.

5. What audience(s) do you usually write for online?

 **GLOBAL CONTEXTS**
Personal and cultural expression

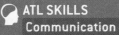 **ATL SKILLS**
Communication
Use intercultural understanding to interpret communication.
Use a variety of speaking techniques to communicate with a variety of audiences.

TOPIC 1

How audience members respond

Audiences in the world of the 21ˢᵗ century face amazing challenges. According to Dr. Martin Hilbert in a 2011 *Science Magazine* article,

> *The average person in 2007 was transmitting the information equivalent of six newspapers each day and receiving 174 newspapers of data (much of that reflected in video and photos).*

Also, according to the New York Times,

> *Yankelovich, a market research firm, estimates that a person living in a city 30 years ago saw up to 2,000 ad messages a day, compared with up to 5,000 today.*

Both of these studies were conducted in 2007 when the use of mobile devices was much less frequent!

With so much information available, improving and utilizing the ATL skills of Information and Visual Literacy has become very important.

 Activity 2   **What do you believe?**

Fundraising advertisements

Following the tsunami disaster that decimated Japan in 2011, many well-intentioned individuals from across the globe watched emotional news reports showing the mass destruction. They immediately sought to donate relief funds. However, with this amount of aid being handed out so quickly, some dishonest and corrupt individuals used the opportunity to create false charities and to intercept audiences by predicting their behaviors, and collected money for their own personal use. Stories of the scams hurt the ability of honest and **reputable** agencies to collect new funds that would have been given by people if they were not frightened of being swindled.

STEP 1 | **Discuss** as a group. Do you think the following advertisement is trustworthy? How could you make sure? What strategies would you use to check the authenticity?

WEB LINKS
To find out more go to www.theguardian.com and enter "Red Cross Tsunami donation scam" into the search box.

The Blair Witch Project

The following website along with the associated videos posted on it was spread online from 1998 until the release of the film footage in 1999. This **documentary** film the college students set out to make focused originally on the legend of the Blair Witch. However, it ended up being an unfinished documentary about themselves and their disappearance.

STEP 2 | As a group, access the web link that follows, view the video footage (be sure to consult your teacher first) and answer the accompanying questions.

Questions

1. Do you believe that the story of *The Blair Witch Project* is true?
2. If it were true, how would you approach the viewing of the documentary? Would you want to see it?

WEB LINKS
The link to the documentary materials that were discovered can be found here: www.blairwitch.com.

3. If it were not true, how would this affect your viewing of the film? Would you want to see it?

4. What evidence can you find that would lead you toward either conclusion?

GLOBAL CONTEXTS
Scientific and technical innovation

ATL SKILLS
Information literacy
Use critical-literacy skills to analyse and interpret media communications.

TOPIC 2

How creators reach different audiences

As Julian Friedmann mentions in his TED Talk "The mystery of storytelling", the formula for reaching an audience in theatre and film has not changed much since Aristotle wrote *Poetics* in 335 BCE:

1. Create sympathy

2. Show pain

3. Create a catharsis or a major release of emotions that is therapeutic for humans

One major aspect of writing has changed dramatically since Aristotle's time. Previously, only the most talented and educated of scholars and artists created material that reached a large audience, with very few exceptions. In today's world, however, anyone who has access to a computer can become published and anyone with a phone can potentially record, photograph, or tweet something of artistic, historical, or social merit.

With so much opportunity, it is important to know how to develop the mindset and the skills necessary to reach your goals as well as knowing some of the tools that are being used to influence you as an audience member.

To discuss what an artist's effect is on an audience, you should first understand what goal they are trying to achieve. Read the quotes from different writers and the example ideas for MYP personal projects to determine their goal.

For each example, identify the creator's goal. What are they trying to accomplish?

Is their goal:

1. to factually recount or inform
2. to persuade/sell
3. to entertain?

Order of activity:

- **Think:** Write down your own answers with a quick note why you feel the way you do.
- **Pair** with a classmate and come to an agreement on what you think the correct answers are and why.
- **Share** your answers with the whole class in a discussion.

5 quotes from writers

1. *Here is a population, low-class and mostly foreign, hanging always on the verge of starvation and dependent for its opportunities of life upon the whim of men every bit as brutal and unscrupulous as the old-time slave drivers...*

2. *Our economic role in this culture of consumerism is to be little more than walking appetites that serve the function of maintaining our economy's throughput (output). Our psychological state is comparable to that of drug addicts needing a fix: buying things doesn't really make us happy, except perhaps for a moment after the purchase. But we do it over and over anyway.*

3. *Gather ye rosebuds while ye may,*
   Old Time is still a-flying:
   And this same flower that smiles to-day
   To-morrow will be dying.

4. *Bayern Munich became the first team to advance to a Champions League final it is hosting, beating Real Madrid 3–1 on penalty kicks Wednesday night when Schweinsteiger converted the final shot after Sergio Ramos skied his over the crossbar.*

5. School Challenge: the power of kids
   For the past five years, school kids around the world have been reinventing Ryan Hreljac's six-year-old dream and making it their own. With imagination leading the way, and the can-do attitude shared by kids everywhere, they work from September until World Water Day in March. They work for other kids who only dream of having clean water to drink and washrooms in their schools.

10 Personal Project products

1. A cookbook of family recipes.
2. A pamphlet explaining scoliosis and how to detect it.
3. A website to convince tourists to visit a country for its tourist destinations.
4. A novel about a dragon who grows up believing she is a duck.

5. A comedy night or fashion show organized to raise money for a charity.

6. A business proposal submitted to a philanthropist to gain financial support for building an orphanage or boarding school in Palestine.

7. A 3-song album created to inspire people to donate time and money to building homes for the homeless.

8. Documentary film about a women's shelter.

9. A YouTube video showing people how to do a variety of juggling and ball-handling tricks with a football or soccer ball.

10. A student standing in a roundabout for rush hour during a given week, holding up a sign showing how many auto accidents had occurred on that street in a year, then determining if traffic accidents decreased.

🌐 **GLOBAL CONTEXTS**
Orientation in space and time

🧠 **ATL SKILLS**
Information literacy
Use critical-literacy skills to analyse and interpret media communications.

 Activity 4   Pantomania

The following is an extract from a Personal Project product written in 2013 by Colegio Franklin Delano Roosevelt MYP 5 student Tracie Horsington. Read the extract and answer the questions that follow.

🔗 **WEB LINKS**
If you are unfamiliar with the English pantomime genre, search www.youtube.com and enter "What is an English Pantomime?" into the search box.

Cinderella

Dame: (To audience) Are you here for the party? I'm afraid you're a tad early. Why don't you help me with something? Alright, I need someone to look after the cake...the one I made special for the prince's birthday. I am putting the cake right here and will leave for a minute to ensure the preparations are complete. I want you to yell "thief" if someone tries to take the cake, alright? (Pause) Good.

(**Lester** enters and tries to steal cake, reacts to audience calling, "Thief!" and hides behind **Dame** after they enter)

Dame: Where?

(**Dame** reacts to audience shouting "Behind you!" then turns to see **Lester**)

Dame: Why you little...get back here!

(**Dame** chases **Lester** with a rolling pin, both exit, **Prince** enters)

King: There you are, my boy. Are you excited for the party tonight?

Prince: Of course, father. I just wish mother were here to see this.

King: I know son, she would have loved to be here too. I met her at a party just like this...

Prince: Really?

King: Yes. It was love at first sight. She was so beautiful...I knew she was the one. (pause) But no use bringing up those sad memories, tonight is going to be spectacular. I ensured that every fair lady in the land has been invited to this party...I hope you choose wisely.

(**King** exits)

Prince: He did what? I can't believe it...well actually I can, that is just what I would expect from father. I really don't want a huge celebration, just the two of us. And all of those screaming girls, fighting over me, trying to take pictures of me to put on Instagram and Facebook...this is going to be an absolute nightmare...and it's not like I'm going to fall head over heels in one night, right?

(**Prince** exits)

Blackout

Scene 3

(Lights go up to see **Cinderella** on stage alone)

Cinderella: What shall I do? I really want to go to the party, but I have no invitation, no dress, and all of these chores to do. (Sighs) I guess there is no hope for me.

(**Fairy Godmother** floats down from the ceiling and lands behind **Cinderella**)

Fairy Godmother: (Taps **Cinderella** on the shoulder) Why, there is hope for you yet.

Cinderella: Who are you? And how did you get in here? Stepmother locked the door.

Fairy Godmother: I am your fairy godmother. I got in here with magic.

Cinderella: You have got to be kidding. Magic? That's impossible.

Fairy Godmother: No, indeed it is not. Observe.

(**Fairy Godmother** points magic wand at a wilted flower pot, the wilted flower is instantly replaced with a beautiful bloom by a stagehand)

Cinderella: Impressive.

Fairy Godmother: Thank you. Now, you shall magically be wearing a spectacular gown that came out of nowhere.

(Stagehand re-enters with a dress and puts it over **Cinderella**)

Cinderella: Amazing.

Fairy Godmother: (Takes shoes from a stagehand) Oh, and here are the shoes that match; you can't have a dress with shoes that don't match.

Cinderella: Thank you, these are amazing.

Fairy Godmother: Now, you shall have an elegant high-class limo take you to the party.

(An old beaten up car cut-out appears, carried by stagehands)

Cinderella: An elegant, high-class limo?

Fairy Godmother: Well, you can't always get what you want... (**Cinderella** climbs in) I'll handle the chores. And sweetie, remember your stepmother will be back here at eleven tonight, so I advise you to come home before then...

Cinderella: Hold on, what happened to her coming home at midnight? (To audience) Figures I'd get the strict fairy godmother...

Questions

- What are some of the tools the creator utilizes to get the audience more involved?
- What are some of the tools used for creating humor?
- What is the effect of having the audience involved in this manner?
- Why do you think children enjoy this type of performance? How are traditional plays different?
- What do you think Tracie's Personal Project goal was?

Just as there are certain tools that are repeated for audience familiarity in English pantomimes, there are also tools that are used in advertising, narrative writing, and virtually any other genre that comes to mind. The key is to learn these tools, develop the vocabulary and conceptual background necessary to identify them and then learn how to apply them.

🌐 **GLOBAL CONTEXTS**
Personal and cultural expression

🧠 **ATL SKILLS**
Critical thinking
Analyse complex concepts and projects into their constituent parts and synthesize them to create new understanding.

TOPIC 3

🔗 **WEB LINKS**
Search for the video "Propaganda Transfer Technique" at www.youtube.com.

Reaching the intended audience

When speakers or advertisers create a message, they use different techniques to convince or persuade their audience, an author uses different tools to entertain her or his audience. The following table shows some examples of these techniques:

Type of technique	Definition	Example
Emotional appeal	Seeks to have an emotional effect on the intended audience. Emotions might include fear, love, patriotism, sympathy, or basically any emotion that can be utilized to prompt some sort of action.	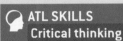 "If we can conquer space, we can conquer childhood hunger."

Propaganda techniques *(Continued)*

Bait and switch	Many adverts will use this technique, featuring a deal that is too good to be true to inspire an audience to come into their shop. When the audience comes, the original product has already been sold out, but a new one, with a lesser deal, is available.	 Shown Reality
Bandwagon	Makes an audience feel like "everyone is doing it" and they should join in or feel left out.	
Glittering generalities	Grand statements that sound really impressive, but do not say anything factual.	I'm Loving it! Open happiness! Impossible is nothing
Name calling	Often used in politics, this technique insults a candidate directly by giving them some type of negative label. This technique borrows from the narrative text type, as it seeks to negatively characterize a candidate or product.	
Plain folks	Used to make an audience feel like a person or product is normal, down-to-earth and everyday.	
Testimonial	Uses a famous personality to sell a product/person.	

(Continued)

Transfer	Connecting a person or product to a better-known person or product, inspiring a similar emotional response.	
Card stacking	Only presenting one side of an argument and intentionally leaving out information from the other point of view.	A soft drinks company states that they are "low sodium", without discussing other dietary areas, like calories. LOW IN SODIUM
Faulty cause-effect	This technique suggests that because B follows A, A must cause B even though the 2 are not logically connected.	A leader of a country is blamed for rising gas prices as soon as he comes into office even though there was a major world issue that actually caused the event.

(Continued)

Activity 5 — Propaganda quiz

Using the **propaganda** techniques and examples from the previous table, categorize each slogan, description or advertisement that follows by the type of propaganda technique being used. Each type of propaganda technique covered in the table is used once.

1. A teenager wants to spend the night at a friend's house. He tells his parents that his friend's parents will be home, forgetting to mention that there is a party across the street with no parents.
2. "Yes we can!"
3. "The best children's film since *Toy Story*."
4. A truck advertisement shows an unknown man in blue jeans and a white t-shirt leaning on their product in front of his farm.
5. Michael Jordan is shown in a trainer/sneaker advert.
6. "Heart disease went down significantly during ____'s (insert name of health official) term in office." (This information is used in an election without mentioning the new heart medication that came on the market during this time.)

7. A specific car is on sale for a greatly reduced rate. When you go to the car dealership they tell you that the vehicle advertised has already been sold, but that there are other cars you should look at. These cars do not have the same sale offer.

8. A politician refers to an opposing candidate as "a waffler"—someone who cannot make up her mind or stick to her convictions.

9. An advertisement shows a large group of people marching down the street toward a banner showing the name of an insurance company.

10. A car advertisement shows a bad automobile (car) accident about to happen, complete with screeching tires. The car's new safety features help avoid the accident.

 GLOBAL CONTEXTS
Orientation in space and time

ATL SKILLS
Information literacy
Use critical-literacy skills to analyse and interpret media communications.

 **Activity 6**   Looking at audiences from a non-literary point of view

Successful businesses always do market research to determine what their audiences want. As entrepreneur.com states, the number one rule before opening a business is

> *Do your market research. Just because you build it or sell it doesn't necessarily mean anyone will buy it. The first essential step is to research your potential market. Who needs what you are offering?*

Yet many MYP students introduce their Personal Project products to their audience very late in the process, leaving little time for evaluation or improvement towards reaching their goal and creating an experience that is different to the authentic world outside of school.

Activity directions: In groups, you will read and respond to the case study on how *Sesame Street* became a popular children's television show. Then use the *Forbes* magazine article to help you to devise a business plan with an intended audience.

How *Sesame Street* reached its audience and can help you reach yours

STEP 1   Watch the video of Malcolm Gladwell reading a segment of his book *The Tipping Point* to a bookstore audience (see web links). Then answer the questions that follow.

The segment from 13 minutes and 38 seconds to 20 minutes and 45 seconds in the clip given discusses the process of making *Sesame Street*, the classic children's program that has been running since 1969. It talks about the key audience research that was done prior to its public release.

 **WEB LINKS**
Search www.youtube.com for "How Little Things Can Make a Big Difference: Malcolm Gladwell on Sociological Changes (2000)".

Questions

1. What do you think Malcolm Gladwell means when he talks about "stickiness"?
2. In your own words, what research did the makers of *Sesame Street* do to better understand its audience?
3. What major change did the producers make prior to the release of the show?
4. What did they learn about their audience that caused them to make that change?

STEP 2 **Creating a sticky business plan**

Silently brainstorm on this topic: What are some needs within your community? (Using a blank piece of paper, everyone in your group writes simultaneously all of the possible products and services you think your community needs.)

WEB LINKS
For a useful article about forming a business plan, go to www.forbes.com and enter "Step 6 For A Successful Startup: Know Your Audience" into the search box.

Community need	Example
Services	
Products	

STEP 3 Evaluation: Which of the ideas has the greatest demand within your community? Which idea is most needed? (Give everyone in your group 3 votes. You can spend all 3 votes on one idea or spread them out across different ideas.)

STEP 4 Upskilling: Now that you have selected the need you wish to address, what skills will you need to utilize or develop in order to run this business?

STEP 5 Target audience: What type of audience are you focusing upon? Think of demographic information (gender, social, economic, students/parents/children).

STEP 6 Make a business plan: Similar to the *Sesame Street* example, what are some strategies you would devise to reach your goal based on your target audience? How could you test to make sure that your audience is interested in your product?

Questions:

1. How did the collaborative strategies (silent brainstorming and 3 votes) you used in this activity work? What were their strengths and limitations? What other collaborative strategies could you have used?
2. This section focused on how creators reach their audiences and introduced some of the tools and decisions that a conscientious creator makes. **Discuss** with someone else, either in your class or in your community, a time where you have intentionally tried to reach an audience and the key decisions you made to reach your goal.

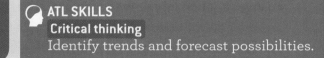
 Activity 7   Final summative application of the concept of audience

Choose from one of the project options that follow, designed to reach the goal of demonstrating insightful understanding of the concept of audience. All of the choices culminate in a 5-minute oral presentation. Your teacher can give you more information on how you will be assessed, as well as help you with any terminology used in the oral presentation options.

Oral Presentation Options:

- **An analysis of how 2–3 comedic writers or comedians create** humor in their videos/movies/writing/stand-up performances. Example: A comparison of how Monty Python, Adam Sandler, and Louis C.K. create humor, discussing the differences in their historical audiences.

- **A sociological and linguistic investigation** into register and communication in your community. This project would require observation and tracking the usual register, non-verbal communication, phrases, vocabulary, colloquialisms, grammar, and/or vocal tone used within a variety of situations within your community. The presentation would present 3–5 different types of interaction and how the change in audience changes the type of communication involved.

- **An inquiry into the tools used to create empathy or persuade an audience** in a film, short story, TED Talk, poem, song/album, novel, or work of non-fiction. Possible resources to refer to are shown below (which you could research further online), but there is no limit to resources in this topic. There is an abundance of literary, cinematography, and rhetorical terminology and tools that are utilized in each.
  - *This I Believe*
  - NPR's Story Corps
  - Sarah Kay's keynote address at the Madrid IB Regional Conference
  - professional storytelling in the ghost story genre

TIP

Presentation: Include visuals to show understanding of the needs of your audience. If you place words on slides avoid using more than a sentence or a small paragraph. Never use your presentation as a script—visuals are only for your audience. If you require a cue card, keep it in your hand and make it bullet-pointed rather than sentences so that you are not tempted to read and will better communicate non-verbally with your audience.

Focus: Make sure you focus on the concept of audience in your thesis. Make sure you state specifically who the intended audience is (the reader, listener, or viewer), the impact or desired response created, and the tools/terminology used to bring out that response.

- **An investigation into propaganda and advertising techniques** used for a specific audience and their overall effects. Example: You could focus on gender or health issues, stereotypical representations of a certain demographic group, definitions of beauty, political propaganda, etc.
- **A business plan analysis:** Utilize someone who has recently put together a business or marketing plan. Break down the major decisions made by the company and their intended effects. Example: You could `create` this as a presentation for shareholders, collaborating with a local business to analyze the effects of a marketing plan they are implementing for a specific audience. (Students choosing this topic should ensure that they are organizing the information, though the company may provide it.)

REFLECTION

1. How did you organize your time and make steps to choose, research, organize, and prepare for your oral presentation?
2. What were some of your examples of perseverance, emotional management, and/or self-motivation?
3. What specific ATL skills did you improve through this project? How are your skills better now than they were before? What do you better understand about yourself or the world now that you have completed the project?
4. Using Howard Gardner's Multiple Intelligences chart, which project did you choose? Did you learn anything useful about what your strongest intelligences might be? How can you apply this personal understanding to new academic and personal challenges?

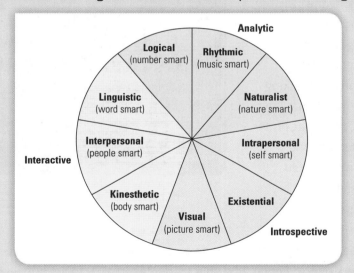

TIP

You may want to discuss this intelligences chart with a teacher or a partner, then apply it to the project you have undertaken.

GLOBAL CONTEXTS
All global contexts apply

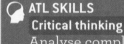

ATL SKILLS
Critical thinking
Analyse complex concepts and projects into their constituent parts and synthesize them to create new understanding.
Communication
Use a variety of media to communicate with a range of audiences.

Summary

Shakespeare's quote from Macbeth, "All the World's a Stage", has never been truer. Anything that you record or that others record of you, any photo you post, update you make, or email you send quickly reaches an online audience and becomes your electronic persona (personality). If you consciously think about the audience that is viewing your information, you can control how the world perceives you, including the universities, employers, and less ethical individuals that might be looking.

Anyone can now publish without the help of a publisher and can become a "viral" success overnight. And anyone can make a difference by keeping in mind the best and most appropriate ways to reach intended audiences.

Regardless of whether you decide to seek out an audience yourself, you will be a member of a day-to-day target audience. It is important that you evaluate the goal of the creators you encounter, analysing the tools they use and what their effects have been. If you are more aware, then practicing and improving the affective skills of delayed gratification and overcoming distractions will be easier and you will make more informed personal choices. With so much possibility and distraction, these skills have become 21st century audience imperatives.

References

Anon. 2012. *Bayern Munich reaches CL final.* ESPN Soccer website, The Associated Press. Retrieved from: http://espn.go.com/sports/soccer/story/_/id/7855684/2012-uefa-champions-league-bayern-munich-beats-real-madrid-play-chelsea-final.

Herrick, R. 1983. *To the Virgins, to Make Much of Time.* In *The Norton Anthoogy of Poetry.* W.W.Norton; Later Printing edition.

Hibbert, M., Lopez, P. 2011. "The Worlds Technological Capacity to Store, Communicate, and Compute Information." *Science Magazine.* Retrieved from: http://www.sciencemag.org/content/332/6025/60.

Homer-Dixon, T. 2008. *The Upside of Down: Catastrophe, Creativity, and the Renewal of Civilization.* 1st ed. Island Press.

Horsington, T. 2013. Personal Project. Colegio Franklin Delano Roosevelt, Peru.

Lewis, S. 2001. *The Jungle,* Dover Thrift Editions.

Mintzer, Rich, 2009, Entrepreneur.com. Retrieved from: www.entrepreneur,com/article/202106.

Story, L. 2007. *Anywhere the Eye Can See, It's Likely to See an Ad.* Article by New York Times. Retrieved from: http://www.nytimes.com/2007/01/15/business/media/15everywhere.html.

INQUIRY QUESTIONS	**TOPIC 1** The graphic novel
	■ **What are the essential components of a graphic novel?**
	TOPIC 2 Creative writing
	■ **What key elements and techniques must be combined in effective creative writing?**
	TOPIC 3 Creative writing: poetry
	■ **What are the key elements and techniques that must be combined in order to create your own sonnet?**

SKILLS

ATL

✓ Evaluate evidence and arguments.

✓ Use critical-literacy skills.

✓ Communicate information and ideas effectively to multiple audiences using a variety of media and formats.

✓ Read critically and for comprehension.

✓ Write for different purposes.

✓ Give and receive meaningful feedback.

Language and literature

✓ Understanding and appreciating graphic novels.

✓ Using and interpreting a range of discipline-specific terms and symbols.

✓ Creating original works and ideas.

OTHER RELATED CONCEPTS

Character	Setting	Structure	Style	Theme

GLOSSARY

Cliffhanger a plot device to hook the reader. The idea is to leave them in suspense so they will read on.

Dovetail to come together in a perfect fit or combination.

Idiom a saying that has its own separate meaning rather than one that is clear from the words that make it up. For example, "caught red-handed" means being caught in the act of doing something. Having red hands is unimportant and completely unrelated to the literal meaning.

Working title a temporary name for something.

COMMAND TERMS

Analyse break down in order to bring out the essential elements or structure. To indentify parts and relationships, and to interpret information to reach conclusions.

Explore undertake a systematic process of discovery.

Introducing self-expression

Self-expression essentially means expressing your personality, feelings, beliefs and ideas. It is something that writers treasure. For example Ralph Waldo Emerson captured the urge for creativity in the following way: "None of us will ever accomplish anything excellent or commanding except when he listens to this whisper which is heard by him alone." The playwright, Oscar Wilde, put it differently. He was famous for his sense of humour and made the following witty comment: "I may not agree with you, but I will defend to the death your right to make an ass of yourself." The urge for self-expression is an essential part of being human; moreover, there are thousands of forms of human self-expression. Some fall elsewhere on the school timetable such as in design, the arts, sport or dance.

Forms of self-expression vary according to the culture in which we live and our individual values. The practice of self-expression is an important part of a balanced life. As the father of modern psychology, Sigmund Freud, once said, "Unexpressed emotions will never die. They are buried alive and will come forth later in uglier ways." Therefore, not having a creative side can lead to a more stunted, limited life. This chapter focuses on two important parts of self-expression: first, the appreciation of the writing and the use of images of others and second, your own original creative writing.

QUICK THINK
Take a look at the images below.

Figure 17.1 Egyptian hieroglyphics, the Bayeux Tapestry and Trajan's column

TOPIC 1

The graphic novel

In this topic you will explore self-expression by analysing *Deogratias: A Tale of Rwanda* (First Second Books, 2006), a graphic novel written and drawn by Jean-Philippe Stassen that tells the story of the Rwandan Genocide of 1994 through the eyes of an adolescent boy, Deogratias, and those who live around him.

⃝ INTERDISCIPLINARY LINKS
In your individuals and societies classes, you will come across the related concept of conflict.

Discuss ways in which each of these images is similar to and different from a modern graphic novel, in terms of the way the story is being told and of the style the artists have used.

Activity 1   Exploring the novel

This activity requires you to read the graphic novel *Deogratias: A Tale of Rwanda*. **Explore** the graphic novel and consider the following points consider the following points. Include the introduction, *From the Depths* at some point in your reading.

Here are some words to give you context.

Genocide: the systematic murder of an ethnic or racial group.

Hutu: the largest ethnic group in Rwanda.

Interahamwe: an extreme, racist Hutu militia who typically armed themselves with machetes.

Tutsi: the second largest ethnic group in Rwanda and the targets of the Genocide.

Twa: an African people of unusually short height, sometimes also called pygmies. They were not Tutsi and were very few in number yet were also targeted during the Rwandan Genocide.

Urwagwa: a beer made from fermenting bananas.

During reading

This story is told in the novel's present, during the Genocide and prior to it; therefore flashback techniques are frequently used. First, focus on the techniques used by the artist:

- How do you know when Deogratias is in the present or the past?
- How do the cartoon borders change depending on the time that image is set in?
- How much actual violence do you see and how much is suggested through facial expressions?

After reading

After you have read the graphic novel, consider character:

- Hero, villain, victim: To what extent do each of these words fit Deogratias?
- Research the name *Deogratias*. In what ways do you consider this name well chosen? Could you consider the name ironic? Justify any comments you make with evidence.
- How sympathetically are the missionaries presented?

For these points and all future comments, justify your comments with evidence.

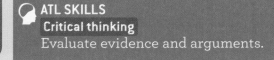

🌐 **GLOBAL CONTEXTS**
Fairness and development

ATL SKILLS
Critical thinking
Evaluate evidence and arguments.

Activity 2   Literary techniques

In this activity you will focus on the literary techniques used in *Deogratias: A Tale of Rwanda*.

At one point in the story the graphics suggest that Deogratias turns into a dog. Do you believe he actually turns into a dog? Is it all in his head? Is it symbolic in some way, and if so, how?

- Consider the motif of poison. In which different ways is this present in the graphic novel and to what effect?
- Consider the portrayal of animals and animal-like behaviour. What is the work trying to say through this?

If you have read the entire novel, answer the following questions about the theme. Justify your comments with evidence.

- To what extent is justice served by the end of the graphic novel?
- What is suggested about the role of western countries in the Rwandan Genocide?
- Consider the way the word *cockroach* is used by certain characters. What does this work say about racism?
- What is said about madness?
- What is said about the survival instinct?

Explore each of these questions to begin working towards one of the assessment tasks for the unit:

To what extent do the writer's style and the artist's techniques combine effectively to create a powerful message in *Deogratias: A Tale of Rwanda*?

Your teacher will choose the format in which you will present your work, and give you advice as to how it will be assessed.

> ### 🏃 TAKE ACTION
>
> At the end of World War Two and the horrors of the Nazi concentration camps, the victorious powers agreed to a convention (an understanding) designed to stop genocide ever happening again. Yet genocide has happened several times since. Find out about the most recent examples of genocide or attempted genocide.

> ### 🌐 GLOBAL CONTEXTS
> **Fairness and development**

> ### 💭 ATL SKILLS
> Information literacy
> Use critical-literacy skills to analyse and interpret media.

Activity 3   Analysing graphics programs

You have been studying *Deogratias: A Tale of Rwanda* in order to analyse how a storyline and visual images combine. Consider this section from *Deogratias: A Tale of Rwanda*. Even a small part tells its own story.

> ### 🏃 TAKE ACTION
>
> Taking action also involves coming to a moral judgment about something. Find out more about the Rwanda Genocide. In particular, why did foreign powers not stop it? Who do you think is to blame for allowing the killings to continue?
>
> You are now going to tell a story of your choice with a compelling message. You will be using a piece of open source software. Some examples are given in the web links box.

In the first part of this activity you will analyse these and other graphics programs available on the web.

STEP 1 **Graphic Program Survey**

Out of 10, where 10 is excellent and 1 is terrible, analyse your selected graphic programs for the following:

- Variety of backgrounds available in the program
- Variety of characters available in the program

Write down any other observations and an paragraph-long assessment of the quality of this program.

What is your overall assessment of this program? (Give a mark out of 10.)

After this, choose a program and begin the next task.

STEP 2 **Planning**

Creating a work like *Deogratias: A Tale of Rwanda* takes many months of work. You do not have time in your language and literature classes to work on something so ambitious.

Your task is to choose an English **idiom** and present it as a story in an exciting and compelling way, using a combination of images and storyline. To select your idiom go to one of the following websites suggested in the web links box.

English has so many idioms so everyone in your class should be able to select a different one.

Answer the following questions to help you to create your plan:

1. What setting will I use to illustrate this idiom?
2. Who will the characters be? (Have just a few.)
3. What will each character's personality and motivation be?
4. How will the storyline develop?

    Setting the scene → Problem/conflict → Resolution + Idiom explained

5. Artistically, how will you distinguish between the characters?

Once you have had your plan approved by your teacher, you are ready to begin.

Your teacher will give you feedback throughout the creative process. This may be ongoing during class time, or your may review a first draft of your work.

GLOBAL CONTEXTS
Personal and cultural expression

ATL SKILLS
Media literacy
Communicate information and ideas effectively to multiple audiences using a variety of media and formats.

Reflection

1. What impact did *Deogratias: A Tale of Rwanda* have on you? How moved were you by the story?

2. What skills did you learn in making your own comic strip?

3. To what extent do you consider graphic novels as literature?

TOPIC 2

Creative writing

One of the best ways you can explore self-expression is though creative writing. In this topic you will analyse a short story by a famous author and, just as you did for *Deogratias: A Tale of Rwanda,* you will then work on your own creative writing.

 Activity 4   **The short story**

In this activity you will consider an extract from the short story *The Secret Life of Walter Mitty*. Read the extract, written by humorist James Thurber in 1939, and answer the questions below.

"WE'RE going through!" The Commander's voice was like thin ice breaking. He wore his full-dress uniform, with the heavily braided white cap pulled down rakishly over one cold gray eye. "We can't make it, sir. It's spoiling for a hurricane, if you ask me." "I'm not asking you, Lieutenant Berg," said the Commander. "Throw on the power lights! Rev her up to 8500! We're going through!" The pounding of the cylinders increased: ta-pocketa-pocketa-pocketa-pocketa-pocketa. The Commander stared at the ice forming on the pilot window. He walked over and twisted a row of complicated dials. "Switch on No. 8 auxiliary!" he shouted. "Switch on No. 8 auxiliary!" repeated Lieutenant Berg. "Full strength in No. 3 turret!" shouted the Commander. "Full strength in No. 3 turret!" The crew, bending to their various tasks in the huge, hurtling eight-engined Navy hydroplane, looked at each other and grinned. "The Old Man'll get us through," they said to one another. "The Old Man ain't afraid of hell!" . . .

"Not so fast! You're driving too fast!" said Mrs. Mitty. "What are you driving so fast for?"

"Hmm?" said Walter Mitty. He looked at his wife, in the seat beside him, with shocked astonishment. She seemed grossly unfamiliar, like a strange woman who had yelled at him in a crowd. "You were up to fifty-five," she said. "You know I don't like to go more than forty. You were up to fifty-five." Walter Mitty drove on toward Waterbury in silence, the roaring of the SN202 through the worst storm in twenty years of Navy flying fading in the remote, intimate airways of his mind. "You're tensed up again," said Mrs. Mitty. "It's one of your days. I wish you'd let Dr. Renshaw look you over."

Walter Mitty stopped the car in front of the building where his wife went to have her hair done. "Remember to get those overshoes while I'm having my hair done," she said. "I don't need overshoes," said Mitty. She put her mirror back into her bag. "We've been all through that," she said, getting out of the car. "You're not a young man any longer." He raced the engine a little. "Why don't you wear your gloves? Have you lost your gloves?" Walter Mitty reached in a pocket and brought out the gloves. He put them on, but after she had turned and gone into the building and he had driven on to a red light, he took them off again. "Pick it up, brother!" snapped a cop as the light changed, and Mitty hastily pulled on his gloves and lurched ahead. He drove around the streets aimlessly for a time, and then he drove past the hospital on his way to the parking lot.

. . . "It's the millionaire banker, Wellington McMillan," said the pretty nurse. "Yes?" said Walter Mitty, removing his gloves slowly. "Who has the case?" "Dr. Renshaw and Dr. Benbow, but there are two specialists here, Dr. Remington from New York and Dr. Pritchard-Mitford from London. He flew over." A door opened down a long, cool corridor and Dr. Renshaw came out. He looked distraught and haggard. "Hello, Mitty," he said. `'We're having the devil's own time with McMillan, the millionaire banker and close personal friend of Roosevelt. Obstreosis of the ductal tract. Tertiary. Wish you'd take a look at him." "Glad to," said Mitty.

In the operating room there were whispered introductions: "Dr. Remington, Dr. Mitty. Dr. Pritchard-Mitford, Dr. Mitty." "I've read your book on streptothricosis," said Pritchard-Mitford, shaking hands. "A brilliant performance, sir." "Thank you," said Walter Mitty. "Didn't know you were in the States, Mitty," grumbled Remington. "Coals to Newcastle, bringing Mitford and me up here for a tertiary." "You are very kind," said Mitty. A huge, complicated machine, connected to the operating table, with many tubes and wires, began at this moment to go pocketa-pocketa-pocketa. "The new anesthetizer is giving away!" shouted an intern. "There is no one in the East who knows how to fix it!" "Quiet, man!" said Mitty, in a low, cool voice. He sprang to the machine, which was now going pocketa-pocketa-queep-pocketa-queep. He began fingering delicately a row of glistening dials. "Give me a fountain pen!" he snapped. Someone handed him a fountain pen. He pulled a faulty piston out of the machine and inserted the pen in its place. "That will hold for ten minutes," he said. "Get on with the operation.

A nurse hurried over and whispered to Renshaw, and Mitty saw the man turn pale. "Coreopsis has set in," said Renshaw nervously. "If you would take over, Mitty?" Mitty looked at him and at the craven figure of Benbow, who drank, and at the grave, uncertain faces of the two great specialists. "If you wish," he said. They slipped a white gown on him, he adjusted a mask and drew on thin gloves; nurses handed him shining . . .

"Back it up, Mac!! Look out for that Buick!" Walter Mitty jammed on the brakes. "Wrong lane, Mac," said the parking-lot attendant, looking at Mitty closely. "Gee. Yeh," muttered Mitty. He began cautiously to back out of the lane marked "Exit Only." "Leave her sit there," said the attendant. "I'll put her away." Mitty got out of the car. "Hey, better leave the key." "Oh," said Mitty, handing the man the ignition key. The attendant vaulted into the car, backed it up with insolent skill, and put it where it belonged.

They're so damn cocky, thought Walter Mitty, walking along Main Street; they think they know everything. Once he had tried to take his chains off, outside New Milford, and he had got them wound around the axles. A man had had to come out in a wrecking car and unwind them, a young, grinning garageman. Since then Mrs. Mitty always made him drive to a garage to have the chains taken off. The next time, he thought, I'll wear my right arm in a sling; they won't grin at me then. I'll have my right arm in a sling and they'll see I couldn't possibly take the chains off myself. He kicked at the slush on the sidewalk. "Overshoes," he said to himself, and he began looking for a shoe store.

When he came out into the street again, with the overshoes in a box under his arm, Walter Mitty began to wonder what the other thing was his wife had told him to get. She had told him, twice before they set out from their house for Waterbury. In a way he hated these weekly trips to town--he was always getting something wrong. Kleenex, he thought, Squibb's, razor blades? No. Tooth paste, toothbrush, bicarbonate, Carborundum, initiative and referendum? He gave it up. But she would remember it. "Where's the what's-its- name?" she would ask. "Don't tell me you forgot the what's-its-name." A newsboy went by shouting something about the Waterbury trial.

... "Perhaps this will refresh your memory." The District Attorney suddenly thrust a heavy automatic at the quiet figure on the witness stand. "Have you ever seen this before?" Walter Mitty took the gun and examined it expertly. "This is my Webley-Vickers 50.80," ho said calmly. An excited buzz ran around the courtroom. The Judge rapped for order. "You are a crack shot with any sort of firearms, I believe?" said the District Attorney, insinuatingly. "Objection!" shouted Mitty's attorney. "We have shown that the defendant could not have fired the shot. We have shown that he wore his right arm in a sling on the night of the fourteenth of July." Walter Mitty raised his hand briefly and the bickering attorneys were stilled. "With any known make of gun," he said evenly, "I could have killed Gregory Fitzhurst at three hundred feet with my left hand." Pandemonium broke loose in the courtroom. A woman's scream rose above the bedlam and suddenly a lovely, dark-haired girl was in Walter Mitty's arms. The District Attorney struck at her savagely. Without rising from his chair, Mitty let the man have it on the point of the chin. "You miserable cur!" ...

"Puppy biscuit," said Walter Mitty. He stopped walking and the buildings of Waterbury rose up out of the misty courtroom and surrounded him again. A woman who was passing laughed. "He said 'Puppy biscuit,'" she said to her companion. "That man said 'Puppy biscuit' to himself." Walter Mitty hurried on. He went into an A. P., not the first one he came to but a smaller one farther up the street. "I want some biscuit for small, young dogs," he said to the clerk. "Any special brand, sir?" The greatest pistol shot in the world thought a moment. "It says 'Puppies Bark for It' on the box," said Walter Mitty.

His wife would be through at the hairdresser's in fifteen minutes' Mitty saw in looking at his watch, unless they had trouble drying it; sometimes they had trouble drying it. She didn't like to get to the hotel first, she would want him to be there waiting for her as usual. He found a big leather chair in the lobby, facing a window, and he put the overshoes and the puppy biscuit on the floor beside it.

QUICK THINK

Thanks to this story, the word "Mittyesque", or the phrase "leading a Walter Mitty-like existence" have entered the English language. What do you think they mean?

Questions

What do you notice about the main character?	How did the writer create this effect? What did the writer add to the story to make you notice this?
What do you notice about minor characters?	How did the writer create this effect? What did the writer add to the story to make you notice this?
What do you notice about the setting?	How did the writer create these effects? What did the writer add to the story to make you notice this?
What do you notice about the message/theme?	How did the writer create this effect? What did the writer add to the story to make you notice this?

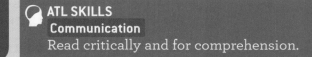
Creative writing: some basic tips

Now begin to plan out your own creative piece.

Below are some points to consider. Read them carefully as they lead into the next assessed activity.

Figure 17.2 Are you ready to get started?

TIP

Refer back to Chapter 14, Purpose, for a bulleted list of the elements of a story.

Don't tell them, show them	Your most important task is to entertain the reader. A reader wants to be active. They want to figure things out for themselves, wherever possible. For example, look at two different ways of saying the same thing: *"Get out of here!" she shouted angrily.* *"Get out of here!" Her face reddened. She was shaking uncontrollably.* In the second example there is a picture for the reader to imagine, so they get involved, whilst the first is a simple, blunt statement.
	Also: ■ Be clear. ■ Try to avoid clichés: overused phrases that lack imagination.
Experiment	Try to stretch yourself. Include more adjectives, similes and metaphors. Use a thesaurus.
Research	■ Write about something that you know well, or have researched thoroughly. Otherwise, your story it will not be convincing. ■ Tie up all loose ends. Make sure you finish the different aspects of the story; leave no gaps.
Point of view	To write your story you need to consider the best way to tell it. Who should be the narrator? What is the best way to get your message across? Here are three of the most common options: 1. First person narrator: tell the story from inside someone's head. E.g., *"If you really want to hear it, the first thing you'll probably want to know is where I was born, and what my lousy childhood was like…"* 2. Third person narrator: reveals a character's perceptions from the third person. E.g., *"Hale knew, before he had been in Brighton two hours, that they meant to kill him…:"*

3. Third person omniscient: a godlike narrator who reveals what all characters are thinking and feeling. E.g., *"It was the best of times, it was the worst of times ..."*

Some things to consider about point of view:

- Make sure that first person narrators only know things that they can perceive for themselves.
- Third person omniscient is an old-fashioned way of writing to many.
- Avoid "mind hopping"—being inside too many heads.
- Consistency of narrative style is key.

Hooks	The three examples in **Point of View** above are also good examples of the ways famous writers have tried to "hook", or grab, their reader's attention with strong opening sentences. ■ How does each of these hooks work? ■ What will yours be?

 Activity 5　　**When you can show it, don't tell it**

Change the sentences below into something creative, imaginative and exciting.

For example, you might change

"I'm thinking of killing myself"

to

"To be or not to be, that is the question."

Someone leaving his or her love might say

"Goodbye, I'm going home now."

or

"Parting is such sweet sorrow."

The sentences below are in urgent need of first aid. Rescue them!

QUICK THINK

Who would write something like that?

1. José felt really, really frightened.
2. Tatiana was very, very angry.
3. The dog was so, so hungry.

4. After the bullet hit him it hurt very, very, very badly.
5. The disease was spreading around her body. She was concerned.
6. Rashid had not washed for days. It did not feel nice.
7. Nothing was happening there. It was boring.
8. She was with him. Diana was jealous.
9. Mei had not slept for days and so she was tired.
10. "I'm going to get you," said the man in a way that was really quite aggressive.

GLOBAL CONTEXTS
Personal and cultural expression

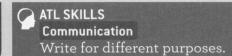
ATL SKILLS
Communication
Write for different purposes.

 Activity 6   Creative writing: oral task

The situation

You want to get your short story published, so you approach a small publishing company. They tell you to meet the editorial board and "sell" your story to them. You will speak for four to five minutes and afterwards take questions and comments. Include the following eight essential elements in your presentation:

- gripping opening: how you will hook the reader from the start
- setting
- plot or storyline
- who the narrator is: first person narrator, inside someone's head; third person narrator, revealing a character's perceptions from the third person; or third person omniscient, a godlike narrator
- conflict of some kind
- characters' names and who they are
- themes – what message you are trying to convey to your readers
- **cliffhanger** so editorial board does not know what finally happens until they read the story

When you are not presenting:

All members of the class and the teacher act as the editorial board, asking questions and offering advice on how to develop the story: things to do, things to avoid, etc. After you finish your presentation, make notes on any advice you receive.

After you complete your first draft, swap your story with a classmate for more feedback. Use the following chart to record your thoughts on the short story you are reading and then share your ideas and comments.

Peer editing and creative writing: your impressions

At the top of the page write the author's name and the **working title**.

Help your classmates with constructive comments that will lead to a polished final piece. Comment on the following and cite the specific paragraphs as you discuss them:

The beginning and the hook: Does this piece grab your attention and make you want to read more? Which parts capture your interest? Can you see ways to add excitement?

The setting: Does it convince you? Is it realistic?

Characterisation: How are the characters? Do they stand out in some way? How? Do you need more on them? How or why?

What themes or ideas have been developed so far?

The ending: Does it convince you? Do you like it? Is there a twist or a surprise? Did the story end how you thought it would? Why or why not?

Is there enough description/imagery? What would you like described in more detail?

Is there anything confusing that needs clarifying?

Describe the overall tone of the story.

What else would you like to say? Also, note any language, verb, punctuation or grammatical points that you would like to see checked.

At some point, your teacher will want to see your draft in order to give you feedback before grading the task.

REFLECTION

1. How many of the eight essential elements in a story do you feel that you got right?
2. Explain what worked in your story for each of the eight essential elements.

GLOBAL CONTEXTS
Personal and cultural expression

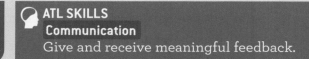
ATL SKILLS
Communication
Give and receive meaningful feedback.

TOPIC 3

Creative writing: poetry

Just as you did for short stories you will analyse and write sonnets in this topic. When completing a textual analysis of a sonnet, you will focus on aspects that are not present in short stories, such as rhyme and structure. In a form of poetry, such as a sonnet, precise rules of construction must be followed. Part of your job is to determine what these are.

Sonnets were first created in Italy in the medieval era. In the 16th century they had spread to England, and they continued to be popular in the 17th century, though as free verse became increasingly popular among poets, they became less common. Nevertheless, they make appearances from time to time in the work of modern poets.

Critical thinking

Read the following sonnets carefully. You will analyse them in the same way you responded to texts in Chapter 14. Refer to the mnemonic from that chapter to help you, and answer the questions that follow the sonnets. Ask your teacher if you are not clear about the literary terms used in the questions.

Death, be not proud by John Donne
Death, be not proud, though some have called thee
Mighty and dreadful, for thou art not so;
For those whom thou thinkst thou dost overthrow
Die not, poor Death, nor yet canst thou kill me.
From rest and sleep, which but thy pictures be
Much pleasure; then from thee much more must flow
And soonest our best men with thee do go
Rest of their bones and soul's delivery.
Thou art slave to Fate, Chance, kings, and desperate men,
And dost with poison, war, and sickness dwell,
And poppies or charms can make us sleep as well
And better than thy stroke. Why swellst thou then?
One short sleep past, we wake eternally,
And death shall be no more; Death, thou shalt die!

When, in disgrace with fortune and men's eyes by William Shakespeare.
When, in disgrace with fortune and men's eyes,
I all alone beweep my outcast state
And trouble deaf heaven with my bootless cries
And look upon myself and curse my fate,
Wishing me like to one more rich in hope,
Featured like him, like him with friends possess'd,
Desiring this man's art and that man's scope,
With what I most enjoy contented least;
Yet in these thoughts myself almost despising,
Haply I think on thee, and then my state,
Like to the lark at break of day arising
From sullen earth, sings hymns at heaven's gate;
For thy sweet love remember'd such wealth brings
That then I scorn to change my state with kings.

Questions
1. Make a list of the words that you do not know and find their definitions.
2. Find the rhyming pattern for both poems. Note that the pronunciation may have changed slightly since these sonnets were written.
3. Count the number of syllables in each line of each poem.
4. Comment on the rhythm and tone of both poems.

5. Look for personification (giving human characteristics to something that is not human), irony, allusion and euphemism (using soft or indirect language in place of stronger words) in the poems.

6. Comment on the imagery that is particularly striking and describe the effect it has on you.

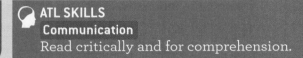

GLOBAL CONTEXTS
Identities and relationships

ATL SKILLS
Communication
Read critically and for comprehension.

 **Activity 8**   Writing your own sonnet

In this activity you will create your own sonnet.

STEP 1   **Writing your sonnet**

When writing poetry consider the following:

- rhyme – the rhyme pattern that you will follow
- themes – message you trying to convey
- imagery – images need to match the themes
- tone/mood – needs to match the themes
- narrator/point of view – perspective the story is Presented from (See the section on short stories for the different types of narrators.)
- characters/setting/conflict – optional
- ending/resolution – everything should **dovetail** work's finish, and everything should have been working to this through entire story

STEP 2   **Assessing your sonnet**

After you complete your first draft, swap your sonnet with a classmate for more feedback. Use the following chart to write out your thoughts on the sonnet you are reading and then share your ideas and comments.

> **Peer editing and poetry: your impressions**
>
> At the top of the page write the author's name and the poem's working title.
>
> Help your classmates with constructive comments that will lead to a polished final piece. Comment on the following and cite the specific lines as you discuss them:
>
> The beginning: Does this piece grab your attention and make you want to read more? How does it gain your interest? Or, can you see ways to add excitement?
>
> Characterisation: If there are characters, how are they developed? Do they stand out in some way? How? Do you need more on them? How or why?
>
> What themes or ideas have been developed so far?

The ending: Does it satisfy you? Do you like it? Is more needed? Why or why not?

Is there enough description/imagery? What would you like described in more detail?

Is there anything confusing that needs clarifying?

Describe the overall tone of the poem.

What else would you like to say? Also, note any language, verb, punctuation or grammatical points that you would like to see checked.

At some point, your teacher will want to see your draft in order to give you feedback before grading the task.

REFLECTION

1. Explain your choices for placing or not placing rhyme in your poem.
2. If you were writing a rationale for your poem, what would it say?

 **GLOBAL CONTEXTS**
Personal and cultural expression

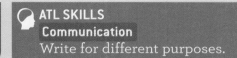 **ATL SKILLS**
Communication
Write for different purposes.

Summary

You have worked on three forms of self-expression. Thanks to human invention and advances in technology, there are other ways of self-expression that have not been covered in this chapter but have been explored in other chapters in this book. Consider the following activities in earlier chapters.

- Making a video in the chapter on theme (Chapter 10) can easily be considered as creative.

- The activities on improvisation and storytelling for purpose (Chapter 14) are other forms of self-expression.

- To what extent does creativity bring balance and health to you personally?

References

Donne J. *Death, be not proud.* The Poetry Foundation. http://www.poetryfoundation.org/poem/173363.

Thurber, J. 2008. *The Secret Life of Walter Mitty.* Creative Education.

Shakespeare, W. *When, in disgrace with fortune and men's eyes.* The Poetry Foundation. http://www.poetryfoundation.org/poem/174357.